Making CRM Stick

Readying Your Organization for Successful Customer Relationship Management

Daniel T. Murphy, Joseph B. Grady, Javad Maftoon

and Andres A. Salinas

www.makingcrmstick.com

MAKING CRM STICK

Copyright © 2005, Joseph B. Grady, Javad Maftoon, Daniel T. Murphy, and Andres A. Salinas. All rights reserved.

The views expressed by the authors in this book are not necessarily those of our employers. While we are deeply grateful to our colleagues for having educated us and giving advice along the way, we solely are responsible for the views and any weaknesses that you might see in the book.

No part of this book may be reproduced, stored in a retrieval system, or transmitted by any means, electronic, mechanical, photocopying, recording, or otherwise, without written permission from the authors.

MAKING CRM STICK

"Whenever you are asked if you can do a job, tell 'em, 'Certainly, I can!' Then get busy and find out how to do it."

– Theodore Roosevelt –

MAKING CRM STICK

MAKING CRM STICK

Contents

About This Book ix

About the Editors xiii

Chapter 1: Introduction 1
CRM 101: Building a Great Customer Relationship Management Strategy
— Peggy Menconi 3
Hitting the Mark with CRM: Beating the Odds and Ensuring CRM Success
— Tom Amerongen 23
Are You Firing On All Cylinders?: A CRM Checklist — Jeremy Cox 33
CRM Reality Check!: Three Questions to Ask About Customer
Relationship Management (CRM) Strategy for Financial Institutions —
Sam Kilmer 43

Chapter 2: Organization Alignment 51
Time for a Tune Up — Helene Mazur 53
CRM Works - Only If You Create the Right Environment: To implement
CRM successfully, you'll have to reorganize around your customer
and change your organizational mindset — William F. Brendler 57
Do You Want to Increase Customer Loyalty? Align Your Organization! —
William F. Brendler 63
Building Support for the Strategic Plan: Aligning Employees with Strategy
— Robert W. Bradford 69
Turn Your Customer Data In to Gold — Raj Menon 77

Chapter 3: Managing Organizational Change 89
Straight Talk on Empowering Change: What your mother never taught you
about change in organizations — Stephanie Cirihal 91
How to Maintain Commitment to New Initiatives — Rick Maurer 93
Building a Foundation for Change: Why So Many Changes Fail . . . and
What to Do About It — Rick Maurer 97

v

MAKING CRM STICK

Chapter 4: Building Commitment at the Top 107
Why CEOs Run Shy of CRM! – Dave Rochford 109
The Preemptive Turnaround: Renewing the Corporation: Body, Soul and Bottom Line – Tom FitzGerald 115
The CEO and CRM – Glen S. Petersen 125
Gaining Visibility and Commitment to Technology Projects (Part 1) – Douglas Arnstein 129

Chapter 5: Making the Business Case for Change 133
Show Me The Money!: Making the Value Case for Change – Daniel T. Murphy 135
Information Technology (IT) and Return on Investment (ROI): Understanding Why, Where and How They Matter – Richard D. Janezic 141
ROI, Cost Benefit and Business Case Analysis: The ABC's of CBA – Understanding and comparing ROI, NPV, IRR, DCF, EVA, TCO and Real Options (Part 1 of a 5 part series) – Richard D. Janezic 159

Chapter 6: Beyond Requirements: Architecting the Future-State Customer Experience 167
Strategic Visioning – Helene Mazur 169
A Quantitative Business Case is Not Enough: Document the qualitative benefits of integrated CRM technology in a future-state customer experience scenario – Daniel T. Murphy and Andres A. Salinas 173
Focus on Late Adopters Series: CRM Technology and the Marina of the *Near* Future – Daniel T. Murphy and Andres A. Salinas 181
Focus on Late Adopters Series: And Would You Like A New Bath Tub With That? The CRM-Focused Plumbing Company – Daniel T. Murphy and Andres A. Salinas 189

Chapter 7: The Old New World of Learning and Development 193
Why Most Training Fails – Jim Clemmer 197
Managing Training-Related Risks in a CRM Deployment – Daniel Murphy, Andres A. Salinas, and Michael Scruggs 201
End User Training: Lessons Learned from Recent Enterprise-Wide CRM Deployments – Joseph B. Grady and Daniel T. Murphy 211
A Bulletproof Model for the Design of Blended Learning – Frank J. Troha 217
When Should Your Organization Use Technology-Based Training? – Terrell L. Perry, Ed. D. 225

MAKING CRM STICK

Are Your Virtual Classes as Successful as They Could Be? – Christina Morfeld 233

Chapter 8: Project Management and Governance 237

How the CEO Should Move the Monkey for Major IT Projects – Walter Adamson 241
Gaining Visibility and Commitment to Technology Projects - Part 2 – Douglas Arnstein 251
Effective Use of a Program Management Office in CRM and Other IT Projects – James Butler and Andres Salinas 255
Why Planning Fails in Middle-Sized Enterprises – Walter Adamson 267
The Challenge of Knowledge Transfer in the New World of Outsourcing and Offshore CRM: The effective transfer of system administrative knowledge requires a formal program where all parties have specified roles and responsibilities – Javad Maftoon and Daniel T. Murphy .. 273

MAKING CRM STICK

MAKING CRM STICK

About This Book

> "Unfortunately, CRM efforts of all types are either foundering or are likely to fall short of their goals. Gartner Group predicts that during the next five years, 55 percent of all CRM projects will fail to meet their objectives. Furthermore, the Data Warehousing Institute recently noted that 41 percent of CRM projects are experiencing difficulty or are potential flops. And, a study by crmindustry.com, revealed that 56 percent of US-based companies have not achieved a measurable return on their CRM investment." (The Road to CRM Riches, Accenture, 2004.)

Whether you are reading this book at the beginning, or in the middle or near the end of a large, complex CRM implementation, you should congratulate yourself for having recognized something important – that there is a certain challenge to being successful with CRM. Projects are getting larger and more complex, nearly always with an outsourcing and an offshore component. Project interdependencies, complexity of data, and a seemingly infinite number of integration points between CRM systems, ERP systems, legacy systems, data stores, etc., have created an unprecedented level of complexity and risk.

Looking around every industry, we see a landscape littered with failed or partially-failed CRM implementations. According to a recent article in the Wall Street Journal "The real news about CRM is its decidedly mixed reputation in the tech world. Some studies show that half of all CRM projects never work out, despite the hundreds of millions of dollars companies sometimes spend on them."

A recent study by Accenture says "However, as many companies have

MAKING CRM STICK

discovered, adopting the right CRM capabilities – and generating significant business benefit from those investments – is not as easy as they first thought. In fact, many industry observers and analysts are quoting failure rates as high as 60 percent for recently completed CRM projects, and are equally bearish on initiatives currently under way." (The Road to CRM Riches, Accenture, 2004.)

According to a recent study by IBM, "Trouble is, CRM is done right less than 15 percent of the time across the globe. In America, Europe and Asia, 85 percent of companies, large and small, are not feeling fully successful with CRM, according to an IBM Global CRM Survey of over 370 companies across industries." (Doing CRM Right: What it takes to be successful with CRM, IBM, 2004).

The good news (if this can arguably be construed as good news) is that the large number of failures has given us great insight into why these projects fail or partially fail. IBM's statistical study of 370 companies has yielded some useful information. For example:

> "Ownership of CRM within companies today is largely in the wrong place. Nearly three-quarters of companies have division-owned CRM, such as Marketing, Sales, IT or Customer Service; only one-quarter of companies give ownership of CRM to Corporate, a senior level team that spans multiple divisions and business units within a company. However, the study shows that when Corporate owns CRM, there is a 25 to 50 percent greater chance of success than with other ownership models."

> "Senior management, in over 35 percent of companies, is actually impeding the success of CRM because it views CRM as useful, not critical. When senior management views CRM as critical or strategic, study results show it is a major contributor to overall CRM success. Viewing CRM as useful, not critical actually detracts from success because it sends a message within the company that CRM is not a priority." (Doing CRM Right: What it takes to be successful with CRM, IBM, 2004).

IBM found that the factors contributing to CRM success varied by geography. For example, in the United States, CRM Strategy and Value Proposition Development was the leading contributor to CRM success (26%), with Budget Management, Process Change, Governance, and

Change Management not far behind (All are addressed in this book). In Asia Pacific, Stakeholder Assessment was by far the leading contributor (38%). In EMEA, Capabilities and Risk Assessment was the leading contributor (19%), with Customer Data Integration Ownership, Process Change, Prioritization of Company Initiatives, and Organizational Alignment not far behind. (Doing CRM Right: What it takes to be successful with CRM, IBM, 2004).

Armed with greater insight as to why CRM projects fail, practitioners across the industry are getting better at mitigating risk. Companies large and small, and individual practitioners, are publishing points-of-view, best practices, white papers, and success stories. There are hundreds of articles on building solid business cases, transferring knowledge, transforming the organization, getting stakeholder buy-in, etc. The volume of intellectual capital seems infinite. This is a good thing. Theoretically, a smart practitioner should be able to read ten or twenty of these pieces, and take some steps to reduce the level of risk of failure of a planned or partially completed CRM implementation.

But where do you start? How do you weed your way through the huge pile of content to find a few gems that will provide some useful insight? As a consultant who is expected to be 90+ percent billable on a project, and with increasingly less time every year allocated to your professional development, where do you find the time to search for these gems. This book has done at least some of that leg work for you.

As senior CRM practitioners and mentors, we were at first interested in being able to provide our junior practitioners with some suggested reading for learning and development – something more than the methodologies, best practices, techniques and templates that are in the knowledge bases of every professional services firm. We tried to imagine ourselves at the beginning of a very large, very complex CRM project. We asked ourselves – "What are some readings that would be useful to put in the hands of the project management team and the work stream leads?"

We tried to picture something like this – At the project initiation kick-off meeting, we would walk into the room with the typical project organization charts, role and responsibility descriptions, initial project plan, etc. But at this kick-off, we would also have a book to hand out – a copy for the PMO team members, with specific chapters flagged for them to read; a copy for the Design Team Lead, with specific chapters flagged for them to read; a copy for the Technical Architect; and so on.

MAKING CRM STICK

Making CRM Stick is intended mainly for CRM sponsors, project managers and practitioners who are looking for insightful ways to increase the probability of successfully implementing CRM. It is especially useful for practitioners who will be stepping into project leadership roles for the first time. For seasoned CRM practitioners, this book is intended to serve as a reference book and a refresher.

We viewed thousands of pages of content and settled on what we believed to be a representative sample of insightful readings. In order to provide a balanced body of content, we organized these readings around a basic organizing framework that we feel accurately assimilates and summarizes the multitude of CRM success factor dimensions identified by top consulting organizations.

We hope this book helps you chart your way to CRM success . . . and we wish you well on your voyage!

MAKING CRM STICK

About the Editors

Daniel T. Murphy is an experienced business consulting Practice Leader, Project/Program Manager, and practitioner, with an emphasis in Sales and Service Strategy Development and Implementation, Customer Relationship Management (CRM) Solution Implementation, and Human Performance and Learning. His clients have included: AT&T; Avaya; AXA Financial; BarnesandNoble.com; Citigroup; Fleet Boston; Manulife Financial; The MONY Group; Nextel; OppenheimerFunds; Sony Pictures; and Verizon. Dan has been a member of four top-tier consulting firms – IBM Business Consulting Services, PricewaterhouseCoopers, Arthur Andersen, and the Renaissance Strategy Group – now The Balanced Scorecard Collaborative). Before becoming a consultant, Dan was a Lieutenant in the U.S. Coast Guard where he served as the Program Manager for Operations Training, and as a Deck Officer. Dan received his Bachelor of Arts degree from the University of Massachusetts and his Master of Arts degree from Georgetown University.

Joseph B. Grady has over eleven years experience in CRM, specializing in Global Networking Organizations and Financial Services at the Vanguard Group (managing Contact Center Operations) and at IBM Business Consulting Services. He has developed and delivered numerous training courses teaching CRM Strategy, Contact Center Operations, and CRM Implementations. He has done consulting work for many Fortune 100 companies, including AIG International, AXA Financial, CitiGroup, and Pitney Bowes, as well as the U.S Government. Most recently Joe led a team in developing a world-wide distance learning solution serving over 30,000 CRM end-users across the globe. Prior to becoming a consultant, he was an active duty Naval Flight Officer on EP-3E and EP-3J aircraft, with the rank of Lieutenant Commander, and held numerous Naval training positions. Joe received his MBA from San Diego State University.

Javad Maftoon has served in multiple leadership roles helping clients improve workforce performance and better leverage knowledge capital to meet business objectives. Javad's areas of emphasis include: CRM strategy, knowledge management, performance support, learning strategies and technologies, knowledge mapping, process modeling and mapping, sales force and contact center automation, change management, program management. Javad has been a member of several top CRM companies, including IBM Business Consulting Services, Learning Matrix, Broadbase Software (now KANA), and the Renaissance Strategy Group. Earlier in his career, Javad was a Program Manager in Digital Equipment Corporation's Consulting division and Educational Services organization. Javad has served as an adjunct faculty member at Lesley University and Lasell College, teaching Educational Media and Technology, Curriculum and Program Development and Information Technology courses. Javad received his Doctorate of Education from Boston University.

Andres A. Salinas specializes in the project and change management of large enterprise-wide initiatives. He has served both as an external and internal consultant, and has directed projects in Mergers & Acquisitions, Divestitures, Sales Force Automation, CRM, ERP, Business Process Reengineering, and System Integration. He has worked in a wide variety of industries, and his clients have included: Federal-Mogul Corporation, Ferguson Enterprises, Inc., Anheuser-Busch Entertainment Corporation, Marriott Corporation, Wachovia Bank Corporation, Central Fidelity Bank, Jefferson National Bancshares, First Citizens Bank and Trust of North Carolina, First Citizens Bank and Trust of South Carolina, One Valley Bank Corporation, Nettel Communications, Entergy Corporation, and the Internal Revenue Service. Andres received his MBA in Marketing from The College of William & Mary in Williamsburg, Virginia, and his BBA in International Business from James Madison University in Harrisonburg, Virginia. Early in his professional career, Andres served as a U.S. Coast Guard intelligence and staff officer.

Chapter 1: Introduction

There are many reasons for the high failure rate among CRM implementations. These range from the strategic to the tactical, from the human to the technical, and from the real to the perceived. Short of natural disasters, war, or other calamity, most can be avoided by senior management with some good project planning, change management savvy, and solid execution.

This chapter is intended to philosophically set the stage for the remaining chapters of the book. The recent studies by IBM, Accenture, Gartner and others have certainly proven that there is an alarming failure rate in the world of CRM. The readings in this chapter underscore the need for thoughtful planning, a focus on value creation, and reflection on successes and failures.

For this chapter, we selected four readings. We felt that Peggy Menconi's paper, *CRM 101: Building a Great Customer Relationship Management Strategy*, is aptly named in that it does explain the importance and fundamentals of a sound CRM Strategy – exactly the things that we would teach in a CRM 101 course. We believe it is a must read for a junior CRM practitioner.

The final three papers in this section have similar objectives, and they certainly have some overlap. Read all three and you will have significantly reduced the probability that your recipe for success may be missing an important ingredient. Tom Amerongen's *Hitting the Mark with CRM: Beating the Odds and Ensuring CRM Success* emphasizes some tactical considerations to consider in selecting an implementation partner. Jeremy Cox's *Are you firing on all cylinders?: A CRM Checklist* emphasizes some things that other professionals do not – For example the need for symmetry

MAKING CRM STICK

between the customers' interests and the interests of the business.

Finally, *CRM Reality Check!: Three Questions to Ask About Customer Relationship Management (CRM) Strategy for Financial Institutions*, by Sam Kilmer provides a structure to think through the question: "What are the right CRM technologies for my company?"

CRM 101: Building a Great Customer Relationship Management Strategy – Peggy Menconi

THE ISSUE: LONG-TERM SUCCESS REQUIRES A GREAT CRM STRATEGY

Business as usual is out. Competitive companies are undertaking the introspective soul-searching necessary to let customers, not marketing or Research and Development (R&D), direct the future. Companies are putting Customer Relationship Management (CRM) strategies into place and are already seeing the benefits: attracting and harvesting customers and making money.

But the strategies have wide-reaching effects, changing the roles of those who deal with customers daily and those who seldom, if ever, speak to them. CRM-focused enterprises mobilize the entire company to serve customers better, locking in long-term relationships that benefit buyer and seller.

A CRM strategy means that operations revolve around the customer and involve much more than installing any one application, embracing a new technology, or even committing to one vendor's CRM suite. It sparks new ways of doing business and provides better insight into customer behavior. Superior implementations merge the so-called front-office and back-office operations, giving employees a complete view of the organization's relationship with its customers, and open up internal systems to customers so they can service and sell themselves. CRM strategies require a cultural shift that aligns a company, its employees, and its systems toward customers and away from traditional product- or process-centric models. Companies that are unresponsive to the shift will soon find themselves scrambling for scraps left behind by those that are. CRM applications and technologies form a base that enables and propels the CRM strategies that companies build to gain competitive advantage.

CONCLUSIONS

<u>CRM Is a Strategy, Not an Application, Technology, or Suite of Products.</u>

CRM is a strategy used in competitive environments that combines the information, systems, policies, processes, and employees of an enterprise in an effort to attract and retain profitable customers. CRM applications and technologies are tools used to implement such a strategy and must be woven into the fabric of a company's business strategy, not bolted on to it.

<u>CRM Is Not a Grassroots Initiative.</u>

CRM must come from the top. CRM is an all-encompassing strategy, and no one department, call center, or Information Technology (IT) manager can drive the cross-functional process changes required. Bottom-up implementations may optimize local needs, but optimizing efforts to benefit customers means that some parts of the business will not be as efficient as they were while others do better. Such choices are made in the boardroom. A recent study showed CEOs were directly involved in successful CRM initiatives more than 40% of the time.

<u>CRM Strategy Is for Business-to-Business and Business-to-Consumer Situations.</u>

Most of us initially think business-to-consumer when we think of CRM, probably because we have first-hand experience. Telemarketers call when statistics say we are likely to be home, such as during the dinner hour, and offer products based upon profiles gleaned from vast marketing databases. We can check savings account and mortgage balances by telephone, fax pizza orders, and find a dream vacation on the Internet.

But CRM strategies also apply to business-to-business situations. With the Internet, sales partners participate as full members of the sales team, and product buyers can place orders, check shipping schedules, and pay bills. When customers use a seller's internal processes as their own, relationships deepen.

MAKING CRM STICK

<u>No One Vendor Provides All the Applications a CRM Strategy Requires.</u>

Given the importance of making the right CRM technology choices, sorting through the myriad applications on the market today can be intimidating and frustrating. Applications can be sorted by the breadth of functionality included, communication channels involved, and size of company they fit the best. No single vendor provides all the required applications, so users must patch together the systems to fit their strategies. According to AMR Research, a great CRM strategy:

Realigns and reinvents business processes
- Requires policy decisions that effect the entire organization
- Opens the enterprise for customer self-sale and self-service

Is based upon the full range of technology
- Enables new business strategies
- Streamlines processes and speeds communication
- Adapts quickly to support business changes

Provides a complete view of each customer

Uses technology to make the most out of each customer contact
- Each contact becomes an opportunity to sell
- Customers can use seller's processes instead of building their own

Puts current applications to strategic use
- Data warehouse stores used to strategic advantage
- Back-office system integrated for customer support

Drives ROI for both users and customers

Great CRM strategies include specific elements, which can be put into a practical checklist. Make sure your strategy addresses five concepts:
- **Realign and reinvent business processes to implement strategic choices.** Since relationships are strongest when they result in mutual advantage, an effective CRM strategy embraces customers and channel partners, weaving them into the fabric of daily operations. Customer-centric operation means letting go of traditional standards in favor of new ones, measuring how often each customer visits and how much is purchased each trip rather than the total same-store sales.
- **Use the full range of technology.** Rapidly advancing technology means rethinking how business is conducted. New communications technology connects remote employees with the rest of the enterprise;

the Internet deepens self-service options, and telephone advances make virtual call-center operations possible. An effective CRM strategy makes technology a base to be used in an iterative process that considers what technology can do and what the organization can do with the technology.

- **Sell the company as well your wares.** A principal CRM tenet is that users see all aspects of their relationships with customers, the so-called 360-degree view. Customers know they buy a supplier as well as product, and now sellers are awakening to find that they sell products, services, and their enterprise. Integrating front-office applications is a step forward, but information held in such systems as accounting, human resource, purchasing, material management, production, and distribution is also important. Customers expect to speak immediately to the right person, who already knows all about them. They want the Website or telephone system to have easy-to-reach, complete information that meets their objectives.

- **Use technology to make the most of each customer contact.** The relationship is everything in Services, and so the industry was an early adopter of CRM technology. Although its models may not fit other industries perfectly, it provides good benchmarks. Service industry leaders are always available and let customers choose which channel they want to use at any particular time. They make each call center or Website contact a selling opportunity by marketing the products a database analysis forecast says that the customer is likely to buy. Websites serve as customer resource centers, with entry pages formatted for each customer, presenting information the customer is likely to want. Website and telephone self-service saves customers time and reduces costs for the customer and seller.

- **Put current applications to strategic use.** Existing systems can further customer relationships. For example, most companies use data warehouses as repositories of transactional data for tactical reporting. CRM applications unlock data warehouses and use them for marketing campaigns. When sifted, the data can be used to develop marketing strategies individualized for each targeted customer. Back-office information is critical to a fully developed CRM strategy, and the boundaries between the front and back offices are blurring. Pop-up screens with information such as a customer's credit standing and long-term financial value to the company, on-time product delivery status, product as-built and as-shipped configuration, and warranty status give call-center agents—often the primary representative of the company—much broader knowledge.

MAKING CRM STICK

ROI Comes From Multiple Sources.

The benefits of a well developed CRM strategy far exceed the cost savings often used to support application purchases. CRM strategies result in increased sales, new ways to differentiate in the marketplace, the ability to absorb new business methods such as the Internet, and other benefits.

RECOMMENDATIONS FOR USERS

- Develop a CRM strategy. Technology-assisted relationship management is a must. A well articulated strategy provides unequivocal direction to employees selecting and deploying CRM applications.
- Use technologies available today creatively to strengthen your customer relationships. Use an iterative process and think about how to apply applications and technologies to make processes better. Then springboard to entirely new ways of working with customers and see how available technology supports the redesigned processes.
- Make information from all parts of the enterprise available to employees who deal with customers. Use information to acquire and sell more to your customers.
- Open your enterprise, making it easy for customers to use your systems. Once they rely on your processes, customers aren't likely to switch to a competitor.
- Evaluate current systems for fit in your overall CRM strategy. Identify critical areas that require immediate attention and plan to replace any systems that don't fit.
- Learn your Enterprise Resource Planning (ERP) provider's CRM direction and the strategies of CRM vendors selling the front-office applications you need. Depending upon the industry, a full system may require multiple vendors.
- Develop new metrics to speed adoption and increase Return On Investment (ROI).

RECOMMENDATIONS FOR VENDORS

ERP Vendors

- Acquire, build, or partner for CRM functionality. Top vendors SAP AG (Walldorf, Germany) and Oracle Corporation (Redwood Shores, CA) lead in such endeavors.
- If partnering, integrate extensively enough to free up all the information employees need and let customers sell to and serve

themselves. Integration must allow automated workflows to trigger events in complementary systems.
- Target your vertical markets first and avoid trying to be all things to all people. Leading CRM vendors are already providing vertical applications.
- Develop, partner, or acquire the sales, marketing, and customer service consulting skills needed to implement CRM.

CRM Vendors

- Make integration to ERP applications and legacy systems easy. Integration should be deeper than the data level and initiate automated workflows.
- Target verticals in which customer service is the end-product and supply chain integration is less important.
- Push the benchmarks higher, adding functionality of such importance it outweighs the cost of integration and subsequent maintenance.

FRONTLINE ANALYSIS

CRM IS A STRATEGY, NOT AN APPLICATION, TECHNOLOGY, OR SUITE OF PRODUCTS

CRM is a strategy to attract and retain customers. A company implementing a CRM strategy must make policy choices that could ripple throughout the enterprise and affect organizational structure, business processes, and information requirements.

For example, a company may attempt to solidify ongoing relationships by making select internal information available to key customers. However, implementing such a decision means new business rules and processes for many parts of the organization. Sales and marketing departments and the call center will need to create customer-specific programs and responses, but so will other functions such as purchasing, manufacturing, distribution, and R&D. Customers will work with people in many parts of the organization, not just the traditional sales and service areas, and will expect all employees to know about them.

CRM applications and technologies present the tools users need to implement a CRM strategy, but they are not strategies themselves. Picking one application, no matter how much pain it solves, is not a CRM strategy. Sales Force Automation (SFA) may help sales managers forecast revenue better, but it does not foster a customer relationship, nor do pop-up screens telling a call-center agent about a customer. Committing to one vendor is not a CRM strategy, either. Suites are broad and cover more and more elements of a relationship, but a CRM strategy is far deeper than supportive tools. CRM is a strategy of attracting and harvesting a customer base by creating and supporting profitable customer relationships.

CRM IS NOT A GRASSROOTS INITIATIVE

CRM is a high-level strategy that re-orients the organization around the customer–a charter much larger than making sales reps productive or presenting call-center agents with more customer data. New ways of thinking about business fundamentals are required, such as considering customers and their lifetime buying potential as assets, more important than manufacturing plants, retail outlets, or traditional sales processes.

Change is far too sweeping to be driven by the IT department or a call-center manager: CRM strategy decisions sit squarely on the shoulders of senior management. Optimizing efforts to benefit customers means that some parts of the business will not be as efficient as before, while others will do better. Roles will change and new measurements will be needed to instill the new strategy. For example, when customers can opt to buy from a Website, through an Interactive Voice Response (IVR) system, or by talking to an agent over the phone, the sales rep's role changes, as does, presumably, the compensation plan. When call-center agent responsibilities rise from completing transactions to meeting a customer's need, rewarding rapid call closure can lead to disaster.

Companies are often reluctant to disclose their strategies because a well designed, crisply executed strategy creates competitive advantage. With so much riding on such an important change, CEOs are getting personally involved in defining CRM strategy, and many turn to consultants to help them work through the out-of-the-box thinking it requires.

CRM STRATEGY IS FOR BUSINESS-TO-BUSINESS AND BUSINESS-TO-CONSUMER SITUATIONS

How do companies manage customers? You're probably thinking of an anecdote depicting your bad or good experience in a business-to-consumer relationship: the Website that took you nowhere, or the bank customer service representative who politely asked if you were settled in your new home, when you called with a question. But CRM is not just for business-to-consumer situations; in fact, 70% of future Internet transactions will be business-to-business, according to one estimate. CRM strategies open the enterprise to trade partners, and once customers use a seller's internal processes as their own, relationships between businesses deepen. Switching suppliers is more expensive and disruptive if buyers must be trained to use a new vendor's system.

Selling Partner Relationships

Companies using channel partners as a part of selling strategies are engaged in important business-to-business relationships. Vendors must support the channel partner customers in much the same way they would a direct sales team.

To have channel partner sales representatives participate as full members of the sales team, sellers make resources available over the Internet. A channel partner's sales reps use a Website to perform the following:

- Get leads that the seller distributes
- Learn of events possibly influencing sales
- Identify active marketing campaigns
- Download marketing brochures
- Prepare quotes
- Enter orders

Sellers also use CRM systems to monitor and measure channel partner activity and sales.

Buying Relationships
Business buyers often work within a series of rules, such as spending limits, defined product sets, and approved vendors. A strong CRM strategy is to make the buying process as efficient as possible, creating an environment that keeps the customer's buyers coming back. Internet or IVR buying lets customers do the following:

- Place orders
- Check shipping schedules
- Check shipping status
- Pay bills

Other Business-to-Business Relationships

When a customer is a business, the relationship involves more than buying and selling, and can include many factors:
- **Supply Chain Collaboration** – At 2 a.m., a Singapore customer's

material planner can update his material forecast, revising a supplier's build schedule.
- **Design Engineering** – A customer's design engineer may search a supplier's product specifications for the tolerance data he needs as he embeds a subcomponent into his product.
- **Customer Self-Service** – Customers may choose to do first-level maintenance themselves, relying on their own service technicians to repair purchased equipment. The technicians can search a supplier's knowledge base for problem fixes, check as-built configurations, identify parts from bills-of-material, purchase spare parts in an emergency, and trigger immediate courier delivery from a parts bank.

NO ONE VENDOR PROVIDES ALL THE APPLICATIONS A CRM STRATEGY REQUIRES

The CRM Application market has exploded, growing from $1.4B in 1997 to a projected $16.8B in 2003. The highly fragmented and rapidly changing market bubbles with mergers, consolidations, partnerships, new entrants, and failures. Vendors are broadening their product line, expanding the communication channels, and designing products to fit more market segments. Given the importance of making the right CRM technology choices, companies are faced with sorting through market dynamics, technology trends, and the products and market strategies of the many application vendors.

Breadth of Operational Functionality

Vendors offer, respective to the business operations they automate, a wide range of products. Generally, products can be grouped in five ways:
- Specialty point products zero in on specific niches. Because the overall scope of customer relationships is wide and the market is highly fragmented, there are literally hundreds of products that address narrowly defined problems.
- Functional suites automate specific customer-facing departments or organizations, such as marketing, sales, electronic storefronts, customer support, and field service.
- Cross-functional CRM suites automate two or more customer-facing organizations and are characterized by shared data and automated workflows, which streamline processes and communications between the supported organizations.
- Enterprise suites, characterized by data elements shared by customer-facing and other internal organizations and workflows that move seamlessly throughout the entire enterprise, are emerging, though they

are not fully functional today.
- Vertical products address the specialized functionality needed in specific industries.

Communication Channels

CRM strategies require organizations to be available through whichever channel customers choose, and vendors are on hand to provide the capability. Some vendors provide applications allowing communication through one specific channel while others consolidate communication through several mediums:
- Internet-based communications, including e-business, self-sales, and self-service
- Telephone communication, including agent-assisted support and customer self-service implemented through IVR systems
- E-mail products, which help users manage e-mail orders, service requests, and general communications
- Fax communication, which is facilitated with fax products
- Kiosks, which are used to extend services to remote locations

Enterprise Size

Applications are offered to support different-sized enterprises and their different strategic imperatives:

Large organizations need applications that automate complex environments, simplifying operations and making enterprise performance data available to management. Applications must be flexible enough to fit operations with minimal customization. Systems consolidating large data volumes are required to obtain a global view of customers transacting business in many parts of the world.

Middle-market organizations, characterized by limited IT resources, require cost-efficient applications that implement best-practices out-of-the-box.

Small companies must solve problems quickly and need basic, very inexpensive applications that are simple to install and use.

CHECKLIST FOR AN ENTERPRISE MOBILIZING TO SERVICE CUSTOMERS BETTER

Great CRM strategies include specific elements, which have been put into this practical checklist. Ensure your CRM strategy addresses five key concepts:

MAKING CRM STICK

- Realign and reinvent business processes
- Use the full range of technology
- Sell the company as well as your wares
- Use technology to make the most of each customer contact
- Put current applications to strategic use

Realign and Reinvent Business Processes

A great CRM strategy provides the opportunity to realign and reinvent processes. While saving your way to prosperity is impossible, it is possible to streamline operations and reduce cost. Looking into an organization with a sound CRM strategy reveals the following:

- Customer information is available to everybody, cutting the need for double entry.
- Communication is faster because systems send automated alerts. For example, a sales rep receives an alert when a customer places yet another service order to repair a newly installed and mission-critical system.
- Internal systems are opened up to customers. For example, most companies want to keep their bills current and are willing to take a look at overdue bills on their own. Over shipments and under shipments, which cause the lion's share of accounts-receivable discrepancies, can often be resolved by the customer alone or through Internet chat.
- Self-service plays a key role. Interactions resolved via IVR cost around a fourth as much as an agent-answered call while Web-based resolutions cost about a tenth as much. The real benefit, however, is not so much in the cost savings as in the convenience customers experience through self-service options available 7 days a week, 24 hours a day.
- Customers configure and place orders themselves. They can sell to themselves at their convenience and create as many self-generated quotations as they like.
- The call center becomes a contact center, the place where customer touches from any and all channels are collected. Intelligent call distribution sends calls to the most qualified available agent, so customers get to the right person immediately. Customers don't have to retell their stories to different agents after waiting in more queues, and the company doesn't pay for redundant agents or additional time on 800-lines.

Important policy choices must be made, and each has far-reaching effects

MAKING CRM STICK

on people, processes, and the organization. You'll need to drive policy decisions throughout the organization, from marketing messages and pricing to the decision rules and workflows that extend out to all contact points. Here is a partial list of choices:

- Treating lucrative customers like royalty and letting those costing you money go away
- The role of the sales rep
- The roles of call-center agents
- Internal data to be made available to customers
- Data that customers should maintain themselves
- Measurements relevant to the new strategy

See the sidebar, "Simple Decision, Complex Result", for a discussion of the effects that a seemingly simple CRM decision, such as letting a field engineer sell parts, can have.

SIMPLE DECISION, COMPLEX RESULT

As processes are changed to service customers better, considering all the second- and third-order consequences of policy decisions is important. A seemingly simple decision can influence many parts of the enterprise.

For example, many organizations feel that field engineers should never sell because a customer may think the engineer was pushing a new sale rather than fixing a repairable unit. But, in the name of customer convenience, it may be best to let field engineers sell customers spare parts or whole replacement units.

However, to do so, the engineer must have current price information and needs knowledge of any special marketing programs that are in place. He must also know if the customer is entitled to any pre-negotiated discounts. The customer is likely to ask when the engineer will come back to install, so the engineer needs to know if stock is available-to-promise and if any special delivery considerations exist, such as handling procedures for hazardous materials or capacity commitments to transportation vendors. The engineer will need to schedule the installation service call with the customer and make plans to come back later to install.

Further implications require additional policy decisions. Will the field engineer's sale count against the sales rep's quota, and does the rep receive a commission? If the field engineer is paid a commission, the human resource and payroll systems must be advised. Which organization funds the commissions, sales or service? If many engineers sell, who forecasts sales volumes so manufacturing capacity can be planned, triggering the supply chain to buy the needed materials?

MAKING CRM STICK

Imagine What Can Be If You Use the Full Range of Technology

Rapidly advancing technology forces organizations to rethink the ways they do business and fosters creativity. ERP systems support every company's fundamentals, such as taking orders, paying bills, and taking in money from customers. CRM systems bring pizzazz, using data to help users and customers work together so both achieve their goals. For example, users can choose automated trigger points and have the system proactively tell them what they want to know. The system can monitor marketing campaigns and push feedback alerts. Systems can advise, for example, that "the hundredth unit was just sold" or "three sold in the first five days" so marketing can tweak campaigns real-time, across all channels.

Technology Is a Base Used in an Iterative Process

For CRM to be effective, organizations must have an iterative process that considers what technology can do and what the organization can do with the technology.

The steps to follow in the cycle include the following:

- Learn about the technologies available today and how they are currently being applied. Find out what advances are predicted for the future.
- Think through how your company could apply the technologies to improve service to your customers.
- Given the process changes, look for quantum leaps. For example, the Internet may let customers register change-of-address information rather than calling in or sending letters or e-mail. But go a step further: Why not open customer records so customers can maintain their own contact data?
- If you decide not to adopt a new technology, imagine a world in which your competition does. Evaluate your risks.

IT Innovations Boost New Business Strategies

When IT transforms data into information, the door to new strategies is opened. A number of these strategies are starting to emerge:

- Database mining identifies ways to customize products and services for each customer. Tailoring product variations, volume discount levels, response times, and delivery commitment windows to fit

MAKING CRM STICK

individual customers helps lock them in.
- Interactions from all channels–telephone, Internet, fax, e-mail, or kiosk–are viewed together so the most profitable customers can be singled out for preferential service.
- Virtual call centers tie together geographically disbursed call centers and can shift calls between them according to business rules. Extended coverage hours, access to multilingual agents, and shortened wait times, for example, can be offered when virtual call centers are deployed.
- Channel strategies are easier to adopt or expand when systems make support easier to provide. Systems should give channel partners the support they need to meet their objectives and report partner activity to suppliers.

The Technology Foundation Must Adapt Quickly to Business Process Changes

CRM strategy must consider today's major events. Mergers bring new customers and products to be woven into the fabric of your customer loyalty plans. The underlying system architecture should be able to handle such major events, making it easier to do the following:

- Use different telephone systems
- Integrate e-mail response systems
- Extend workflows to disparate systems
- Address back-office integration to multiple systems
- Analyze data from multiple sources

Sell the Company As Well As Your Wares

Organizations with CRM strategies now realize that when customers buy products, they have implicitly agreed to the way the vendor does business, as well. Customers think about a supplier in terms of their total experience, which includes price, quality, flexibility, technology use, financial terms, on-time delivery, risk tolerance, availability and ease of doing business, how closely the supplier's strategy fits their own, and how critical the vendor is to their success.

Suppliers must be able to consider customers in similar terms, not just as a sum of transactions. The IT structure supporting your CRM strategy should include the wherewithal to see customer relationships in their entirety–the so-called 360-degree view.

MAKING CRM STICK

Customers want the Website or telephone system to have complete information that is easy to reach and helps them meet their individual objectives. They expect to speak to the right person immediately and for a seller's employees to know all about them.

Certainly call-center agents must have transaction-related information at their fingertips, such as who the caller is, her phone number, where she is located, and so on, not to mention what products the caller owns, which products are under warranty, and what, if any, service calls are open. It's helpful if agents know if there are pending sales and if their CEO is visiting the customer's headquarters today.

Other dimensions of the relationship, not contained in the front office alone, exist that agents need to know:

- Whether a customer is considered critical and has high lifetime value
- Whether a customer pays bills on time and is never delinquent
- Whether you shipped products late and the customer had to wait
- Whether the customer completed your product training
- Whether the customer rated your company average on the last vendor rating matrix, so there is a risk of losing it to the competition
- That the customer uses the e-commerce site heavily and has explored certain pages before calling

Use Technology to Make the Most of Each Customer Contact

Be Open for Business

Be available always and let customers choose which channels they want to use at any particular time. Consolidate the contacts from telephone calls, Web visits, faxes, e-mail, and chat sessions into unified queues, giving an overview of activity and automatically distributing transactions for resolution.

For example, the system identifies the caller and that he is calling about an invoice dispute, not product information or order status, from choices made on your IVR menu. Then, because it is after 8 p.m., the system routes the call, IVR choices, and account status to an accounts receivable agent in California, who answers in Spanish, the caller's preferred language.

Deal With Customers, Not Transactions

Make sure employees work in the context of the total relationship rather than the current interaction.

Make the Most of Customer Self-Service

Self-service saves customers and suppliers money. Using the Internet, customers can register questions or problems, search for answers, or better yet, have the system predict solutions. Systems can track the clicks made during a search and trigger alerts if predefined paths are followed (for example, signaling specialty sales or technical support to contact the customer).

A good Web store offers a complete buying experience. Customers can browse through products or quickly search for a specific item. They can configure an order, making sure their purchase is complete and compatible with products they already have, and get a price. They can even negotiate prices during the visit, settle the bill through credit card or purchase order, and get a delivery date.

Make Your Website a Customer Resource Center

Let customers decide what they would like to see when they enter your site and let them define the format. Share some of the key performance indicators you watch and present data that the system predicts the customer is likely to want.

Use Each Contact as a Selling Opportunity

Even a complaint can be a sales opportunity when agents are skilled in customer management techniques. If the agent judges that a complaint has been positively resolved, she can choose to offer a product that the system predicts can save money or create convenience for the customer.

The customer's entry Website page can be used to post reminders that it's time to reorder consumable products, according to history. It can also be used to advertise upgrades or items from other product lines that research shows the customer may buy.

Put Current Applications to Strategic Use

Back-office systems hold a wealth of information that can improve relationships and support customers better.

MAKING CRM STICK

Give Your Data Warehouse a Strategic Role

Most companies use their data warehouses as repositories of transactional data to be used in tactical reporting. Unlock the data warehouse store and use it for strategic, targeted marketing campaigns.

A CRM Strategy Is Not Fully Developed Unless It Uses Back-Office Information

A CRM strategy mobilizes the entire enterprise to service customers better, not just employees in customer-facing jobs. It is impossible to have a complete customer view or to implement other points of a CRM strategy without using information held in back-office systems. For example, call-center agents will know a lot more about callers with integration to back-office systems:

- They know the financial value the customer brings. Flags tell agents the marketing department targeted the customer for more business.
- If you also buy from the customer, what's the status of the relationship?
- Your on-time product delivery status is also known. Is your performance a plus or minus to the customer's supply chain?
- Call-center agents can be alerted if a critical shipment is on quality control hold and given scripts to follow in making outbound advisory calls. Shipping personnel and transportation vendors can be advised of the delay, and installation engineers can be rescheduled.
- Call-center agents can access manufacturing histories, bills of materials, training documents, shipping logs, and other back-office information to help answer customer inquiries.

In forming an opinion of a vendor, customers consider their experiences with all aspects of an organization. Suppliers must seamlessly draw together all systems, supporting front- and back-office operations as they move to CRM strategies. Boundaries between front- and back-office systems will blur and become meaningless as the entire enterprise begins to march to the tune its customers play.

CUSTOMERS AND SUPPLIERS REAP ROI BENEFITS
If the goal of customer-centric enterprises is to lock customers into mutually beneficial long-term relationships, customers as well as suppliers must gain ROI benefits. Because CRM strategies influence so many aspects of customer relationships, the returns from investment in CRM applications permeate buyer and seller organizations.

MAKING CRM STICK

Supplier revenue may be enhanced by:

- Faster customer acquisition cycles
- Visibility of marketing campaign effectiveness
- Marketing campaigns that are consistent across all channels
- Marketing campaigns that are tweaked in response to automated status alerts
- Extended selling environments, including 24x7 self-sales
- Identification of profitable and unprofitable customers
- Individualized targeted marketing campaigns
- Improved sales representative productivity
- Distribution of best-practices to all sales representatives in all channels
- Better channel partner management
- Long-term customer retention

Customer satisfaction may be enhanced by:

- Reduced sales and service cycle time brought by self-sales and self-service
- Faster response by appropriately skilled call-center agents
- Immediate access to stored knowledge, marketing materials, product documentation, order status, and other supplier information
- Customized products
- Reliance on a supplier's infrastructure rather than building systems internally, such as systems measuring delivery performance
- Faster on-site problem resolution

Cost Savings Accrue From:

- Low-cost customer self-sales and self-service through the Internet, telephone, and kiosks
- Reduced call-center labor and 800-number costs, driven by IVR self-service, faster routing, and better agent information
- Reduced product development and marketing costs as customer needs are forecasted more accurately
- Reduced development and marketing costs when customers specify the customized products they will buy
- Reduced warranty costs derived from early field feedback
- Process workflows that speed communication and reduce or eliminate manual efforts
- Shared data and streamlined processes that reduce or eliminate redundant activities

MAKING CRM STICK

- Better scheduling and productivity of field engineers and spare parts inventories

2004 © Peggy Manconi, Inc. All rights reserved.

MAKING CRM STICK

MAKING CRM STICK

Hitting the Mark with CRM: Beating the Odds and Ensuring CRM Success – Tom Amerongen

Depending on what publications you're reading these days, the success rate of CRM implementations is around 30%. That's an astonishing 70% failure rate. So why am I pointing out this unflattering statistic?

Because you can greatly improve your chances of a successful implementation by following the lessons of companies that make up the winning 30%.

Many factors can influence the results of your CRM initiative. Based on our extensive background and experience with CRM implementations, iFusion Solutions has compiled a white paper containing 20 concise yet powerful lessons to ensure that your CRM project starts off right and stays on track for success.

CRM Experience Counts

Would you hire your Dentist to perform heart surgery?

CRM is not simply a software installation for your IT department, nor is it merely a project for your hardware provider, your web developer, or your financial software consultant. CRM is both an enterprise-wide management strategy and solution that impacts all the stakeholders, systems and processes that touch your customers. CRM stakeholders include your employees (particularly Sales, Marketing and Service), your partners and most importantly your customers. When properly implemented a CRM solution helps your company improve sales and marketing effectiveness, increase customer loyalty and optimize profitability. To successfully reach these goals you need an experienced project team with a solid CRM background. The experience of the CRM consultants you select has a direct impact on your success.

CRM is not just about Technology

Implementation is about strategy not software.

In order to turn a company's CRM goals into true results, your CRM strategy must be considered holistically and with a long-term view. When implemented correctly, CRM benefits your entire company - its people, process and technology. It is your employees, partners and customers that drive your business processes through the customer lifecycle. CRM software is only a tool for these stakeholders and while it can offer many benefits it is not a silver bullet. Stakeholder requirements are a critical input for the design of your CRM solution, as are your company's policies and procedures, often referred to as your "business rules". Executives responsible for front office departments must drive and manage your CRM initiative, with IT playing an important advisory and supportive role. A successful, long-term CRM strategy must look beyond the technical considerations of CRM software installation, and focus on its implementation, expansion and continuous improvement.

Build a Solid Business Case

Why CRM? What do you aim to achieve?

You need to determine the business pains that have put you on a course towards CRM, then gain consensus from key stakeholders regarding those issues. Set project goals and critical success factors that are realistic. You should also define high-level metrics used to evaluate your CRM return on investment (ROI). Consider both hard metrics that are quantifiable such as cost of sale, and soft metrics that are more difficult to quantify such as customer loyalty. Determine a high-level project scope and a solid action plan. Work closely with your CRM consultant to develop a realistic implementation approach that considers your budget, resources, timeline and project goals. Ensure that CRM aligns with your company's overall business strategy.

Develop a Realistic Budget

Consider more than just the software cost.

Since CRM is not solely about technology, it cannot be installed as easily as word-processing or contact management software. CRM requires a structured implementation. The cost of implementing enterprise software is commonly calculated using a ratio of software to services cost. The ratios vary from 1:1 to upwards of 1:7 for large-scale implementations. For small to medium sized companies you should consider a cost ratio of between 1:1 and 1:2. An accurate cost estimate might not be possible until a detailed project scope and requirements are established. It might appear that monetary cost is the only component of your budget, but you must also properly budget and allocate adequate time and resources. Consider the Total Cost of Ownership (TCO) for your CRM solution, which includes not only software and consulting services, but any required infrastructure, training, support and maintenance. TCO should be a key component when deciding which CRM software to purchase. Monthly fees for hosted software, for example, may have a higher TCO over time than purchasing an "in house" solution.

Proactive Executive Sponsorship

Effective change is driven from the top.

Ensure that your management team has strong consensus and firm support for this initiative. You must have a senior level "Champion" to oversee and guide the project from start to finish. Much of the project sponsor's focus should be to ensure that the CRM solution and a Customer-Centric vision are promoted across your entire company. IT leadership often initiates the CRM project or is tasked with researching CRM and making recommendations. This is generally a result of IT's greater awareness and knowledge of the power of CRM, however, it is still essential that the "business side" of your company take a leadership role. Effective project sponsors come from the departments most impacted by a CRM solution - Sales, Marketing and Customer Service. These executives stand to gain the most from CRM and are in the best position to sell the initiative to their front office departments. Consider forming a CRM Steering Committee made up of executives from these departments and IT management. This committee will work with the project sponsor to ensure that the project is aligned with corporate goals and all key stakeholder voices are heard.

Proven Methodology is the Key

Strong project management must be at the helm.

CRM is an enterprise software application which means that it impacts your entire organization, as well as your partners, suppliers and customers.

MAKING CRM STICK

An initiative of this scope and importance requires a proven methodology that will produce a detailed project plan to ensure that all necessary tasks are completed on time and on budget. The methodology should be structured, yet flexible enough to accommodate varying approaches such as a phased implementation. It should be composed of best practices, including effective tools and timesaving templates. It should also reflect your consultants' background and expertise with CRM implementations. A strong project manager is crucial to ensuring that the implementation adheres to the methodology and project plan. They should also play a major role in helping you take advantage of the lessons in this guide.

Control Scope - a Phased Approach

Project risk increases with scope and duration.

Project scope refers to many aspects of a CRM initiative. Items to consider include company departments and locations, CRM software modules and functionality, and possible system integration. Project scope states which of these items will be part of an implementation and in what phase the items will be included. It may also specify items that are specifically out of scope. Determining project scope requires careful consideration and planning. Create a balanced plan that incorporates the need for change and improvement with the need to respect the constraints of your company. A phased approach is the most logical and effective strategy. Each phase's scope must be clearly defined and signed off by the project sponsor. Scope creep should be an anticipated risk and must be mitigated with strong project management. Any major scope change requests require serious consideration and must be evaluated against the impact they will have on the budget, schedule and resources for the current phase and overall project. A phased approach will help ensure that your project roadmap is followed correctly and allow key stakeholders to properly budget and allocate resources.

User Adoption: Buy-In, Input, Acceptance

Prepare for and embrace change.

Your employees already believe they have a system, processes and roles in place. Whether they realize the need for change or not, their buy-in and adoption are critical. You must sell CRM to your employees as a means of working smarter, not harder. Ensure that you tactfully gain employee input prior to starting the implementation process. Set realistic expectations and provide them with regular updates on the project and its progress.

MAKING CRM STICK

Anticipate resistance and plan for it, particularly with sales users, who are traditionally independent-minded and often lack previous experience with CRM software. Work with your CRM consultant to create an effective training and deployment plan. Consider motivating employees in the first months after deployment by promoting early gains and using incentives.

Maintain Momentum and Take Ownership

CRM is an integral part of your company.

Transforming your company into a truly Customer-Centric organization that uses an effective CRM solution can be a trying process. It is essential that everyone maintains focus on reaching your CRM goals and takes ownership of the new system - from the executives and project sponsor, to the project team, and ultimately the end users. During and after the project there will be CRM-related responsibilities across your organization. For instance, management must continually guide CRM strategy and measure its impact on your company's performance. Front office executives must ensure user adoption, while employees are responsible for ensuring that data stays accurate and clean. The project team might own the solution at the start of the project, but by the time it is deployed the CRM solution should be an integral part of your company's strategy and operations. Consider choosing a CRM Champion from your management team whose role will be to continue to promote CRM and a Customer-Centric approach throughout your organization and guide your long-term CRM strategy.

Communication, Collaboration and Cooperation

3 "Cs" critical for CRM project success.

CRM initiatives are led by a project sponsor and implemented by a project team with CRM consultants, but implementations need to involve the entire organization. Regular and effective communication between the project team and stakeholders is essential. This includes progress reports and key milestone announcements. The project team should represent a cross-section of your employees. They will collaborate as a new unit for the duration of the project. An effective project team has a critical balance of skills, compatibility and authority. The project team requires the cooperation of all employees in order to properly define, implement and deploy the CRM solution. Avoid over reliance on CRM consultants. While employee time constraints and job responsibilities are a valid concern, no one knows your business better than your employees.

MAKING CRM STICK

Improve Business Processes

Don't pave the cow path.

Your business processes are critical to the alignment of your goals and strategy with your people and supporting technology. So before you start an implementation, you need to seriously consider your existing business processes. Do you have well defined sales, marketing or service processes in place? Are your processes as efficient as they could be? Do certain processes even need to be automated? Surprisingly, many companies planning to implement a CRM solution do not have defined processes and unfortunately those that do often automate the existing bad processes. Conduct a thorough Process Review with your CRM Consultant to analyze how business is currently being conducted. Determine the changes and improvements required to meet the goals of your CRM strategy. Consider the best practices of leaders in your industry. Align your process improvement with the functionality of your CRM software, as well as with the requirements and capabilities of those stakeholders impacted. Business rules for your processes should be defined and configured in your CRM software. A Process Review is invaluable and will result in employees gaining a greater awareness and appreciation of your complete customer lifecycle, as "silo thinking" is replaced with a holistic and cross-functional understanding of you company's operations.

Customer-Centric Focus

Time to start thinking like your customer.

To become a truly Customer-Centric organization you need to look at your company as your customers do. Ask yourself (and your customers) questions such as "How do they want to be served?", "How can we better meet their requirements?" and "What are other suppliers doing for them that they like?" Define and measure the customer experience you are currently providing. Remember that acquiring new customers is more expensive than keeping existing ones, so loyalty and satisfaction equal profitability. The quality of the relationships you have with your customers is a direct reflection of how well you listen to them and understand their needs. Utilize CRM to create detailed customer profiles, track preferences and measure customer experience. Refocus your employees and realign your processes from a product to a customer perspective using CRM strategies such as segmentation. Drive a "customer first" philosophy throughout your organization that effectively balances the goals of operational efficiency with improved customer loyalty and satisfaction.

MAKING CRM STICK

Key Performance Indicators

Strive to benchmark, measure and benchmark again.

In addition to the high-level metrics defined in your CRM business case, you should also establish key performance indicators (KPIs). During the process review define the KPIs you will use to gauge improvement and measure success. Since "you can't improve what you can't measure", you must first determine measurements and set benchmarks for KPIs in the current period. In order to set realistic targets for your company, try to gather benchmark data from top industry performers. As CRM is a long-term strategy, its true gains will come over time. Schedule periodic measurements of your KPIs and continue to set new benchmarks as you strive for continuous improvement. These measurements play a major role in validating your CRM business case so their importance cannot be understated.

Data Cleansing > Data Standards > Data Quality

Remember to take out the garbage first.

If you know the old expression "Garbage in - Garbage out", then you understand the importance of data quality. Imagine the ramifications of poor data quality when you attempt to query your data in order to segment customers, conduct a direct mail campaign or generate a sales forecast. Data quality begins with ensuring that clean data is migrated into your new CRM system. Data cleansing is always a major task that is too often underestimated. It allows you to identify the common problem areas within your existing customer data and to determine which records are actually needed for migration. Establish data entry standards that will be reflected in the design of the new CRM system and ensure that you communicate these standards to end users during training. Implement and enforce a data maintenance plan to ensure that your data stays accurate and clean. Consider assigning the part-time role of CRM Data Champion to an end user who will manage and promote clean data and adherence to data standards and conventions.

Knowledge Transfer and Effective Training

CRM solutions are only as powerful as the people using them.

In order to truly own and benefit from your CRM solution, your employees need to understand both its capabilities and its purpose within their company. This ownership process includes the transfer of knowledge from your consultant to the project team. Your project team must work closely with your CRM consultants to fully understand the capabilities of the CRM software, as well as thoroughly review all project deliverables and CRM documentation. Knowledge transfer works both ways. Your project team must effectively relay your company's CRM requirements to your consultants. Together both groups must work to properly align your people, processes and technology, and effectively deploy the new solution to your stakeholders. Effective training and documentation are crucial for knowledge transfer to the employees who will ultimately drive your CRM solution. Avoid the tendency to cut the time and budget allotted for training, as this tends to have a negative impact on the entire project. Instead, plan and budget for additional training in the weeks following your deployment to ensure that your CRM system is being utilized effectively.

Segment the CRM Strategy

Not all customers are created equally.

You may have noticed Pareto's Principle at work in your company - 80% of your revenue comes from 20% of your customers. You may already have service levels, account teams and processes in place that reflect this ratio. Utilize CRM to analyze your customers based on their actual and potential profitability, and other qualitative criteria. From there you can identify your most profitable customers and segment them into "tiers". Segmentation allows you to better allocate resources and focus so that you can initiate cost saving measures, yet still improve productivity and performance. Define and implement a plan to ensure that this segmentation remains accurate, and make certain that the plan is reflected in the design of your CRM solution. Consider aligning your front office departments with the customer tiers that you create. When initiated in conjunction with a Customer-Centric focus, segmentation enables you to analyze, interpret and report on your customer data with greater accuracy. This allows you to effectively evaluate corporate performance and make agile business decisions to determine future strategy.

Expand the value of CRM

Share data with your back office.

As the core of your front office operations, CRM serves as the hub of

MAKING CRM STICK

Sales, Marketing and Service data for your entire company. CRM integration with your financial and ERP software increases the value of these systems through the exchange of records and information. Customer Service, for example, could gain access to important account information such as payment history, while Sales could benefit from access to information such as inventory levels to help ensure accurate order fulfillment. Back office departments such as accounts receivable can benefit from the ability to automatically receive sales orders from CRM, thus eliminating the need for manual re-entry into your financial software. This invaluable exchange of information between departments provides your employees with greater insight, empowering them to make timely and informed decisions, and also helps to ensure data integrity. Technical complexity, budget, required resources and strength of business case are key considerations when determining the appropriate phase for front and back office integration. Once considered a dirty word, "integration" is increasingly becoming more realistic due in part to improved technology, a more simplified process and lower costs.

Best Practices for your CRM Solution

Take a lesson from your competition.

CRM and independent software vendors offer vertical applications for a variety of industries including banking, energy and transportation. Vertical software applications are designed to incorporate industry specific functionality and best practices. They are often developed using the industry experience gained from the vendor's past implementations. A vendor's best practices offer a valuable tool for your CRM project as you strive to gain a competitive edge through cost savings and greater efficiencies. Vertical applications provide industry specific templates, functionality and automation not present in your "out of the box" CRM software. This can reduce the amount of customization required for your CRM system, as well as provide a time and cost savings jump start to your CRM implementation.

Extend Front Office Functionality

Continue to build your CRM solution.

Horizontal applications have a broad applicability to business users regardless of the market they work in. These solutions build on your CRM foundation by providing existing users with additional applications and functionality (i.e., time and expense tracking and contract management).

MAKING CRM STICK

Certain horizontal applications extend CRM's benefits to other front office departments such as field service. Carefully determine the appropriate phase during which to integrate horizontal applications with CRM. Business Intelligence, for example, requires that you have a mature CRM system in place with an extensive and clean data set before it provides its intended value with CRM. Where integration exposes your CRM system to external stakeholders, such as customer self service via the web, ensure that your company has first fully embraced CRM and a Customer-Centric focus. This will minimize the risk of revealing any shortcoming to these external stakeholders.

Continuous Improvement

Become a believer in the world of "Kaizen".

This Japanese management strategy roughly translates as "the act of continuous improvement or uninterrupted, ongoing incremental change". Once your CRM system is deployed, you need to continually gather and act on employee, customer and partner feedback, measure performance, and manage and promote continuous improvement. Learn from your KPIs, metric evidence and the data captured in your CRM system to continually refine corporate strategy, set new goals and develop action plans to achieve them. Create a team of employees who will regularly examine your business processes and implement improvements. Put in practice a well defined process for managing changes to your CRM system. Keep vigilant to ensure user adoption and data quality, and continue to promote CRM and a Customer-Centric focus across your organization. Look to extend the power of your CRM system in future phases through the addition of new modules, integration to other applications and the rollout to additional stakeholders.

2004 © Tom Amerongen. All rights reserved.

MAKING CRM STICK

Are You Firing On All Cylinders?: A CRM Checklist – Jeremy Cox

Customer Relationship Management as a strategy and business architecture is now well within reach of most companies, but the path to progress is strewn with obstacles and misunderstandings. This article is intended as a navigational aid to help the board find the right path to success, avoiding many of the pitfalls that have bedevilled corporate enterprises.

Introduction

Various analysts put the success rate of CRM as low as 40%. The main reason for this lack of success is that CRM deployments to date amongst many corporate organisations have been IT led and executed in a piecemeal fashion with few measurable business objectives and no governing strategy to achieve them. The climate has changed substantially over the last year and now more than ever clear accountability and a real return on investment must be demonstrated. Whilst most firms have embarked on customer related initiatives, experience shows that to generate a real return from them and move forward, the whole business strategy around CRM needs to be re-addressed. It is our contention that by doing this systematically, firms irrespective of industry, will generate measurable business returns. This checklist looks at the key elements that need to be on your radar screen, if you are to do this successfully.

CRM Definition

CRM is the core business strategy that integrates internal processes and functions, and external partner networks, to create and deliver value to targeted customers at a profit. It is grounded on customer selection, high quality customer information and is usually enabled by information

MAKING CRM STICK

technology. (Professor Francis Buttle 2003, Macquarie Graduate School of Management, Sydney.)

What this definition recognizes that many do not, are three things:
1. There should be symmetry between the customer and the firm's interests.

Advocates of 'buyer centricity' tend to forget this and weight it too much in favour of the customer. This is both unrealistic, and unsustainable except for charities and philanthropists

'Traditional' adoptees of CRM software on the other hand, fail to recognize the importance of the customer and worry more about targeting customers with offers via campaigns, cross selling and up selling. The key goal here tends to be to sell more at lower cost, but with little insight into customers' changing needs, this only delivers peripheral benefits.

2. Customer Value increasingly requires alliances with third parties and internal cross product/organizational collaboration.

In B2B markets especially, the ability to meet and exceed a customer's expectations often requires a solution that can only be fulfilled through partnerships or a network of firms. These can be ad hoc or planned. Firms that take a strategic approach to this will tend to create innovative solutions and offset commoditization with higher margins. The software industry treats this as a separate item – Partner Relationship Management or PRM. Our contention is that this is a vital subset of CRM and if treated separately is unlikely to be successful.

Advice from most CRM authors or 'gurus' ignores this vital network dimension. The assumption made is that all firms have full control over their value propositions, but increasingly networks are competing with other networks. Airlines are an obvious example.

Large companies in particular are poor at collaborating across product groups and find themselves targeting the same customers in an uncoordinated way. This irritates the customer and sub-optimizes demand generation investment.

3. Customer Selection is deliberate.

The aim is not just to acquire customers, and retain them for the hell of it. Financial services firms tend to be more consistent here, but many focus on

MAKING CRM STICK

churn with little thought to profitability of customers. This is especially true of Telecom companies.

Rarely do we find evidence that a firm has as its goal a clearly articulated objective focused on which customers to acquire, develop or retain. The reason for this is that many are unable to measure their current customer profitability, and so don't bother. This is a mistake.

Sponsorship & Leadership

Without doubt, a CRM program which is sponsored and led from the top has a much greater probability of success than one without such leadership. For CRM to work effectively, it requires the value creation and delivery mechanisms to be working in synch with each other. The promise of fine customer service and specific benefits must be matched by the ability to deliver; therefore the supply side must be directly driven by the demand side of business. Michael Dell (CEO Dell Computers) refers to this as velocity.

Few other companies have managed this level of integration and coordination of effort. For this to happen, someone with responsibility across the organization must take charge. Where CRM is driven by a departmental advocate – sales director or marketing director, this cross company collaboration is difficult to create. The challenge is all the greater where third parties are involved and it is difficult enough for resources controlled by the company, but which have been parceled out to different departments or product/category managers. Each has its own objectives which may not be line up behind company goals.

Insurance companies appear to be very poor at achieving this cross organizational collaboration. By offering an insurance portfolio deal, targeted at strategically important customer segments, for a lower overall cost, these firms would significantly enhance the lifetime value of their customers, win advocates amongst them and lock out the competition. Why don't they do this? The answer is partly to do with accounting on a product basis, and also a lack of customer focus; and finally no real insight into customers' needs and the customers' context, which drives them. This is further compounded by a lack of internal collaboration.

Customer Profitability Management

The business goal of CRM should be to grow the profitability of the customer base or portfolio. This drives shareholder value, as firms which

MAKING CRM STICK

have a credible growth strategy win the backing of the stock market and existing shareholders. For privately owned businesses, this impacts future cash flows, profitability and the size of the overall business. If your current CRM strategy does not have this as its core driver, then it is unlikely to demonstrate a measurable return. Jay Curry of the Marketing Institute in Holland has a simple refrain which is: 'Get 'em in, move 'em up (value to the firm – revenue and profit) and keep 'em'. He has developed a simple modeling tool which demonstrates, (once completed), the profit impact of migrating customers from occasional buyers to more ardent users. Accounting systems do not capture the cost to serve customers. Support is normally needed to help extract these costs and attribute them to customers.

In B2C markets, where consumers are often transitory, this is even harder to do. Numbercraft, a specialist mathematical modeling company, has developed statistical analysis techniques using advanced mathematics to predict customer movements. What this enables retailers and CPG firms to do, is identify customers at risk of defecting, based on their buying patterns. Kitshoff Gleaves, a specialist portfolio analysis consulting firm have also developed techniques to quantify customer profitability. Their experience shows that most organizations are simply unaware of the underlying negative profitability of many of their customers. In one case some 600% of the profit contribution came from less than 10% of customers. What this meant was that the rest were costing more than they were contributing. Most firms do not realize just how many of their customers are profit takers, without some analysis of the cost to serve, as well as the product usage. On many occasions we have found that the old Pareto effect that 80% of revenue and profits comes from 20% of the customer base is too optimistic. It's much worse than that. This is little more than a comfort blanket, which allows firms to avoid the effort of a more rigorous analysis which is required.

Customer Context & Customer Intimacy

The weakness of buyer centricity at the moment is its impracticability. Its strength though, is in its relentless focus on understanding not just the buyer's wants and needs, but also the actual context which creates them. For a business customer, this means understanding the underlying issues and challenges which the customer faces and which have created the demand for your product or service or both. Good marketing practices have always sought to do this. During the early 90's IBM lost touch with its customers and came in with the biggest loss in corporate history. Lou Gerstner came to the rescue, first driving as much unnecessary cost out of the business as possible, and then reorganizing the company to focus on key customer segments. This was an attempt to understand customers and build insights into the businesses which would drive product demand. This required new skills and processes, one of which was a strategic market management process which ensured that business plans were directly linked to the customer context.

On a very recent assignment with a mid sized American software company, focused on retail banking, we were asked to develop this strategic market management process and coach the solutions teams through it. After 6 weeks, it became clear that if the firm wanted to flourish and grow profitably, it would need to organize itself differently and acquire new capabilities, to meet the needs of mid sized banks for more 'packaged' products. It could acquire these capabilities through partnering with appropriate organizations, which were then identified. Those partnerships are now taking root and very detailed joint execution plans are in place to avoid the fate of so many alliances, which look good on paper but are easily blown off course. By segmenting customers and determining their specific contexts – drivers, needs, wants, and behaviors, a firm can determine the best way to create and deliver value. This process also flushes out the information requirements that are needed to support the development of customer intimacy. Rarely is this information found in accounting systems.

Customer Value

A fundamental goal of CRM is to generate superior customer value. Mindful of the symmetry expressed earlier between customers and shareholders and other stakeholders, such as employees and partners, the big question here is:

'What constitutes value?'

The real arbiter is the customer. Most firms like to think they offer value for money, with one or two notorious exceptions like Gerald Ratner. Value is one of those terms we think we understand but when pressed we all find it very difficult to articulate, unless we have the kind of insights generated by understanding the customer context. Richard Branson is a past master at building businesses on the strengths of this understanding, and shattering the status quo of traditional self serving practices, whether it is airlines, banking or retail products.

There is no generic standard method of developing customer value, but the

MAKING CRM STICK

following areas are worth exploring, some less obvious than others.

Benefits Delivered

Customers or consumers buy products not for their intrinsic value but in the benefits they expect to gain by using the product. This ties back to understanding the customer context. As basic products become increasingly commoditized, they can sometimes be augmented to deliver greater benefit to the customer. This might involve wrapping advice and guidance on usage of the product, or a reduction in complexity to make it easier for the customer to derive the anticipated benefits.

Price Paid - Easyjet and Ryanair have grown on the back of this strategy. Their pricing model, based on a first come lowest price basis, attracts early bookings and improves utilization of their assets. Sometimes a higher price can be of value. Stella Artois sells its product on the basis of it being 'reassuringly expensive'

Convenience - Internet banking and shopping on line is of value to individuals who lack the time or the inclination to visit shops. A group of normally competing butchers in Ludlow Shropshire UK, has banded together to sell their meat products all locally produced, online, forming the Ludlow Sausage Company. They have been pleasantly surprised by their success, and have collaborated with other local producers in Shropshire such as Hobson's Brewery to extend their value proposition.

Reassurance - Where there is a feeling of risk attached to a particular purchase, often the brand name provides the reassurance needed to help the customer buy. Other forms of reassurance are: tradition, guarantees, references, sale-or-return, and risk sharing.

Innovation - Sooner or later all products and services are copied by competitors. Firms which constantly innovate, tend to replace their low margin products on a more consistent basis than the more conservative firms. Being innovative and making this work for customers relies very heavily on deep customer insight as well as creativity. Domino, a UK manufacturer of printing technologies both laser and inkjet has led innovations in date stamping of perishable food, drink and pharmaceutical products. Their deep understanding of their customer requirements, including close collaboration with them, has helped them maintain this lead and they have been rewarded with growth. Their very strong customer driven philosophy and culture is a strong contributory factor in their success.

MAKING CRM STICK

Reliability - In many industries this is a basic requirement, and no longer much of a differentiator. In recent years in the financial services industry reliability has come under increasing scrutiny, where pensions, investment policies have been miss-sold or have underperformed as in the case of many endowment policies.

Image - Marks & Spencer has invested heavily in updating its image to make its range more attractive to younger customers. Swatch, built its business on the fun image associated with its watches backed up with lean manufacturing techniques. Many corporate firms have been fixated on brand development and portraying a particular image or position to attract customers from particular segments. As firms collaborate more with each other in order to create and deliver value, they are careful to develop alliances with firms which enhance their image or share similar values.

Quality - This continues to preoccupy firms, but like reliability is not always a great differentiator. In the case of food, the provenance of the product is becoming more important, as we acquire the more discerning eating habits of our European neighbors, and demand fresher, more authentic foods. The Ludlow Sausage Company is selling 'Shropshire', and competes successfully against larger supermarkets, because customers are looking for a better quality sausage and other locally produced meat products.

Support and Responsiveness - Sony Viao support line for consumers is not only very easy to navigate, but their direct follow up to ensure that the customer's problem is solved encourages loyalty. BTOpenworld provides its customers with a downloadable self diagnostic to help solve problems quickly. As a user, I found the easy ability to email my problem and see that an individual with a name had been assigned to support me, very reassuring and responsive.

Relationships - Relationships are especially important in many business-to-business markets. This tends to be of greater value to customers where there are inherent risks involved in the purchase and its importance to the company is high. The experience and insights that the supplier can provide as well as their empathy towards the customer's context help nurture loyalty and reduce the risk. As products become better understood, by the customer, and more packaged, the importance of a relationship can diminish. This also impacts how they buy and understanding the underlying principles of this will help firms develop their online and offline channel strategies. Getting this right significantly enhances

MAKING CRM STICK

productivity.

Organizational Readiness

People and change are at the heart of a successful CRM execution. Significant change needs to be managed effectively. The battle for hearts and minds is even more important than the decision on which technology to adopt. This is where leadership plays a vital part. The first hurdle is to convince employees that the desired change is in the interests of customers and that they
have a vital part to play which is worthy of their efforts.
New skills may need to be acquired as well as new mindsets. If the CRM program is not led at board level and if there is not demonstrable 'walking of the talk', then this can only increase cynicism. Measurement systems and rewards should also encourage the desired new behaviors. Communications of early successes as well as the overall plan are important.

Functions & Processes

A key change will be in the new roles and responsibilities that people have. The most notable change is likely to be a demand for much greater cross functional collaboration. This involves breaking down the traditional departmental barriers and refocusing objectives to ensure that the common purpose is met. In most cases this will require the development of new processes or the capturing and synthesizing of best practices, into a consistent approach and process. Experience shows that simply adopting a software 'solution' without laying this foundation, is likely to generate 'push-back'. Ownership is very important, and by including the champions of good practices in the design of these process and expectations of who will perform what, where and when; buy-in is enhanced. The common dilemma that many firms face is:

- Do we develop our own processes or
- Do we take the 'out of the box' processes advocated by the software vendor?

The answer is very often a hybrid between the two. Automating bad practice is a mistake. Many CRM software vendors have developed in the first instance processes more attuned to B2C environments rather than B2B. This was the case with one of our client's a major computer company. The strategic decision had been made in USA to adopt a particular software application in support of 'closed loop marketing'. We successfully represented the real underlying business needs to the vendor and they changed their application to support more relevant processes.

IT Support

Much of what you will read about CRM spends 90% addressing IT and only 10% on CRM strategy, people, and processes. We would argue that the 6 previous topics provide a path for successful adoption of IT. There are now more than enough applications out there in the market, to suit virtually any situation. Our guidance is to address the first 6 topics, and then use this to drive IT, not the other way round.

Benefits of getting it right & measurement

There are four major benefits of getting CRM right:
A growing and increasingly profitable customer base
Greater customer satisfaction and an enhanced experience
More motivated and satisfied stakeholders – employees, partners, shareholders as well as customers.
A business which is sensitive to change and is therefore more adaptive has a distinct and sustainable competitive advantage

Measurements should support the goals and be associated with each of these benefits as well as milestones to track progress in executing the plan.

Summary Checklist:

- Board level sponsorship and involvement in setting the vision
- Develop a customer portfolio goal to drive the strategy
- Understand the customer context
- Create customer value based on this context and examining different elements of value
- Organizational readiness – people, structure, incentives, communication
- Drive functions and process design based on the above items
- IT now has something clear to support. There may be some trade-offs between perfection and price to consider
- Track the benefits and execution.
- Finally, as nothing is static and the bar of competition is being continually raised . . . Learn from the experience and improve.

2004 © Jeremy Cox. All rights reserved.

MAKING CRM STICK

MAKING CRM STICK

CRM Reality Check!: Three Questions to Ask About Customer Relationship Management (CRM) Strategy for Financial Institutions – Sam Kilmer

While unfortunate, many financial institution executives equate hearing the letters C-R-M with a wince of hype. Some technology marketers have been misleading and others, even if well intentioned, are misguided. Application providers claiming the next greatest "CRM technology" provide a confusing landscape for financial institution managers trying to assess the fundamental question – do they have a compelling need to change the way they do business? After sorting through the case for a change to a CRM business strategy, the next logical question is what technology – or more importantly, what functionality – will enable the business strategy. Lastly, what type of implementation hurdles are involved?

First Question: Is CRM a compelling business strategy?

First and foremost, it is clear that Customer Relationship Management (CRM) is a business strategy. In fact, CRM is one of many potential business strategies that underscore the need for any financial institution to identify and leverage its primary competitive advantage. Treacy and Wiersema, in their widely accepted Discipline of Market Leaders, point out that leading businesses have one of three primary competitive advantages which are identified and leveraged.

1. Operational excellence
2. Product leadership
3. Customer intimacy

MAKING CRM STICK

While all financial institutions need a minimum capacity for all three abilities, there is one of these three that should be the discipline in a successful business. Operational excellence typically involves both the productivity and the scale of a large organization, allowing the benefits to be passed along to the consumer. This is arguably reserved to the very largest financial institutions. Product leadership is a difficult proposition in what has become an arguably homogenous financial products market. This leaves Customer intimacy as the most viable primary competitive advantage for most financial institutions. In the view of the pre-eminent industry researcher on the topic, Robert Landry of the Tower Group, the choice is clear.

"Banks are going to have to gain the scale to be a low-cost producer or follow a relationship strategy aimed at expanding wallet share", notes Landry. Simply put, a financial institution's board should pursue one of two alternative courses of long-term strategic action: Leverage a CRM business strategy to be the custodian of the customer or consider the necessary mergers or acquisitions to become a large national provider. For most banks and credit unions in the U.S., that choice makes CRM the compelling business strategy.

Second Question: What type of technology – or functionality – do I need to implement a CRM business strategy?

Customer Relationship Management is truly a pervasive change in the way of conducting business for a typical bank or credit union. It takes quite a bit of coordination – enabled by technology – to pull off the strategy successfully. According to Tower Group's Kathleen Khirallah, "The Financial Institution with a CRM strategy should be constantly asking itself about how it handles the next interaction with each customer regardless of the point of delivery. What experience do we want this customer to have?"

And, according to Gartner's Kimberly Collins, "To develop a CRM strategy that generates a profit, a financial institution will have to consider a variety of applications". But, sorting out these applications is a challenge.

Applications in the functional areas of front-end or platform, business intelligence or analytics, and customer interaction management are seldom described cohesively and in their entirety. This picture is not always painted clearly by many technology providers, because very few of the providers offer the technology in its entirety. It is important to understand, however, that certain functionality, which crosses these areas, is absolutely required to implement a successful CRM business strategy in a typical financial institution. Some software providers, including Harland Financial Solutions, have packaged and integrated these applications. But clearly, without this "CRM base functionality", it would be difficult or impossible to undertake a CRM business strategy. You might even say that without these requirements, it cannot truly be CRM.

CRM Base Functionality

Relational CRM

Most financial institutions recognize the value of their personal interaction time with their customers. When it comes to positively molding the customer relationship, the discussion usually starts with empowering employees with better information and processes to improve the customer experience.

Relational CRM applications focus around the idea of interactions between employees and the customer or prospective customer. The Front-end CRM application is interfaced to and complimentary to the core processing solution. Whereas core processing applications tend to focus on financial transactions, relational CRM applications tend to manage interactions through a combination of contact management functionality, flexible displays of key client indicators, and follow-up workflow. The relational CRM application is interfaced to and complimentary to the core processing system.

A full documentation of service and sales interactions, referrals, follow-up, ticklers, escalated issues, and resolutions is managed. Normally integrated with email and the company intranet, all client correspondence is documented enterprise-wide. Performance management goals for both service and sales can be tracked to catch customers falling through the cracks, improve customer interactions in aggregate, and increase individual and group employee performance.

Whether in branches, call centers, departments, or a combination of these, relational CRM applications empower the employee to proactively deliver a consistent and always-improving experience to the customer. Since they tend to have a large number of in-person interactions, community bank and credit union executives usually have this functionality in mind when discussing CRM. Be aware that with a fully mature CRM business strategy, customer expectations are increased and, therefore, relational CRM applications become mission critical. Successful interactions become as important as successful transactions in day-to-day operations.

Analytical CRM

To proactively manage customer relationships, there is a critical need for information about customers, which is not generated natively in front-end contact management applications or core processing environments. Usually, this intelligence – routinely stored in batch-oriented MCIF systems, profitability systems, data marts, data warehouses, or other "repositories" – has passed through validated analytical processes which aid in decision-making and personalizing the customer experience. For the purposes of the Customer Relationship Management business strategy, there are at least four analytical pieces of business intelligence necessary: Householding, Profitability, Demographics, and Propensity Information.

Often overlooked, a consistent householding of account information from all sources is essential to a successful CRM strategy in financial services. Institutional information is often disparate and the core processing environment might not even be aware of credit card, trust, investments, or other information. Even if so, core processing environments do not typically aggregate accounts across the family household or business relationship. Highly profitable households can appear to be unprofitable customers and key decisions are negatively affected with devastating results. Or, a valued money market account holder can be mistakenly targeted as the perfect candidate for an embarrassing offer to open a money market account. With a CRM business strategy, mistakes like these are not options. Householding is mission-critical to the analysis.

Understanding the profitability of customers and the entire household relationship, likewise, is essential. Often, a CRM business strategy calls for segmenting and protecting the organization's most valuable customers. Much like the airline industry's gold and silver delineations, this understanding of "valuable" must be accurate, consistent, and appropriately used. While profit segmentation information has historically been used for research purposes in banking, the CRM business strategy often brings it front-and-center, on a per-client basis. Calculations of revenue and costs should be client and activity-specific and a funds transfer pricing methodology will usually need to be employed.

Consistently refreshed demographic information, such as age/income, presence of children, and homeowner/length-of-residence are extremely helpful in the process of proactively managing a customer relationship. Not to be confused with the static demographic information captured manually at a typical account opening, this information is normally obtained through a validated third-party and refreshed routinely to identify changes in customer lifestyle. Historically, this information might have been used for "segmentation" to categorize customers. Now, demographics are essential to business intelligence because of statistical modeling's ongoing ability to create "segments of one". Demographics are among the most dependent variables for statistical models that aid decisions in financial services. In short, lifestyle information is critical in making proactive decisions about next steps with customers.

Lastly, information really began to take on meaningful action with the proliferation of statistical modeling's ability to find propensity information. Modeling answers many of the big sales and service questions – Which customers will likely buy which products?, Who will probably defect or leave the institution?, Which unprofitable clients are most likely to be profitable?, Who is most likely to respond using which medium? – with total automation and with accuracy much greater than human analysis and judgment. This type of "artificial intelligence" is important because the customer relationship changes so often and those changes bring opportunities that only models can efficiently and consistently find.

Interactive CRM

A financial institution's customers utilize a mix of delivery channels. Interactive CRM, sometimes called Customer Interaction Management or Personalization technology, aims to consistently deliver the CRM business strategy across all delivery channels. It is the glue that connects the analysis and the message to the different points of presentation in the financial institution.

"CRM must be enterprise-wide and it must include your electronic delivery channels" according to the Tower Group's Khirallah. While Relational CRM applications address the needs of employees dealing with customers, a host of other applications usually manage the ATM, interactive voice response (IVR/VRU), Internet Banking, statement and mail rendering environments. Customer Interaction Management technology provides the universal business rules and standard messaging interfaces to ensure a consistent and effective experience across the enterprise.

MAKING CRM STICK

Interactive CRM technology could be viewed simply as the organizational traffic cop. What are we going to do next with this customer? Driven by Analytical CRM, but with real-time contact management and knowledge of the delivery channel being utilized at the time, the experience is personalized with information or media stored centrally or called at the individual delivery channels. The key point is that the message is determined centrally and coordinated, in real time, with other efforts throughout the organization. The next experience at any point of delivery will be changed, for example, if a customer responds to an offer on another point. Customer retention, service, and sales efforts are optimized and the results are measured for effectiveness.

In summary, Relational, Analytical, and Interactive function sets, working in concert with one-another and with the core processing environment, enable a CRM business strategy.

Third Question: What Implementation Hurdles Are Involved?

Gartner estimates that companies implementing a CRM business strategy, to date, have spent three to five times more on implementing the technology than they have on acquiring the technology itself. Couple this with Gartner's estimate that half of all CRM implementations have failed to meet their objectives, and it becomes clear:

Implementation is Everything

Among others, there are three key factors that determine the expense and success of an implementation of the CRM business strategy: Employee/cultural issues, customization issues, and system integration issues.

First, many CRM application technology implementations have arrived as part of an early sales force automation movement that has expanded its presence into a more operational, customer service focus. In many cases, the technology has arrived with an inherent sales tracking and incentive-planning objective. While sales tracking and performance incentives are consistent with a CRM business strategy, they bring many organizational and cultural issues to the forefront in the process of implementation. However, CRM application technology implementations that focus first on the customer, customer service, and improving the customer experience can avoid many of these cultural issues. Performance Management as a discipline is increasingly important and, certainly, organizations may wish to review and optimize their compensation plans to include meeting defined service and sales objectives. However, wading these cultural waters take time and implementations should not be drowned by them. The focus of a successful CRM implementation needs to be about service first.

Second, customizing a CRM-related application, particularly the Relational CRM application, is an iterative process. However, for many organizations, it is an overwhelming task just to get out of the gate. When an application technology has been designed to cross industries, fit various data models, and all screens need to be customized, the implementation and its resources can drag on for months and years. There is more than a subtle difference between a "customizable" application and a "customized" application. Banks and credit unions are remarkably consistent in the types of interactions and workflows they have. A "customizable" application can take months to sort out even redundant contact management tasks while a "customized" industry solution can be implemented quickly with minor changes to parameters and workflow.

Third, systems integration can be a struggle without either the right resources or the right support. A solid understanding of the connection between core processing, Analytical CRM, Interactive CRM, and Relational CRM applications environments is absolutely critical. Some providers have much of the systems integration complete which can minimize both time and resources. This approach to implementation can have the effect of inverting the Gartner estimate where implementation costs can be a fraction of the technology acquisition costs.

Ultimate Reality: CRM is Compelling, Can Be Practical, and Can Be Mission-Critical

Financial institutions are discovering the compelling nature of the CRM business strategy. Protecting valued customers is synonymous with protecting future earnings as an alternative to being acquired or gaining massive scale.

Solutions providers are beginning to make CRM a reality by leveraging both new and existing applications technology, packaging and integrating them, and bringing implementation costs down to a fraction of the costs of acquiring the technology. Systems integration and support will continue to be an ongoing priority.

Customer Relationship Management business strategies are coming of age in larger organizations at a time when they are now being born in credit unions and community banks. According to many industry veterans and some weary consumers, it's not a moment too soon. Disconnected efforts within financial institutions are a barrier to maximizing and protecting profitable customer relationships. Without a clear CRM strategy moving forward, there will be a diluting effect on a financial institution's ROA. As organizations are introduced to more realistic means of implementing technologies and as consumers truly begin to see tangible benefits, the CRM business strategy will be as pervasive in the financial services industry as it has become in so many others. Only time, and a review of shareholders reports, will tell.

© 2002 Harland Financial Solutions, Inc. All Rights Reserved.

MAKING CRM STICK

Chapter 2: Organization Alignment

> "Most companies truly believe they are customer-focused, but most companies are still very product centered—they still develop products and services and then search for customers. The challenge, then, is to shift their thinking to a more customer-focused world—where they create new products and services that follow the customer's lead. This is the primary basis for competition and competitive advantage. To make that shift, however, companies will have to change their core-operating model." (William F. Brendler and Sharon Vonk, www.crmguru.com, 5/9/2002).

Realign around your customers! Realign around your strategic objectives! Become more customer-centric! Don't pave the cow path! All this sound-bite advice is enough to make your head spin.

IBM's recent *Doing CRM Right (2004)* study showed that process change and organizational alignment together were key drivers of CRM success. Think for a moment about the other success dimensions mentioned in this book: *Managing Organizational Change*; *Building Commitment at the Top*; *Making the Business Case for Change*; etc. You can easily imagine a project plan behind each of these dimensions. With a little experience and a little imagination, you can probably articulate the project tasks behind those success dimensions.

Organization Alignment is different. Of all the CRM success factors to be considered, Organization Alignment is the most challenging. It is very easy to say, "We're going to change from being product-focused to customer-focused." But how is it accomplished? These days, the term 'customer centricity' conjures up all the same mystic images in one's mind

MAKING CRM STICK

that the terms 'change management' and 'reengineering' conjured up a decade ago. Customer centricity must be an art! – Something that the MBA professors talk about in class. But nobody has really done it, have they?

Organization Alignment, in the world of CRM has many different meanings. In some cases, it is about changing an organization's structure, and reorganizing around customer segments or channels or business objectives. In other cases, the realignment may be more a cultural realignment, or skills realignment. We have not attempted to define or prescribe Organization Alignment in this book. But we have tried to provide some thought-provoking readings to emphasize that for CRM to be truly transformational (albeit, transformation is not always the objective), change must be extended beyond the technology and processes. Transformational change (and dramatic results) requires a change in the nature of the organization – changes in the structure, culture, skills, measures, rewards, etc.

We selected five papers for this section. We liked the philosophy of Helen Mazur's *Time for a Tune-Up* – a reminder that a leader in an organization must consistently revisit the objective and realign as necessary. We felt that William F. Brendler's insightful *CRM Works - Only If You Create the Right Environment* provided some much-needed clarity around what it means to align around the customer. We also liked Brendler's key message in *Do You Want to Increase Customer Loyalty?* – enrolling a critical mass of employees behind a widespread change is the first lesson in organization realignment.

Robert W. Bradford, in his *Building Support for the Strategic Plan: Aligning Employees with Strategy* prescribes visible overlap of the new business strategy and the structure of the organization and future-state jobs. Finally, Raj Menon's *Turn Your Customer Data Into Gold* focuses on the concept of customer centricity. According to Menon, analyzing your existing customer data will help you develop a consistent, firm-wide understanding of your customer. Knowing exactly what your customers are worth is the first step towards developing specifically targeted and customer focused strategies.

MAKING CRM STICK

Time for a Tune Up – Helene Mazur

Direction

If you aren't getting to your desired destination quickly enough, it might be time to check the engine. When was the last time you evaluated your direction and alignment?

Many of us know someone right now who is treading water while they ponder their options to look for a new job, stick it out in a position that no longer brings satisfaction, or to start a business. Paralyzed with indecision, they do nothing.

At the other end of the spectrum is the business or professional that is trying to focus in too many directions at once. Afraid of missing an opportunity, they operate without a clearly defined product or a sharply defined target market. Trying to be everything to everyone, they dilute all efforts.

What is the best way to determine where to focus, and when to take a leap? While some people get lucky, the strategic planning process creates an opportunity to work through possibilities without wasting precious time or resources. When the process is done right, the result is a forward-thinking set of strategic objectives that builds on values, vision, and strengths in a way that will make you stand out.

The planning process starts by asking what you are doing today and what were the assumptions you made when you adopted the strategy? Check the assumptions and see if anything has changed. Throw out assumptions that are no longer valid, add new assumptions that make sense in the current environment, and check in with your heart. If you really don't care about what you are doing, you won't fool anyone.

MAKING CRM STICK

Strategic Alignment

It is nearly impossible to succeed without the support of others. Who is involved in your success - customers, employees partners, others? Do your business partners share common goals with you? Do they understand your strategy and share common values? Is your future direction ambitious enough to motivate, yet realistic enough not to discourage?

Good strategies depend on good implementation. Alignment within a business will fuel a strategy forward. Alignment requires agreement between interdependent people, processes, resources, and departments, with a focus on the customer. Some of the benefits that come from strategic alignment include:

- Reduction of conflicting tasks and initiatives;
- Time and resource savings;
- Easier decision-making;
- Clearly targeted external messages;
- More easily understood internal messages;
- Clear expectations, which translate to greater employee satisfaction;
- The ability to attract the right people;
- More successful execution

If there is conflict between any of the parts, success will be difficult. You may want to implement a new process in your business but have not developed people to respond positively to change, or your structure makes change difficult. If people have the knowledge necessary to create positive change but your processes make it too difficult for them to do so, the status quo will become easier. You can create motivation with an inspiring vision, but if the structure in your organization restricts innovation, motivation will be temporary.

Choosing a direction and aligning all efforts to match that vision takes confidence and commitment. Measuring progress in each area is an important part of the process.

Let's look at an organizational example:

ABC Company has a core strategic goal to increase revenue by selling additional products/services to their client base. The following type of questions will help them assess how well aligned this initiative is within the organization.

MAKING CRM STICK

Strategy

Does everyone within the company know that cross selling is a strategic goal, why it is important to the business and them? Are targeted results defined as revenues alone? What are the values the business represents that this goal supports?

When personal values are furthered at work there is no limit to the amount of energy that will be expended. When personal values are in conflict with work, there will be a halfhearted effort at best.

People

Does the organization have the competencies, resources and strengths needed for successful execution? Do the skills, and attitudes of the entire team support the goal? Are activities prioritized so that this goal is realistic and attainable? Who owns the responsibility of collaborating with clients in new areas?

Process

Does everyone have knowledge of the full line of products and services? Is there a training plan? Is there a fact-finding method or tool to uncover client needs? Is a team process is place to support the client with cross-functional services? Are systems accessible that reflect current client information?

Measurements

Are they measuring progress on cross training goals such as the status of product training, the number of cross sell conversations, and new revenues from existing clients?

Rewards and recognition

Are rewards and incentives tied to the achievement of key targets? Do performance reviews and compensation reflect the successful achievement of these goals?

Whether you are driving yourself or an entire organization forward, make sure you are headed where your values want you to go, and that you have a fully aligned support system.

MAKING CRM STICK

Copyright 2004 by Helene Mazur. All rights reserved. Helen Mazur is the President of Princeton Performance Dynamics, a business coaching company.

CRM Works - Only If You Create the Right Environment: To implement CRM successfully, you'll have to reorganize around your customer and change your organizational mindset – William F. Brendler

The complexity of modern business and the need for quick responses to changing conditions don't allow employees to go through channels anymore. But many companies have a hard time combining information, action and interpretation across old structural boundaries. Often, the result is decisions so untimely as to be irrelevant, no matter how technically correct they are.

When CRM works, it helps to solve this problem by meshing everyone together and focusing the entire organization on the customer. Often, people are forced to cross old organizational boundaries and to deal with others they barely knew before, collaborating to make decisions that affect the customer.

But here's the rub: If this process of integrating employees around the customer is not done well by the leaders of the organization, the results can be explosive. Ideally, of course, your company is already integrated around the customer and you are seeing the advantages of working in cross-functional teams. If not, CRM will force those issues in ways that previous waves of business change, like Total Quality Management (TQM) and re-engineering, never did. TQM and reengineering won't shut your business down-losing your customers will.

The new customer challenges demand dramatic changes in how you are organized. To ensure CRM is successful, integration is the watchword. And for some, this will require a large leap of faith.

MAKING CRM STICK

Barring the CEO, managers often don't have a cross-functional perspective on what is needed to change to a customer centric organization. The fact is that many managers are comfortable in their traditional, functional silos. Most were trained as functional specialists. What's more, many management systems further encourage and reinforce this functional specialization.

This traditional, functional view optimizes individual functions at the expense of customers and the whole business. This narrow scope, to which so many want to cling, leads decision-makers to attack symptoms in one function but miss the causes rooted in another. This happens all the time in the silos–sales, marketing and customer service. Making CRM work often depends on your openness to change and your determination to reorganize teams around your customers.

Today's losers are internally focused, functionally managed and management-centered. The future requires a new mindset. It will take nontraditional thinking for you to look at the way in which your company does business with your customer. Traditionally, customers have had to do all the work to get their problems solved. In many companies, the business units designed to serve the same customers rarely interact, and when they do, they seem at odds about how to handle problems or complaints.

A New Approach

To remedy this lack of agreement, you need to look for ways to improve cross-functional communication. Some assign customer accounts to teams of employees from various areas where contact with customers is paramount–for example, sales, marketing, product design, customer service and accounts receivable. A single company contact might have responsibility for all inquiries regarding credit, purchasing and order fulfillment.

Eliminating the layers of bureaucracy between customers and those employees best equipped to solve their problems is the first step in building cross-functional cooperation. As successful companies have discovered, the best way to streamline customer service is to provide a cross-functional team structure and training so that these teams understand the entire customer cycle–from the first contact with the company to the follow-up that accompanies a sale or an order.

Federal Express is another example of cross-functional cooperation. To

MAKING CRM STICK

achieve a more accurate focus on customer needs, FedEx integrated two groups of employees that usually never talked to each other, creating teams made up of information technology (IT) experts and sales representatives. In addition, senior management participated with the employees in this process.

This inventive approach improved the speed and accuracy of customer information by 30 percent. By bringing their different skills and opinions together, the teams were able to better define the needs of the customer and deliver the right services and products.

USAA, a worldwide insurance and financial Services Company for the military community, forms cross-functional teams who go to where the customer dissatisfaction problem surfaces. They focus on both fixing the problem and retaining the customer. The key is the teams are empowered to get it done, whatever it takes.

One of the major challenges in implementing CRM is resistance to change. Change does not occur in isolation. Only committed people implement CRM successfully. For a collection of people cutting across organizational boundaries to create the coordinated set of actions necessary to implement CRM, they must feel connected to each other. Building relationships across function increases trust, and when trust is increased relationships are increased. This is a mutually reinforcing pattern. If the people that impact the customer improve their relationships by working effectively across functions, they learn how to do that with the customer too.

Connected Means Committed

When it comes to understanding what goes on in the entire company, most people would say they know their jobs and the work in their groups. In my experience, most people don't understand the larger system in which they work. When customer problems arise, this unawareness can cause major challenges for the customer. The customer is often passed around like a bouncing ball because no one understands the whole picture and the extent of the problem, which often includes a number of different functions or silos. Issues are often solved in favor of one organizational silo, not for the good of the customer.

A company I know conducted classes for customers on its manufacturing process; its managers believed that having more knowledgeable customers would improve relationships. The thinking was that if the customers knew how the manufacturing process worked, they were able to interface more effectively with their counterparts in the manufacturing organization.

Unfortunately, people who worked within the company were not given the same opportunity to learn about how the whole manufacturing system worked. Some people had worked for 20 years in the same department; they were experts in their part of the system, but had little knowledge of what happened once work left their unit. They understood in only the most rudimentary way the impact their actions had on the rest of the system and especially the customer. They also did not know the impact their work was having on the rest of the organization. Because the organization failed to make the whole system more visible across silos, creating cross-functional cooperation, the entire relationship effort failed miserably.

When the whole system is visible and people can work across functions, a number of things occur. First, people experience themselves as a part of a larger whole. They are no longer just a job or a role, but connected to the whole system-for the customer. Second, they see where they fit in the system and how they impact the customer. They understand how the work that preceded theirs enables them to do their job effectively, and how their job affects the work of those who are next in line. They actually see the processes that impact the customer. Third, when people see where they fit, they are able to make connections with other people in different parts of the system. These links smooth the flow of the work and have a major impact on improving customer relationships.

Changes facing companies today require collective effort. I've never seen a change work that was mandated. People must be willing to make it happen. The desire to become a willing participant must come from within that person. To get CRM to work, the people who are implementing it must be willing to make it work.

Setting the Stage for Action

So here is the dilemma. Companies by their very nature need predictable outcomes. On the other hand, we know that it takes people who are willing, to make these companies work. Without people who care about whether CRM works, the company implementing CRM will never meet the goal of predictable outcomes regarding their customers. Caring about customers is a function of consent, not control. So, is it possible to create action that is based on consent in an organization that is designed to control people and outcomes? The answer is yes.

A barn raising is a perfect example of how a common task and collective

MAKING CRM STICK

effort causes predictable outcomes. In a barn raising, members of the community come together to help a neighbor build a barn. The community voluntarily assists their neighbor because they know that this task cannot be accomplished alone. As people work together to build the barn, the experience in turn strengthens their bonds to each other. When people commit to a course of action, they are willing to hold themselves and others accountable. They are often willing to put forth extraordinary amounts of time and effort. Committed people make things happen.

If you get nothing else in this article, make sure you get this: Logic and facts are nice, but that's not what's needed. Don't get me wrong; statements of facts –market share is declining or our customer service is terrible–can and do influence people. But that's not enough.

I have seen leaders speak eloquently on the case for CRM, with flashy slides, only to meet with yawns. Their belief that logic would win the day caused them to ignore the other more important element–the people's hearts. CRM means customer relationship management, and establishing a great customer relationship comes from the heart. Their people commit to action primarily because of their relationship with the customer and their own personal values. They commit to change when it is consistent with their own personal values.

This is why we have had so much trouble implementing CRM. The mistake leaders make when they seek to gain commitment is just focusing on the logic. They mistakenly believe that once people know the facts they will commit to making the necessary changes.

To give you an example, I work with a company that is implementing CRM and experiencing a great deal of difficulty. Customers are very dissatisfied. The top executives presented data to attest to these facts ad nauseam with little result. What they have failed to realize is that at the value level, people wanted to be a part of an organization that worked–one in which the current system, rules, inefficiencies and waste did not make sense. The logical arguments about customers and market share never addressed these issues. It was not until the change effort began to address these issues–did the people come alive and engage in the effort.
Coincidently and not surprising, there was a direct tie-in between these emotional issues and the logical issues of declining market share, cost and customer satisfaction, but it took the emotional issues to make the logical ones come to life.

Ultimately every organization must address what it's going to do

MAKING CRM STICK

differently so it can respond more effectively to its customers. This understanding cannot be spoon-fed. It occurs when people are actively engaged. I have seen repeatedly that as people come to understand the issues that are affecting them, they become excited about the possibilities for doing things differently. Creating this environment equalizes power. That's what makes CRM work.

If you want to implement CRM successfully, you have to create this environment. There are no "ifs," "ands," or "buts."

2004 © William F. Brendler. All rights reserved.

Do You Want to Increase Customer Loyalty? Align Your Organization! – William F. Brendler

The promised payoffs are high. Many companies have made large investment in Information Technology only to see the promised payoffs disappear into a black hole of organizational conflict.

What's missing? Organizational Alignment – the ability to link people practices to that same organization's business performance. It is a fact: Aligned organizations outperform their competitors by every major financial measure. It is the way you operate with your existing customers that has the most effect upon your ability to improve loyalty. The following case illustrates the challenge.

A Real Case

When the new CEO was hired he announced that the functional silos were coming down and everyone would work on teams focused on resolving serious customer problems. One top manager said, "The Company is losing customers at an alarming rate."

On the CEO's arrival, I was asked to help him and his direct reports find out why the company was losing customers and why they were having so many problems implementing the new CRM technology. I spoke with one of his direct reports who summed up the mindset of the top management group well when he said, "Some organizations like to embrace change to maintain market leadership, and others, like us, resist change until their customer's drag them into it."

MAKING CRM STICK

The CRM solution got lost in a tangle of blame, resentment and resistance.

It became very obvious to me that the new CRM technology was not working. They were losing customers for the same reasons their CRM technology wasn't working. As I began to interview people in the organization – the culture was clearly the roadblock. The sales people were complaining that few knew how to use the new CRM system. The customer service people felt it wasn't doing what they were told it would do by the vendor. Many were continually running to the IT group for help. A number of meetings ensued between the IT professionals, the vendor, and the management to discuss many misunderstandings. The management thought that by buying the new CRM technology it would solve many of their customer problems.

As they began to implement the new CRM technology, everyone was annoyed with everyone else. Many felt they were doing their part, working hard, and doing a fine job given the problems they had to deal with. The CRM solution got lost in a tangle of blame, resentment and resistance. One customer service professional said, "It is not hard to see why we are losing customers."

In one example, the company was having customer problems due to poor cooperation between the customer service and the logistics departments. Both departments reported through senior management in another city and had little direct communication between the two groups. They thought they could mediate the relationship electronically. But they found, as one manager put it, "There are no technical solutions for people problems." They learned that technology couldn't compensate for the lack of people interaction and participation when that interaction is needed for the success of a new technology.

What happened here was mostly a people problem. The customer service people hadn't been brought into the initial CRM project development phase and had to deal with the new system that was dropped in their laps. The technical people were given the technology and told to make it work, without any established strategy for resolving issues that might arise. The sales people were told to figure out how to uses it quickly to save customers they hadn't lost yet. The top management team saw the CRM technology as another IT project – that should be managed by the IT department.

MAKING CRM STICK

"I never realized the extent of the change we have to make."

When I talked to the management team they were very frustrated about the amount of resistance they encountered. They clearly did not think that by bringing a new CRM technology in they would need to ask their employees to change. One top manager said, "I never realized the extent of the change we have to make." One of the sales professionals said, "People are strongly resisting because they have no way of knowing if they'd like the new way better than the old or if their status would remain the same. They think they're going to lose their comfortable work systems."

What they all found out late into the implementation was that not only did they have to deal with significant elements of the change process – they also had to shift their understanding of what their work would be. The changes now required that they had to work across functional silos to successfully implement the new CRM technology. Even though the CEO said the silos are coming down there was so much resistance it caused a great deal of difficulty communicating with other departments. A sale's professional sum up the challenge, "How do they expect us to deal with this mess when the management team doesn't know how to resolve conflicts. The whole company lacks a common method to work together to reform our customer problems." Another said, "Hoarding information is the norm here. Individuals within units don't speak with each other and divisions don't share information."

One of the managers said, "We were not given any training on teamwork, so everyone had differing ideas about what teamwork means and still do. When the new CEO took over one of my colleagues simply announced, 'Now we're going to work on teams and here are the issues.' What ensued was chaos. We all wondered why everyone is very frustrated – it's because we never interacted with each other in teams, there was little trust."

The new CEO realized that he had to align the culture and the strategic direction if he was going to change customer defections. He also believe he had limited time to accomplish this feat. He turned to a new approach a series of workshops that focus on aligning the organization in real time rather than 12 to 24 months.
The workshops are short, intense collective efforts to telescope time frames and promote new behaviors that the company needed to achieve to solve their customer retention problems. For instance, the first workshop was charged with reversing the erosion of market share by changing the culture. The second workshop was charged with improving customer retention. But instead of two years to analyze the plan the new CEO gave the workshop

MAKING CRM STICK

groups 60 days to produce results.

In effect, the new CEO created a way to stop and get off the merry-go-round to take time to change the company. Composed of cross-functional and multi-level participants reflecting the stakeholders groups that would implement the solutions, the workshops were headed by informal leaders and assisted by our facilitators who helped clarify the workshops charge to break through ingrained mind-sets and assumptions that would hinder change. No one had the answer – the workshop groups were told they must generate it.

The CEO said, "For our people to thrive in this workshop environment we must first give them a chance to air their concerns and get their input regarding what needs to change. Our people need to be encouraged to discuss their personal issues, fears, annoyances, and hopes. To me these include questions such as:

- How will my job change?
- Will we work together in teams?
- How will the teams be formed?
- What will my job be once the new CRM process is a part of our daily work system?
- How will I address issues about my job if I'm uncomfortable with the new changes?
- What if we have problems working together – how do we resolve them?

Our main objective as a leadership team is to incorporate our people's personal issues with their professional issues into a dialogue about improving our customer problems."

The workshops fostered a team environment that diffused dysfunctional conflict and created a cross-functional environment that could be transferred to their real organization.

Everyone has heard the old truth about human nature. People are more likely to cooperate with a plan they helped develop. For this organization to succeed they needed to learn how to change. They needed to experience real collaboration. The workshops fostered a team environment that diffused dysfunctional conflict and created a cross-functional environment that could be transferred to their real organization. This process enabled a large group they selected to develop a set of strategies that they would themselves implement. It is a fact that an organization that effectively collaborates is aligned.

MAKING CRM STICK

Participants needed coaching to get through the eye of this emotional needle and gain the confidence to pursue bold and original ideas. The first workshop began to build strength by gathering a base of facts that strengthened cohesion. Regular debriefings fostered a daily mixture of hardships and insights. Developing an initial team point of view was the jumping- off point for action. It is a fact – the faster the participant's get into action the faster they learn.

While the CEO saw these workshops as a "safe haven" for participants, in the beginning, it was a pretty uncomfortable place to be. They usually felt they were walking on a tightrope between results that were too timid or overly bold. This group followed the same pattern as other workshop groups did – nine times out of ten the workshop participants take the courageous route.

They suddenly hit on an idea. They proposed acting out a strategy in cooperation with two of their best customers and inviting senior management to take part. The workshop group spent an exhausting and exhilarating week packaging its menu for services, notifying parties of the offering, and setting up a simulated facility, complete with business services and refreshments. Senior managers were kept in the loop and were invited to see the idea put to the test. On the appointed day the group sold double the normal amount of services and products at premium prices.

Hardly a surprise, once the customers had tasted their V.I.P. service, they wanted more, prompting the company decided to roll out the services to their most profitable customers. This now contributes ten times more to the total net income – and the delivery team is known for its innovation and responsiveness.

The final result came last year where they had a net gain of customers. They finally got the CRM technology running only to find out it wasn't what they needed to improve customer loyalty. The CEO said to the group, "What else is possible if we put this kind of effort into everything we do."

From this experience both the workshop participants and senior management learned a crucial lesson: enrolling a critical mass of employees behind the widespread change is the first lesson in aligning an organization. Each took full responsibility for changing the culture by grounding its work in the reality of action. As one participant said, "That's the only way we would have ever changed." Another participant said, "We're not following a predetermined plan forced on us by management."

MAKING CRM STICK

Increasingly, corporate leaders are realizing they need something that will help them create breakthroughs, not just in the current ways of doing business, but also in rethinking what their businesses could become. That is, companies that want to internalize the disciplines of the workshops will become not simply more successful but more capable to respond to new opportunities. The workshops proved to be an essential means of breaking the gridlock that prevents organization alignment and significant business results.

Copyright © 2004 by William F. Brendler. All rights reserved.

Bill Brendler teaches managers and teams how to align their organizations to improve customer loyalty. He helps companies turn around customer retention problems through his organizational alignment strategies and techniques. Bill has written numerous articles and is quoted extensively in top business publications. He has written a best selling online book and is a keynote speaker at industry trade shows around the world. The workshops sited in the article are designed and implemented by Bill's firm – Brendler Associates in Austin, Texas.

Building Support for the Strategic Plan: Aligning Employees with Strategy – Robert W. Bradford

One of the most common difficulties companies face in strategic planning is turning their vision into a reality. To transform your organization into the one you envision takes more than great strategy and implementation, you also need to make the strategy an integral part of the very fiber of your organization. When we speak of this idea, we usually use the phrase "strategic alignment." Aligning everyone in your organization with your strategy is one of the most important things you can do beyond formulating and implementing great strategies. Alignment will make it much easier for your management team to push the organization in the direction you intend. Without good alignment with the strategy, every bit of forward motion will be a struggle.

As an example, consider a retail computer store. If you are running such a store, you probably want employees who appeal to specialty customers. Helpful, cheerful and courteous employees will encourage these customers to return, even if the prices are a little higher than other stores nearby. Rude, sullen employees who don't know how to help customers will drive customers away. If you have a good staff in a store, you won't have to work as hard to get customers to return. If your staff is really excellent, you may even get some word of mouth advertising. While this may cost a little more in terms of the compensation you offer employees, you will get a payoff in the form of a loyal specialty customer base.

Aligning everyone in your organization with your strategy is one of the most important things you can do . . .

Specialty stores need specialty salespeople - this much is obvious - but your strategies may introduce a twist into your thinking. Let's say there are

MAKING CRM STICK

two kinds of specialty computer stores: those that appeal to neophytes and those that appeal to technologically oriented users. If your strategy is to be a neophyte-oriented store, you want your staff to be good at hand-holding, explaining technology, and patiently answering simple questions. Deep technical knowledge may be less important than the ability to reassure customers who might otherwise be fearful about computers.

At the more sophisticated store, you want a very different sort of employee. Employees who are very knowledgeable about the product will be much more valuable, and a willingness to figure out answers to difficult questions will keep the specialty "power user" coming back. The wrong person in the wrong store will be a disaster in either case, despite the fact that both might be specialty computer stores.

Imagine a new computer user encountering a sales person who is just right for the Techie store. The Techie salesperson will overwhelm the neophyte with information about AGP slots, frontside bus clock speed, and BIOS configurability (most of which most computer users don't need to - or want to - know). The new user will likely go along with this, but may not make the purchase, simply because the salesperson has only convinced him or her that this is indeed a very complicated purchase. Even if he or she does buy that day, you may never see that customer again (if there is a choice) because the experience was more frightening than reassuring. This is a problem in three ways: it's bad for your store, it's bad for the customer, and it's bad for the career of a salesperson who would be really good - in another store.

How do we get this alignment? There are five basic steps that you must take to assure your employees are aligned with your company's strategies.

First, employees must have the conceptual tools required for good strategic thinking about their work.

Second, employees must understand the strategy.

Third, strategic alignment needs to be built around the structure of the organization.

Fourth, strategy must be reflected in the structure of individual jobs - especially those in critical areas.

Fifth, you must have buy-in to the strategy.

MAKING CRM STICK

Let's look at each of these requirements.

First, strategic alignment can only work if the employees already have the tools required for good strategic thinking. This is because employees must be capable of making decisions with strategic impact in order to be aligned with the company's strategy. Anything less than this calls for a strategy that treats people as machines. While such strategies have worked in the past - one could argue they were the foundation of the industrial revolution - they cannot work in places where labor costs are above the absolute minimum. These tools include examples, role models, and training. This does not mean that every employee needs to be a great strategic thinker, but employees must be able to understand how their work fits into the success of the organization.

Another thing to do to get people on board is to make sure your people understand enough of the basics of business that they can see how the strategy is going to make them better off, increase their job security, increase the likelihood that they get promotions, and how it will increase the likelihood that they see pay increases in the future. Without these conceptual tools, it will be much more difficult to get buy-in and intelligent support of the strategy from an employee. Several companies with whom we have worked have had well-designed performance compensation systems fail simply because the employees didn't understand income statements.

The second item, understanding the strategy, can only happen if employees have the conceptual tools covered in the previous paragraphs. This is mostly necessary because good strategy requires focus. There are three main ways to satisfy customers: price, quality (in the broad sense, including product features, technology, packaging and a host of other value-adding features), and service (again, in a broad sense, including delivery, support, etc.).

In a strategically focused organization, there are fewer ways to satisfy the customer. In simple terms, a company that targets specialty customers will excel in quality and/or service, but will likely be middle of the road or worse at price. Commodity companies excel at price; but usually fall down on quality or service, and sometimes both. "Front line" employees - those that have contact with customers - often want to please customers by offering satisfaction in these three ways, but to fit with the focus of the company usually should be willing to leave some customers dissatisfied (for example, a Rolls Royce salesperson should not get upset that a customer didn't buy because he/she did not like the price). Without a clear

MAKING CRM STICK

understanding of the strategy, this kind of alignment is impossible, especially when "front line" employees are far removed from the strategic planning process.

It's very important that the way you hire, train, compensate and retain the employees you have in key strategic areas works with your strategies.

Third, organizational structure can greatly help or hinder strategic alignment. There are several ways this can happen, but let's look at one example. It's very common in larger organizations to find a "silo effect", where the organization is very effective vertically within a department or division, yet lacks efficiency and flexibility in activities which require cross-departmental cooperation. This effect will play in your favor if you create these "silos" around areas which may become separate strategic business units, but may present obstacles to integrating an acquired company, or tackling organization-wide strategic change in areas like quality or IT, which typically require cross-functional teams to succeed.

Some very successful organizations, such as Hewlett-Packard, have taken this concept into account by creating "matrix" organizational structures. These structures attempt to break down "silo" walls by creating reporting structures by both operational function (i.e. manufacturing, accounting) and market or product (i.e. home office printers, banking industry).

The fourth item, job structure, is a pretty broad topic. It's very important that the way you hire, train, compensate and retain the employees you have in key strategic areas works with your strategies. If you target commodity customers, for example, you definitely want all these things to reflect your commodity orientation. For example, in your hiring you want to be hiring people with an eye towards the fact that they might be driving costs up or down through their skills. Your commodity outlook is going to be reflected in one of two ways: either you want high-quality people who by virtue of their quality and productivity keep your costs down or you want cheap people who will keep your costs down simply because they cost less to pay.

Any place where you are hiring smart expensive people, you want to be sure you can use the skills of those people to drive your costs down; otherwise all you're doing is driving your cost up. On the other hand, if you have a specialty strategy, you definitely want to be looking for people who add value to your product or service, so smart expensive people in your company will need to add value commensurate with the cost of hiring them. At the same time, you may have ways to add value with inexpensive people and if you do, you need to manage them to think about the customer and the product or service the right way. This is especially important because inexpensive people may have difficulty understanding certain specialty marketplaces. In any case, you need to remember that you will be challenged by the cost of rejecting otherwise well-qualified job applicants who won't fit with your strategy.

A major challenge that companies face beyond this is the tendency to use specialty people in places where they should use commodity ones - or vice versa. In a commodity company, this drives costs up, and the potential for added value is lost on the targeted commodity customers. In specialty companies, commodity people and commodity job structures drive value out, which will devalue your offering and drive specialty customers away. There is no question that matching employees and their jobs to strategy has a big payoff.

Fifth item: buy-in. If you have an employee who thinks the strategy isn't good, you won't have alignment no matter what you do. The first two items, tools and communication, will go a long way towards getting buy-in, but there are people who just won't buy into some strategies - especially if they are smart. The techie salesperson in the new-user computer store may not buy into the strategy of targeting new users as a market. This makes sense, as the strategy doesn't fit with the salesperson's skill set - but it will create problems for both the employee and the company.

Often, this kind of buy-in problem arises as the result of a failure to fit the job design to the strategy, or some related activity, such as hiring. Occasionally, however, you will find some employees just don't buy in to the strategy. In a non-strategic position, it might be possible to overlook a lack of buy-in, but this can be a real problem in a strategic position, especially one on the "front line". It's always useful to ask yourself if the lack of buy-in stems from a valid objection to the strategy (front line employees do have a unique perspective on the customer, after all). If this is not the case, you - and your employee - will be best off parting ways as soon as possible, since such a basic strategic conflict won't be good for either your company or the employee's career.

Even if the employee performs, not adhering to strategy will cause basic problems and conflicts which will hinder that person's growth. Achieving buy-in is a toughie, because, unless people come up with the idea themselves, it is going to be very hard for them to feel bought in. In addition, it's hard to get people to feel bought into a strategy that might not always be in their best interest. It is also difficult to get people to feel

MAKING CRM STICK

bought in to a strategy that doesn't improve their job security.

Getting people to buy into a strategy means, in part, you have to get them to believe in it. This means the strategy itself has to have some credibility with your employees. It's much easier to add credibility in a company where management puts the money where their mouth is and is willing to spend a little extra money to make employees happier and make working conditions better for people. Probably the most difficult situation is when you're in a company that has a lot of employees who are paid at the lower end of the pay scale. Often, input from these people is strategically critical and they have a critical effect on the way your products or services are created, delivered and perceived by your customers. The fact that these people aren't making a lot of money to begin with usually means that they're willing to consider anything management says as suspect. It's hard for these people to believe that management is on their side.

An interesting challenge for you as a leader in this position is to ask yourself "How could I be happy paying these people a lot more than they're currently getting paid?" What would it take? It doesn't always take pay, but if you can't offer pay, you need to offer a real and valuable substitute.

Let's say you are in a situation where you just can't offer pay. For example, if you're facing heavy price competition from overseas, extracting extra value from the marketplace may become significantly more difficult. It's easy to get people really excited about strategy if they participated in creating it. Also people may be very excited about your strategy if they understand and believe in the concepts involved. Of course an ideal way to get people aligned with strategy is to make it their strategy. Buy-in is much easier if you can actually make your strategy a strategy that employees made up themselves. This is one of the reasons why we push for involvement in the strategic planning process for as many people as is practical.

There are limits to what is practical. We have always taught that it's really difficult to have effective, efficient strategic planning meetings when you have too many people as well as when you have too few people. What you want to look for are ways to make people feel like they are contributing to the strategic decision-making process, even when there are not directly involved in the decision-making part of the process.

Our experience has been that companies that take these few simple steps to build alignment between their employees and their strategies find greater success. Clearly, you will find better support for implementation of your

MAKING CRM STICK

strategies and more effective day-to-day use of your strategies at all levels of your organization when you achieve alignment. This will make the difference between struggling to make your vision a reality and smoothly flowing into the future you have defined.

Copyright 2004, Center for Simplified Strategic Planning. All rights reserved.

MAKING CRM STICK

MAKING CRM STICK

Turn Your Customer Data In to Gold – Raj Menon

Surviving in Tough Times

You are probably in the same boat as many businesses all over the world today. The global economy has turned considerably sluggish and many companies are facing issues like excess capacity, a significantly reduced sales pipeline, and more demanding customers asking for not only cheaper, but also better and faster at the same time. Management teams in the United States as well as elsewhere in the world are faced with the prospect of cutting costs in every department from sales and marketing to operations, human resources and administration. Managers are actively evaluating options and considering opportunities to extract greater bang-for-the-buck from their marketing dollars or euros or rupees.

Are you concerned about any of the following?

- Increasing firm-wide profitability
- Increasing revenues from existing customers
- Getting more bang for your marketing buck
- Getting better customer satisfaction ratings
- Developing a consistent understanding of who your customer is
- Understanding Customer Lifetime Value
- Figuring out your Most Valuable Customers
- Setting a framework for consistent growth
- Focusing each and every employee and each and every activity to create Customer Value

It has been consistently and repeatedly shown that focusing on the customer's perspective and building deeper and more meaningful business relationships with customers almost always results in higher growth and usually results in higher profitability.

As you deal with the realities of the current market conditions, you have probably recognized the need for developing and/or refining a coherent corporate vision for customer focus. This vision should be internalized by all departments in the organization and should be understood by every employee. Then, and only then can each employee implement specific tactics in their day-to-day jobs in a manner that is consistent with, and that will facilitate achievement of the corporate mission.

This white paper outlines a framework for analyzing your existing customer data which will help you develop a consistent, firm-wide understanding of your customer and the notion of customer value. Knowing exactly what your customers are worth is the first step towards developing specifically targeted and customer focused strategies. We also outline seven habits of highly customer focused organizations - strategies used by successful companies to become and remain profitable.

THE IDEA OF CUSTOMER CENTRICITY

At first glance, the notion of Customer Focus seems to be a very obvious and ubiquitous one. After all, management guru Peter Drucker noted several years ago that, "There is only one valid definition of business purpose: to create a customer."[1]

So what, then, is the big deal?

Well, customer focus goes beyond simply focusing on existing customers and serving their needs. A customer focused or customer-centric organization is one in which every asset or resource of the organization is fully geared towards figuring out the specific needs of current as well as potential future customers and then aggressively, efficiently, and effectively fulfilling those needs. Every decision in such organizations is made after asking the question, "What difference will this decision make for the customer?"

The organizational structure of a customer focused company is defined not by some "convenient" or "arbitrary" internal definition of product lines or service lines or geographic divisions. Rather, it is based purely on the customers' view point. In other words, the company organizes itself not by products and services, but by customer needs.

MAKING CRM STICK

A CUSTOMER FOCUS FRAMEWORK

Our Customer Focus Framework, shown below, will allow you to develop a common, firm-wide understanding of who your prospects are, of who truly is your customer, and of how a contact with a prospect turns into the start of a relationship with a customer. The framework then allows you to develop a holistic view of the entire customer lifecycle and track the customer from acquisition through delivery (of product or service) and from customer support all the way through retention and referral.

Customer Identification

A consistent understanding of who exactly is your prospective customer (or prospect) is key. Whether you are in a consumer oriented business or a business-to-business company, your end customer needs to be uniquely identified. Also, realize that your prospect may not necessarily be the decision maker in the sales process. For our framework, we like to define "the customer" as the smallest entity that derives (and therefore defines) "value" from our product or service.

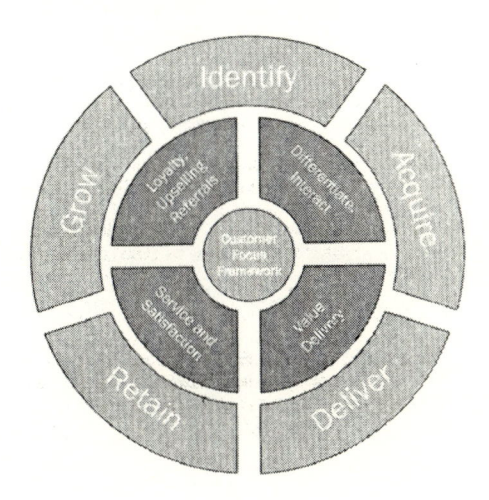

Customer Differentiation

As soon as a prospect is identified, most companies will have a database, preferably electronic, where information about this prospect and the interactions with this prospect can be maintained. Based on knowledge about the prospect and her needs and preferences, the prospect is automatically differentiated into one of several buckets or customer segments.

MAKING CRM STICK

This segmentation and any information you have about the prospect results in a set of established preferences associated with the prospect. For example, if the prospect signed up on your website, you may note that electronic interactions are preferred. Or if the prospect visited your trade show booth and requested more print literature about your Widget A or Service B, you know that is a preference and a need that the prospect has identified for you.

Customized Interaction or Personalization

Personalized, customized and consistent interactions with prospects are essential for developing a one-to-one relationship with a prospective customer. Personalization means that customers provide you, the seller, with "personal" information about their preferences and habits and you in turn agree to use that information in all interactions with the customer in order to serve them better.

According to Don Peppers and Martha Rogers, the one-to-one marketing gurus, successful customer relationships are ones in which the customers preferences are solicited, remembered (in an electronic database, for example) and consistently honored in every interaction with that customer.[2]

Remember, uniqueness is reciprocal. Just as you want your customers to see your company as being uniquely positioned vis-à-vis your competitors, so also each of your customers expect you to treat themselves as having unique needs. If your products or services are customized or personalized for your customers, it is an efficient economic exchange and the inherent elimination of waste can be beneficial for you as well as your customers.

Customer Acquisition

If you have done everything right till this point, there is a good chance the prospect will become a customer. You have identified her needs, solicited and recorded her preferences (and continue to do so throughout the life cycle), and you have a solution that solves her problem.

Value Delivery

The next logical step in the interaction is the actual delivery of goods or services to the customer. Most companies take this step for granted – because their product or service is what they are good at; that's what they produce and deliver, and that's the one thing they know and understand well. However, you must remember that as you deliver your product or service, in exchange for revenues, it is most important to remain focused on value delivered to the customer. Here, we define value delivered as the value gained by the customer through her interactions with you and your company in excess of what she paid for it. Note that there is no focus on pricing per se. As long as the customer gets a positive, non-zero value from the interaction, price is not really an issue.

To be sure, value is an evasive term, but what is important is that it is always in the eyes of the beholder (i.e. defined by the customer). Companies that want to remain customer focused are always obsessed with delivering superior value to the customer. Successful companies excel at finding the right mix of customers for whom the purchase of the companies' product or service results in a high positive value. Creating and sustaining increased value for your customer (while remaining profitable yourself) is the sine qua non of a sustainable, mutually rewarding business relationship.

Customer Service and Satisfaction

Superior customer service is often what differentiates one company from another – especially when the product or service itself is a commodity in the marketplace. Customer service includes all activities that are above and beyond the direct product or service that is sold. This could include things such as telephone support for a software product or convenient invoicing and payment terms for a service.

CUSTOMER RETENTION

Building customer loyalty implies repeat customers that come back to buy your products or services, and keep coming back. Loyal customers expect to be identified and treated differently, and will provide you with information about their preferences in return. They will try new products, offer suggestions for new products and services. They will trust you and tell their friends about your products and services. Classic examples of loyalty programs include Frequent Flyer Programs at Airlines, and Frequent Buyer Clubs at grocery stores.

Customer Referrals

Companies tend to systematically undervalue the power and importance of customer referrals. Referrals can be one of the most effective means of marketing to prospective customers, and as such it is important to recognize the referral component of CLV – Customer Lifetime Value. In other words, even if a customer is not directly responsible for a lot of revenues, s/he may be valuable because of the referrals s/he provides.

In the foreword to a recent book, Geoffrey Moore, author of "Crossing the Chasm," talks about the four levels of deepening customer relationships as being: Maintenance, Referenceability, Participation, and Evangelism. [3] When you have the ability to reference customers, you have a passive level of support or passive referral. But at the deepest or most meaningful level of a customer relationship – your customers may provide hyperactive support by proactively marketing your product or service without any urging on your part. Clearly this has huge economic implications.

CUSTOMER FOCUSED STRATEGIES [SM]

There are many definitions and interpretations of the term "strategy" in use in the business literature today. There are various popular definitions and interpretations of the word. However, the broadest and most general meaning of the word is synonymous with the word "plan" and involves answering the question "HOW" to reach a goal or an objective. Strategy has been compared to a bridge that links businesses from "where they are" to "where they want to be."

Michael Porter's famous article in the Harvard Business Review[4] defines competitive strategy as "being different. It means deliberately choosing a different set of activities to deliver a unique mix of value."

"Customer Focused Strategies" extends the notion of being different from your competition. We formally define customer focused strategies as follows:

A *plan* or a *road-map* for businesses and organizations to structure or re-structure themselves such that they become fully geared toward continuously figuring out and serving the specific, unique needs of each individual customer or customer segment,

and/or

A *vision* and *methodology* to ensure that all of a company's plans, activities and decisions will always address the needs of one or more customers and that any changes to plans or activities will be made after evaluating the impact of such changes on one or more customers.

Thus, organizations that are customer focused constantly refine their strategy by choosing a different mix of activities for each customer segment.

SEVEN HABITS – WHAT WORKS…

The following paragraphs outline seven steps that you can take or recipes you can follow to increase customer centricity in your organization. One or more of these steps may be particularly relevant or appealing in your specific case. *Go ahead, order à la carte, mix and match as you like it!*

1. Create a vision, align the troops

According to author Richard Whiteley, "A vision is like an artist's rendering of a building under construction."[5] Creating and maintaining a coherent, customer-centric vision for the company or organization is perhaps the most important step in the process. It is convenient if this vision comes from the very top of the organization. However it does not always have to be that way. What is important is that the customer focused vision provides an exciting inspiration for a future state for the company and that it acts as a guiding light for each and every decision made within the organization.

2. "Listen" to your customers' perspective

One piece that is often overlooked is tracking customer satisfaction. In fact, a May 2002 study summarized in the Harvard Business Review showed that surveying customers and asking them for their opinion alone increased profitability over the long term.[6]

Another valuable piece that is often ignored is the impact of employee empowerment. I know of one organization where there were a lot of good ideas and changes that were constantly proposed by junior employees on the "front lines" of the company. These ideas were based on customer interactions and customer feedback and were generated through direct contact with the customers. However, most of these initiatives never reached the boardroom because the top executives were perceived to be "closed" to receiving inputs. Thus the initiatives were never implemented and the company eventually lost a significant portion of their customers and market share because the whole company did not effectively "listen" to the customer.

This is extremely challenging to implement and is hard work. The bottom line is that you have to give your customer a voice within your company. And that voice needs to be echoed constantly throughout the hallways of your organization and should manifest itself in every decision that you make. And most important, what you don't hear is as important as what you do hear. Too often, companies see customers leaving "for no apparent reason" – because they have not paid careful attention.

3. Gather, organize and analyze your customer data

Ask any manager or executive where their biggest revenues come from and they will rattle off the names of their largest accounts. However, if you ask them for the names of their most *profitable* or most *valuable* customers – it is usually quite a different story. For most small- and medium-sized companies, it is just a matter of compiling data that is already available from your accounting department. A good start is to create a sorted list of all your customers by revenue for the current year, the immediately past full year and for the past five years.

These lists can also be partitioned by business unit or geographical region, regional office or even down to the specific salesperson, as applicable.

4. Build customer value models

The term "customer value" is probably one of the most misused terms in marketing literature. There are two possible interpretations of the term, both of which are equally important. One of course refers to the "lifetime value" of a customer which is the net present value (NPV) of all future expected profits from that customer. The other definition, of customer value, to which we referred earlier, is the net value that the *customer derives* from transacting with you. This is the differential of the value that s/he derives from purchasing goods or services over whatever the customer has to give up (i.e. the "price") to acquire those goods or services.

Needless to say, successful customer focused organizations concentrate on both of the above metrics and seek to maximize each for sustaining mutually beneficial as well as progressively deepening relationships with customers.

A relatively newer, and probably more appropriate term is a firm's "customer equity" which is defined as the total of the discounted lifetime values summed over all of the firm's customers.[7]

MAKING CRM STICK

Some experts like the Peppers and Rogers Group recommend identifying your Most Valuable Customers (MVCs) as well as your Most Grow-able Customers (MGCs). This latter group of customers is the most important ones to retain. You may not be making much revenues or profits from these customers today, but these are among the most profitable customers in the industry – and you would do well to steer them towards you.

Professor Ronald Rust (formerly of Vanderbilt University) and his colleagues discuss the perils of being slavishly product focused as opposed to being customer focused.[8] They define Customer Equity (the value of a firm's customers) as being the most important metric for driving strategy. You can read more on this topic in an upcoming white paper from Raj Menon.

5. Create your customer pyramid

There are innumerable ways that companies choose to segment their customers. Of these there are a handful that are commonly used. However, two of the most fundamental ways to segment customers are (i) by customer need and (ii) by customer lifetime value (or profitability). Successful companies as well as entire industries (such as banking) have recognized that segmenting customers by profitability can be a very useful tool which can provide valuable insights into overall company profitability.

"All customers are created equal, but some are more equal than others "

We have found that in many cases customer revenues and profits follow the famous Pareto principle. As a rule-of-thumb, only 20% of your customers are usually responsible for 80% of your revenues. Profits are split the same way as well – although it is quite common to find that the top 20% of your most profitable customers generate more than 100% of your total profits! That is because there are usually several customers at the bottom of your profit pyramid that cost too much to serve and are usually loss generators.

Jay Curry's well known Customer Marketing Method[9] is a very useful tool to start segmenting customers by profitability. Using this tool, it is possible to identify your most profitable customers and more importantly, to track these customers by department, by office or even down to the sales person level. Thus you can measure, motivate and reward your sales and marketing organizations for bringing customers into your profitability pyramid, moving them up the pyramid (so that they generate more revenues, and usually contribute a higher profit margin) and keep them in the pyramid.

6. Track retention, loyalty, and referrals

Customer Loyalty has been an area of much hype as well as much analysis recently. Sure, it sounds logical that loyal customers are great. And there certainly are benefits to building deep relationships with loyal customers. However, it is critical to examine this in the context of your own business. Every business is unique and would be well advised to build and analyze customer loyalty models which help identify the relationship between loyalty and profits. This was highlighted in a recent study on loyalty published in the Harvard Business Review, where four companies' customer databases were examined vis-à-vis customer profitability.

More important than retention and loyalty *per se* is to understand the reasons and motives behind customer loyalty – i.e. understanding the customer's loyalty profile.[10] As discussed in a recent McKinsey Quarterly article, by focusing on patterns and reasons for customer migration (i.e. from a highly satisfied customer who spends more to the downward migrators who spend less) companies can increase loyalty in a meaningful way.[11]

7. Appoint a Chief Customer Officer, but eventually get rid of the position!

According to recent estimates, as many as 40 percent of major companies globally now have a "board-level champion responsible for customer-relationship management and the customer experience. Hewlett Packard calls the position 'First Vice President of Total Customer Experience,' whereas Kintana refers to the 'Vice President of Customer Value.'[12] The titles may vary – but having a high level person within your organization as an advocate of the customer's perspective makes a lot of sense. He or she is basically the custodian of your most valuable asset – your customer base.

However, customer focus is not an attribute of the marketing department or the sales force alone. Done right, it is an attitude that permeates the entire organization in a concerted manner. The role of the Chief Customer Officer is to coalesce the customer focus activities in the organization, to make the entire organization self-aware of the voice of the customer and to energize the organization into maintaining its customer focus on a sustained basis. If the CCO is truly successful, his or her position should

MAKING CRM STICK

eventually become redundant!!

SUMMARY

Today, businesses operate in a very complex and rapidly changing world where the rate of change is not only the fastest it has ever been, but is also increasing. Companies of all sizes are facing a hyper-competitive environment where they are forced to provide higher service at lower cost. At the same time, the general expectation of what is *good* customer service has gone up dramatically. Market leaders such as Amazon.com, Nordstrom and Charles Schwab have raised the standards for all companies. The demands for Better, Faster, or Cheaper are now made concurrently, such that the operating word is not "or" but "and" as in: Better *and* Faster *and* Cheaper.

We have discussed the notion of a customer–centric or customer focused organization and discussed some reasons why this is so important today. Applying a customer-centric approach to all aspects of a company's operations is a foreign concept for many organizations – but one that is gaining rapid approval and acceptance as more and more companies successfully implement such strategies and notice a difference in their bottom lines.

Finally, advances in technology, have made it possible and quite economical for companies to invest in any one of a broad array of systems and tools to implement customer focused strategies via a whole host of (often confusing) software applications for automation, data gathering, data analysis, personalization, cost efficiency, and productivity improvement. Such technological advances have made it relatively easier and cheaper to provide personalization and customization in the online environment. These advances have been some of the key drivers for the movement towards greater customer-centricity or customer focus in the late 1990s and the early 21st century.

References:

[1] Drucker, P.F., "The Essential Drucker: In One Volume the Best of Sixty Years of Peter Drucker's Essential Writings on Management," Harper Business, June 2001.
[2] Peppers, D., and M. Rogers, "One to One B2B: Customer Development Strategies for the Business-To-Business World," Doubleday, May 2001
[3] Ibid.
[4] Porter, M., "What is Strategy," Harvard Business Review, November-

December 1996.
[5] Whiteley, R.C., "The Customer Driven Company," Addison Wesley, 1991.
[6] Dholakia, P.M., and V.G. Morwitz, "How Surveys Influence Customers," Harvard Business Review, May 2002.
[7] Rust, R.T., V.A., Zeithaml, and K.N. Lemon, "Driving Customer Equity: How Customer Lifetime Value is Reshaping Corporate Strategy," The Free Press, 2000.
[8] Ibid.
[9] Curry, J., "The Customer Marketing Method", The Free Press, 2000.
[10] Reinartz, W., and V. Kumar, "The Mismanagement of Customer Loyalty," Harvard business Review, July 2002.
[11] Coyles, S., and T.C. Gokey, "Customer retention is not enough," McKinsey Quarterly, No. 2, 2002.
[12] Buss, D., "The new CCO: Delivering Customer Care," BrandChannel.Com, June 2002.

2004 © The Menon Group. All rights reserved.

Chapter 3: Managing Organizational Change

After all these years, and our increased understanding of resistance and change, we still have many projects that founder due to lack of basic blocking and tackling of organizational change. We found hundreds of articles and white papers that covered this topic area, so it was difficult to choose which to include in the book. In the end, we settled on three readings that, although they do not provide the fool-proof approach for managing organizational change, they do provide some insights that will help you think like a Change Management practitioner.

A large complex CRM implementation requires a carefully planned and executed Organizational Change program. If there is not enough budget for the Organizational Change program, then the CRM program should be canceled until there are sufficient resources to do the job *right*! Whether it is called Organizational Change, Change Management or Change Enablement, there are several characteristics that experts say are imperative in the program:

- Organization Change should be a project work stream in and of itself, interlocked with the other project work streams via the integrated project plan;
- Responsibility for Organizational Change should be assigned to seasoned Change practitioners. It should not be a part-time job for the project managers, PMO, training team, etc.
- All components of the Change program (e.g., communications, training and development, stakeholder management, organization redesign, job design, knowledge transfer, user acceptance, etc.) should reside together under one whole Change program;
- Sponsorship is key! – The Change program supporting a large

complex CRM implementation requires executive-level sponsorship at the highest level. Look on the project plan for tasks assigned to executives. Don't see any? Then you should be concerned.

We felt that Stephanie Cirihal's paper, *Straight Talk on Empowering Change*, was an appropriate attention-getting introductory paper, since it addresses commitment and change from the human-level, and raises some of the key questions that are addressed in the follow-on papers. Rick Maurer's two papers, *How to Maintain Commitment to New Initiatives* and *Building a Foundation for Change: Why So Many Changes Fail . . . and What to Do About It* address some of the basic tenets of resistance, commitment and change that we believe every CRM business practitioner (not just the Change Management people) should understand. Maurer provides some useful tools to help put some structure around what most people consider to be the 'soft stuff'.

MAKING CRM STICK

Straight Talk on Empowering Change: What your mother never taught you about change in organizations – Stephanie Cirihal

If I have learned nothing else as a certified problem-solving Six Sigma Black Belt, I have learned how to empower others to accept change in their professional world (and hopefully their personal world as well.) The most important things I have learned about change have nothing to do with change models, but are based on a simple understanding of how people react to change. That understanding has led me to live by the "Three Truths of Change" that I would like to share with you here.

But first, the simple understanding of how people react to change. Simply put, very differently, depending on three factors:

- How much the change will disrupt their expectations or perceptions;
- How willing and capable they are to accepting the change, based on the above;
- Their individual level of control in the situation.

Additionally, most people either have a positive or negative predisposition to change, which means that they experience vastly different emotional states while going through change (you did know change is a process, complete with different stages, right?)

Regardless of people's predisposition, or the above factors however, you can minimize the negative impact of change by increasing the individual control and level of involvement of those who will experience the change. That's where the "Three Truths of Change" come in handy. In no certain order, they are:

People do what they create - the best solutions and changes I have implemented have involved the process owners, or those who end up actually doing the work, FROM THE VERY BEGINNING. So much implementation energy can be spared by just identifying those who will be most affected by the change, and letting them help design it.

Some people will NEVER go along - this goes back to people's predisposition to change as well as their willingness to change. This creates a bell curve of change classifications, and up to 16% of people will hide underneath their desks and hope change will go away, no matter what you do. Your energy is better spent addressing the people who will accept change, with the right approach.

Killing the messenger kills change - I have seen countless leaders punish people for simply telling the truth, which insures that a change culture will never get off the ground. If you want to know how to effect a culture change, for instance, stop looking at how to change the culture and instead evaluate what the barriers are to changing the culture. You must ask for and be prepared to hear the truth.

Finally, the first step to effective change management is to identify your stakeholders. List them all - everyone who will be touched by your proposed change. This includes internal functions and external customers as well. Then determine where each group stands on your change. Who will benefit from the change? Who will not? Look at the benefits and losses for each stakeholder group. And then ask yourself some questions about managing your stakeholders:

- How can you gain the support of unsupportive stakeholders?
- How can you maintain the support of supportive stakeholders?
- How can you use the support of supportive stakeholders to your benefit?

Doing the work up front to understand likely reactions and manage stakeholder expectations goes along way towards smooth sailing down the road when it really counts. Just think what your mother could have done if she had known that!

Copyright © 2004 by Stephanie Cirihal. All rights reserved.

How to Maintain Commitment to New Initiatives – Rick Maurer

While some might think that progress is linear – one thing building on another – change actually happens in a cycle. Each stage of the cycle builds momentum for the next stage. There is little information about the need for change, just some Random Incidents.

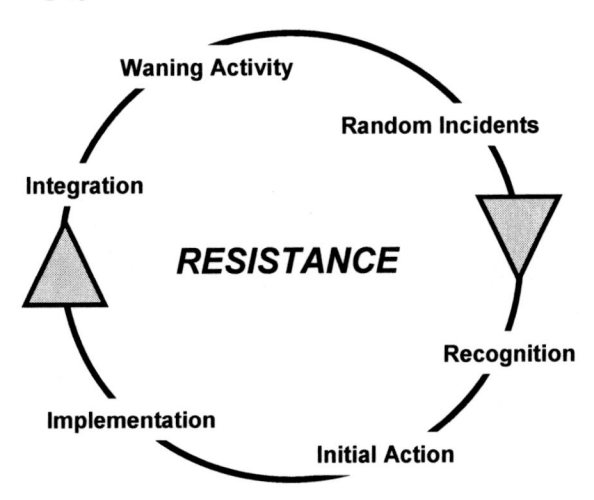

This cycle is adapted with permission from the Cycle of Experience developed at the Gestalt Institute of Cleveland.

- Recognition that there is a problem or an opportunity
- Energy builds as Initial Actions begin.
- The idea is rolled out during Implementation.
- The change is Integrated as a way of doing business
- The change runs its course and Activity Wanes.

MAKING CRM STICK

Keeping energy high as changes move through this cycle can be a major challenge. Once we recognize the need for change, energy builds during the Initial Actions stage and we want to get busy and do something right away. But, this initial excitement often wears off and interest and commitment begins to fade before we get to the Integration Stage.

To make sure that the change becomes an integral part of the way your organization does business, momentum must continue to flow and the organization must remain committed to implementing and integrating the idea. While there are no easy answers or quick fixes to do this, the following must be in place to sustain commitment to change:

Leadership: Someone needs to lead the change. This "czar" is given the authority and resources to make the change a reality. While the czar need not be a senior manager, he or she must have clout in the organization and must be an influential player.

Clear Contract: The czar needs to say, "I will lead this change if certain conditions are met," delineating what he or she thinks it will take to be successful. This means that the czar must have a clear contract with the leaders of the organization, identifying specifically what the leaders will do if, and when, the unexpected happens, and what support he or she can expect from them throughout the life of the project.

Beware of "scope creep": Many projects move beyond their initial scope. To help keep things under control, plan for the unexpected up-front by determining what you will do if the scope begins to shift or if conditions change. Unless the situation changes dramatically, it is important to stick to the original plan. If you must deviate from it, do so, consciously and purposefully -- reexamining resources, assignments to the project, and so forth.

Speed: Determine how fast you can begin to implement the change and still get the level of commitment you need. Does everyone need to be trained before implementation? Do all systems have to be in place at the outset? Sometimes, needed changes fail simply because the organization moved too slowly.

Ownership: Make sure that enough people within the organization support the initiative and that they feel a sense of ownership of the change. If you feel you do not have enough commitment and ownership to move beyond the initial enthusiasm for the change into actual implementation, then slow

MAKING CRM STICK

down and concentrate on getting more people on the bandwagon and committed to moving the change forward.

Copyright © 2004 by Rick Maurer. All rights reserved.

MAKING CRM STICK

Building a Foundation for Change: Why So Many Changes Fail . . . and What to Do About It – Rick Maurer

A significant number of organizational changes are doomed to fail. Recent surveys reported the following success rates:
- reengineering efforts: 33%
- mergers and acquisitions: 29%
- quality improvement efforts: 50%
- new software applications: 20%

These grim statistics represent a tremendous cost to organizations in terms of money, resources, and time. Failed change initiatives also take a human toll. Employees are left feeling discouraged, distrustful and reluctant to participate in the next round of failures.

What often goes wrong? Intelligent people develop a plan that includes a sound business reason for the change. The objectives are clear, time lines are spelled out, and budgets and staffing requirements are calculated. Everything seems on target. But, it's what's not in the plan that creates problems. What most plans lack are strategies for building support for the change.

According to a survey of Fortune 500 executives, the primary reason that changes fail in organizations is resistance. And yet, we seldom figure out ways to transform opposition into support. Face it, resistance is real. No matter how brilliant or needed an idea, resistance will occur. It is a natural reaction to change. It protects people from what they think will harm them. Leaders who close their eyes to resistance are inviting disaster.

There is a better way: Build a foundation for change. Rather than assuming people will automatically love your idea, add strategies to your plan to build support for the change. To do so, four steps should be part of every plan.

- Conduct a Change Readiness Assessment
- Get Others Involved
- Plan for the Inevitable
- Monitor Support

Step 1: Conduct a Change Readiness Assessment
A change readiness assessment answers the question, "Where are we today?" It looks at both past practices and the current situation. Below is a questionnaire that can help you begin that assessment. Ask a cross-section of people in the organization to complete it. Often, your own vantage point allows only you to see a portion of the whole picture; other departments and levels within the organization will give you a more complete view of where things stand.

1. History of Change: What's our track record handling change?

Low 1_____2_____3_____4_____5_____6_____7 High

The past is the best predictor of the future. If your ideas were met with cheers in the past, then it might be reasonable to expect that a new initiative will meet with similar applause. However, if past changes were nothing but headaches – if you had to fight, manipulate, cajole, and make back room deals to push your ideas through – then expect much the same this time. Low scores indicate a strong likelihood that this change will be resisted with great force. You will need to demonstrate repeatedly that you are serious – and that this change is important. People are likely to be very skeptical, you will need to be persistent.

2. Direction: Do people throughout the organization understand and accept the direction the company is moving and the values that fuel that vision?

Low 1_____2_____3_____4_____5_____6_____7 High

Low scores could indicate a conflict over values and overall direction. The people who must support the change may not believe they share much common ground with you. This is a serious problem. It almost guarantees that any major change will be resisted. Without shared values and vision, people lack a context for the change.

On the other hand, low scores simply may indicate a communication problem. In some organizations, values and visions remain secret. People don't know where the organization is going. Senior management hangs onto these documents as if they were sacred texts that only they, the high priests, can interpret. This is a communication problem that can be easily resolved by getting the word out.

3. Cooperation and Trust: Do people share information and deal with each other openly and with respect?

Low 1_____2_____3_____4_____5_____6_____7 High

Low scores indicate very serious problems. It is difficult, if not impossible, to build support for major change without trust. Since the opposite of trust is fear, a low score almost guarantees strong opposition. When people are afraid, they will either fight or lie low: neither response will give you the commitment you need to be successful.

4. Culture: Is this an organization that supports risk taking and change?

Low 1_____2_____3_____4_____5_____6_____7 High

Mid-range to low scores indicate that it may be difficult for people to carry out the changes even if they support you. Your systems and procedures hinder change. You must examine these deeper structural issues.

5. Resilience: Can people handle more change?

Low 1_____2_____3_____4_____5_____6_____7 High

People in many organizations are simply worn out by the number of changes and transitions they've been asked to weather in recent years. No matter how worthy the change, their opposition to it may stem from a lack of resilience, and not from some objection to the idea being proposed.

Low to mid-range scores probably indicate that people have lost their capacity to respond to another initiative. Even though workers may see the need for this change, they may have little energy to give to it.

So, keep two important questions in mind:

Is this change really necessary at this time? If so, how can you support people so that the change can be implemented with the greatest ease?

6. Rewards: Do people believe this change will benefit them?

Low 1_____2_____3_____4_____5_____6_____7 High

One well-used truism: What gets rewarded gets done. Unfortunately, its counterpart doesn't get as much attention: What gets punished gets avoided. For example, organizations that say they want teamwork but reward individual achievement, shouldn't be surprised when cooperation falters.

Obviously, low scores indicate strong potential resistance. After all, who would support something they think will harm them? If employees' perceptions are accurate, then you have a difficult challenge: You must find a way to move forward with the change and find ways to make it rewarding for others. If the low scores indicate a misperception, then you must let people know why they are misinformed. Remember, as anxiety increases, our ability to listen diminishes. It is likely that this message will have to be communicated repeatedly (especially if trust is low as well).

7. Respect, Control, and Saving Face: Will people be able to maintain dignity and self-respect?

Low 1_____2_____3_____4_____5_____6_____7 High

Low scores probably indicate concern over loss of respect, status or face. You must find ways to make this a situation in which all can win.

In my book on building support for change, Beyond the Wall of Resistance, I explore various levels of resistance. Leaders often hope that all resistance will be Level 1: opposition simply because people don't have all the facts. Unfortunately, most resistance to major change is Level 2. This deeper resistance stems from a fear of loss. Our slick Powerpoint presentations cannot deal with these deeper and more emotional issues. You must engage wary people in conversation. Be open and listen to their concerns.

8. Impact on Status Quo: How disruptive will this change be to the status quo?

Low 1_____2_____3_____4_____5_____6_____7 High

High scores indicate that people view this change as very disruptive and stressful. Get people involved because when they have some control over changes that affect them, the less likely they are to resist.

9. Skill at Managing Change: How adept are leaders at planning and implementing change?

Low 1_____2_____3_____4_____5_____6_____7 High

The people leading change need to be adept at such things as:
- creating alignment among diverse interests;
- listening: getting concerns, fears and interests on the table;
- articulating a compelling vision (or working with others to create a shared vision);
- anticipating and responding appropriately to resistance;
- communicating: keeping people informed.

If scores are low in this category, consider how you can develop change management skills as you proceed with the change. There is no shortage of books on the market that cover the needed skills. Consider working with mentors, men and women who have a proven track record, to learn their secrets. Training may be beneficial as well, but choose courses that demand you practice using change management skills.

Interpreting Overall Results

High Scores: Indicate that you are in good shape for this change and suggest that your organization knows how to work well with its people.

Mid-Range Scores: Reveal potential danger and signify the need to look into what is behind these scores. For example, mid-range scores on a category such as Cooperation and Trust might indicate a problem that is slowly developing. Take these scores seriously. You have an opportunity to tilt the balance in your favor by addressing these issues.

Low Scores: Point to serious trouble. The lower scores, the more likely it is that you will face intense resistance. But even a single low score can pose a problem. Treat any low score seriously because raising low scores helps to build stronger relationships with other individuals and groups.

In interpreting the results, remember that the actual scores are less important than the reasons people chose the scores they did. Responses to

MAKING CRM STICK

the questionnaire should act as a springboard for conversation about change and resistance. Conversations should focus on the experiences and feelings that accompany these scores. For example, if the CEO rated everything a seven (high), middle managers scored in the three to five range, and non-management staff rated everything low, there are a lot of issues that need to be addressed. In doing so, consider the following questions:

- What interests you about the scores?
- Where do you see patterns?
- Where are the points of greatest agreement?
- Where are the points of greatest disagreement?

Step 2: Get Others Involved

Everyone who has a stake in the outcome needs to be deeply involved in the change and should have an opportunity to explore and influence the goals and/or their part in the implementation. Anything less and you risk failure or delay.

Change strategies that get people very involved tend to do better than the more traditional methods that rely on raw use of power, manipulation, or overriding opposition. It is counter-productive to look at resistance as a wall that must be destroyed -- doing so may even make the gap between you and the resisters bigger.

Sure, you have probably used at least one of these tactics when faced with resistance -- everyone has. But, overpowering or destroying resistance implies that your way of doing things is right and others must be persuaded or forced to go along. Tension is created and resisters believe that for you to win, they must lose. Naturally, they fight back. So, while you might think these traditional battle tactics will destroy the wall, they actually reinforce it.

To move beyond the wall of resistance, don't battle it -- embrace it. You may fear that getting everyone involved and openly talking about resistance will only invite trouble. That's not the case. Applying the principles or touchstones listed below will not create problems; instead, the process will allow you to engage in relationships and strengthen support for your ideas.

MAKING CRM STICK

Using Touchstones to Involve Everyone

The most successful strategies to move beyond resistance and build support for change have six principles in common; I call these principles the "touchstones."

Build strong working relationships: Most resistance is linked directly to the quality of the working relationship: the better the relationship, the less resistance. HR professionals are busy; but, you must take the time to create relationships that are strong and based on mutual respect and understanding.

Maintain a clear focus: When resistance emerges and others attack your ideas, it's easy to lose sight of your original goals. Be careful to keep your goal in mind while simultaneously paying attention to the concerns of those who have a stake in the outcome. If you only focus on your goal, you will miss mounting resistance. If you only concentrate on the opposition, you will never know when you have enough support to move ahead.

Embrace resistance: You cannot move beyond resistance unless you let down your guard and open yourself up to those opposing change. Embracing resistance encourages employees to talk about their concerns and why they feel that way. When you are open to learning more about another person's view of the situation, you can find common ground and discover ways to transform the negative energy of resistance into positive support for change.

Listen with an open mind: People who fear they have something to lose are naturally reluctant to share their questions and concerns. By creating a climate of trust and openness, resisters will see your commitment to listening to them with an open mind and heart -- and they will tell the truth. I have seen resistance melt simply because the person implementing the change was always honest and forthright with people.

Stay calm to stay engaged: It is difficult to open yourself up to a flood of criticism. That's one reason why we may avoid those who resist us. The key is to stay calm and relaxed -- and centered on the issue at hand. As people raise questions about the changes, listen attentively and draw them out. Do not attack nor give in to them. Instead, use what you have learned to begin seeking common ground.

Join with the resistance: It is important to seek a neutral zone that attempts to include the interests of everyone. Asking three questions will help you do this: What's in it for me? What's in it for you? What's in it for us?

Listen for common fears and anxieties in the answers. Build on those similarities to find a solution that addresses the concerns of all parties. By doing so, you can transform opposition into support.

Step 3: Plan for the Inevitable

You've gotten people deeply involved in the new plan and they are enthralled with its potential. And then something happens that rocks the boat. Perhaps it's a disagreement over which department will get to control the project, or perhaps someone fails to live up to an agreement. Old animosities flare.

This scenario can be avoided with a little planning for the inevitable. Asking a variety of "What if?" questions will help you address things that could go wrong. It's easier to devise a solid approach to a problem before it surfaces than when it is staring you in the face. "What If?" scenarios allow you to step back and calmly play with possibilities without the risk.

Here are some ideas to consider:

If the groups have worked together before, identify times when they were in conflict. If they are new, ask people to draw on their own experience to identify potential conflicts that might occur during the change. Do not assign blame. The goal is to identify issues that could come up during the current change, not dissect past events.

Form mixed groups that contain representatives from a cross-section of departments and levels of the organizations involved. Have those groups take on the issues identified in Step 1 and develop strategies to address these problems should they occur.

Consider the five touchstones as you develop strategies. Groups should address the following questions:

- How can we keep our focus on the goal if this issue occurs? (Maintain focus)
- How will we summon the courage to stick with it, even if the going gets extremely tough? (Maintain Focus)
- What can we do to ensure mutual respect in the midst of this issue?

(Respect)
- What can we do to ensure that all the critical issues get out on the table? (Embrace Resistance)
- How can we stay relaxed in the midst of this conflict? (Relax)
- How can we promote the development of common values? (Join Resistance)

Have subgroups report to the entire group all questions, comments, and suggested changes.

Encourage the entire group to decide together which of these strategies it can fully support. By addressing potential resistance before it occurs, you often preempt it. People get the critical issues out on the table and make agreements before anyone feels a need to put up a wall or attack others.

Step 4: Keep It Alive

Although planning for the inevitable should reduce a significant number of problems, the unexpected will still occur. To be prepared, an effective plan should include the following:

A Way to Include Those Who Were Inadvertently Left out in the Early Stages

One organization did a fine job of getting various interested parties involved, but after the proposal was well into implementation stage, the folks in the mailroom balked. The mailroom! The leaders had never thought about the mailroom when they planned for this change. Those things happen. But, when they do, you have two options. You can keep on moving, crying "Tough luck, Charlie" as you forge ahead. Or, you can apologize for the oversight, and try to gain the support of those you overlooked.

A Way to Engage Those Who Have a Change of Heart

Often people will agree to a change during the early stages, only to discover that they aren't too wild about the idea later on. While it is easy to get angry with these people, this will do nothing to build support for your plan. People often change their minds once they see how much the new program will cost in time and resources.

MAKING CRM STICK

A Way to Monitor Progress

Your plan will no doubt include a way to gauge progress versus deadlines and budgets. But it is equally important to have a way to monitor whether support for the change is building. Some questions to ask include:

- How will we know that support is building for the plan?
- What will support look like?
- What level of commitment will we need at each stage of the project?
- How will we measure active commitment?
- Finally, Pay Attention

Most plans for change are linear: A leads to B, followed by C. It all seems so rational and sane. Unfortunately, support and resistance are ruled by intangibles such as enthusiasm, commitment, energy, fear and threat. These emotional issues don't lend themselves to neat A + B + C plans. Be prepared to work with resistance at every stage of planning and implementation. And, be prepared for support that comes as a gift out of the blue. Good things do happen. Paying attention to what's going on today is the most important thing you can do.

Attending to these four steps will not only help you build support for this change, but will enable you to begin to develop stronger working relationships with those who must support you. In other words, the next change should be easier, since you will have already begun to build bridges between departments and with key individuals.

The Israeli statesman, Abba Eban, once said, "Men and nations may behave wisely once they've exhausted all other alternatives." Applying these four steps allows you to begin to behave wisely before you've run through all the approaches to change that don't work.

Copyright © 2004 by Rick Maurer. All rights reserved.

Chapter 4: Building Commitment at the Top

"There are several critical factors behind CRM's underperformance. One of the most prevalent is the failure of many companies to obtain and maintain executive support for the CRM project. Consider the typical scenario. A group within a company decides that it could benefit from new CRM capabilities. It begins to study the issue, momentum builds, and soon there's strong grassroots support for the effort. Unfortunately, when the time comes from senior management to sign off on the sizable investment required, no executive is willing to do so. Too many times, a group planning a CRM effort fails to ensure – early in the process – that executives understand the initiative and the business case for it; are clearly convinced of the need for CRM; and are willing and able to proactively support the initiative, especially at critical junctures of the project (e.g., securing funding)." (*The Road to CRM Riches*, Accenture White Paper, 2004)

We selected four insightful readings for this section, and we feel strongly that they should be read by CRM project managers, project sponsors, and executive stakeholders all the way up to C-level. The key message – If a large-scale CRM initiative is not receiving a large amount of attention from the executive leadership team, there is likely to be a problem.

As CRM consultants, we continue to be surprised by the lack of C-level sponsorship on enterprise-wide CRM projects. Ten million dollar projects are being delegated down to the middle-management level! Fifty million dollar projects are being delegated down to the middle-management level!

MAKING CRM STICK

We are flabbergasted by the number of CRM project sponsors and project managers who only half-heartedly try to engage the C-level executives in the project.

We were recently involved in a very large enterprise-wide CRM implementation where the CEO and CFO simply did not get engaged. All of the dialogue between the CRM project management team and the C-level executives was funneled through a single project sponsor, who communicated with a color-coded 'dashboard' portraying project tasks completed. The CFO was not appropriately engaged until the project was three-quarters complete. The small amount of time that should have been spent with the CFO *at the beginning of the project*, agreeing on how the business case would be constructed, was instead spent in a panic at the end of the project, trying to convince the CFO that ten million dollars was not going down the drain. Bottom line – When a company truly considers CRM to be strategic, the CEO and the executive leadership team are deeply involved in the project.

In *Why CEOs Run Shy of CRM!*, Dave Rochford sees CRM as a missed opportunity for many CEOs and senior executives. In *The Preemptive Turnaround: Renewing the Corporation: Body, Soul and Bottom-Line*, Tom FitzGerald addresses change at the executive-level. We believe his thinking around the 'spirit' of a company residing in its management corps is thought provoking, and very applicable for the leader of a business transformation project.

According to Glen Peterson in *The CEO and CRM*, CRM cannot be delegated to middle management. The CEO must recognize CRM as a major organizational change initiative, and the initiative must be firmly rooted with organizational goals and have specific success metrics and criteria. Petersen's advice is right on target, given the findings of the recent studies by IBM, Accenture and others.

In his paper entitled *Gaining Visibility and Commitment to Technology Projects - Part 1*, Douglas Arnstein nicely sums up the key success factor for this chapter – That stakeholders, especially at the executive-level, must be included in the process, they must understand the project needs and benefits, and they must be given a chance to voice the matters that are important to their support of the project.

MAKING CRM STICK

Why CEOs Run Shy of CRM! – Dave Rochford

Customer Relationship Management - Is it a fad or do we ignore it at our peril?

Many CEOs seem to run shy of CRM and pass it on to their Service or IT Directors to deal with, but Dave Rochford argues that whilst CEOs may be justifiably concerned, if not paranoid, about the hype and hysteria, nonetheless they are missing significant opportunities. He explains that with the right attitude and approach, such paranoia can be transformed into significant profit and competitive advantage.

CRM – Perpetuating the Paranoia

Current research reveals that most companies don't have a CRM strategy and whilst most have plans to invest in it the vast majority of CRM initiatives continue to fail. We read every day of companies spending millions on a CRM solution with little to show for it, and many are still burdened with processes, systems and people in apparent disarray and disharmony. Why is this so?
An underlying reason is that this is a complex subject and many companies still do not have a real appreciation of their customer needs and what really happens at customer interaction points. As a result channels to market are not utilized effectively, nor integrated sufficiently to enhance customer convenience and value added.
CRM measurement is also still in its infancy. Most companies still rely on quantitative rather than qualitative information and do not know precisely the full costs of service nor which customers generate profit or loss.

Finally, few CRM projects have well defined business cases with an assigned ROI.

No wonder then that CEOs appear disillusioned, disenchanted and disinterested, when CRM is mentioned. How then do we turn this apparent paranoia into profit?

MAKING CRM STICK

Proceeding from Paranoia to Profit

In setting out on a profitable and successful CRM journey, adherence to the following three abiding principles is vitally important.

The CEO and management team should all be involved and committed and significant emphasis should be placed on communication of the objectives and benefits. This is the first hurdle. Without this the project is doomed from the start. Also the benefits must be delivered early, and management operating systems should be put in place to measure what gets done.

But how do you convince the CEO and senior management in the first place, and how do you get started?

As with all other investments CRM should initially be treated as a project and as such it should be clearly defined, clear in scope, and clear on benefits.

To facilitate this and put it into a business context the CRM project should commence with the completion, and sign off, of a Project Initiation Document that interprets the vision and key objectives of the business as well as define the deliverables and benefits from CRM. In doing this it should also contain a CRM route map explaining the "what and when", a business case explaining the "why" in financial terms, and detailed implementation plans and structured project management arrangements explaining the "who".

In implementing CRM it is helpful to "think big but act small", and be "customer" and not "organization" or "system centric". In the early stages of the project, effort should be placed on understanding and working on end-to-end processes that support the customer, rather than focusing perhaps on the software or on how the solution may fit the organization.

Abiding by these simple but pragmatic principles should significantly improve the chances of success as well as deliver a good return on investment.

Making it Happen

Principles are one thing, but making it happen is another. Below are the critical factors that make for a successful CRM implementation.

MAKING CRM STICK

Getting the right balance

As CRM is to be treated as a project, it should have a clear scope and well-defined objectives, robust plans, a sound business case, and a measurable and assigned ROI. Relevant, detailed analysis and evaluation is key to this. Often organizations either fail to give this sufficient weight and attention, resulting in a weak analyses and justification, or overdue it, with the result that people will not buy in to it.

Getting the balance right is important - that is balance between seeing the big picture and detailed analysis, balance between people, systems and processes, and balance in terms of needs and what can be done.

Thinking big but acting small" is key to making it happen. Whilst it is important to set out a CRM route map that aligns itself with the vision and objectives that the organization wishes to achieve, when eating the CRM elephant one should do it in small bite-size chunks that can be swallowed easily.

Therefore, whilst the CRM route map will outline a logical sequence of changes that are required to processes, systems and organization to improve customer management and profitability, the quick wins and improvements that can be implemented easily in a short time scale are key to organizational buy-in and bottom-line success.

Thus, it is important that CRM is seen as a central part of the business, that it delivers early and demonstrable benefits, and that there is alignment with short and medium term business objectives.

Changing the Processes

Understanding and mapping of the key processes and systems involved in contacting and managing customers is also important. The people responsible for particular processes or systems should undertake this work. As it is customer focused it will invariably be cross - functional in scope and may require the appointment of process owners to manage it.

Process owners must have delegated authority to effect change. Furthermore, mapping should not take 6-12 months to complete, as is often the case. In its simplest form "brown papers" (sheets or rolls of paper) can be used to document the existing key processes, systems, organization and interactions, often in a matter of days.
From these maps of existing processes and systems, white papers

documenting the "to- be" or proposed CRM model can be developed, and from gap, evaluation and risk analyses, a route map and plan can be developed to implement the required changes, including quick wins.

Quick Wins – the route to success

So as the CRM route map and plan are essential guides to chart the overall journey, the quick wins are the immediate improvements that should deliver significant and demonstrable benefits. The quick wins will help to obtain buy-in to, and pay back on, the project. They will also provide management commitment and a financial contribution to the next stage of the project.

What can be measured gets done

All of this work will depend on capturing accurate and comprehensive information not only on customer needs and how they wish to be served, but also on current service performance, and the costs and profit involved in doing business with customers.

Clean and comprehensive data is a pre-requisite - a factor often overlooked and which leads to project delays. It is key to obtaining reliable information and acceptance of baselines on performance, which should be put in place from day one of the project so that improvements can be monitored against them.

Some investment in a database management system is also often required to consolidate and present a single view of the customer, which can then be seen by all relevant managers and staff.

People -making it happen

People make it happen and the core CRM project team should have representatives from different functions. The core team should also be full time and individually accountable. Insufficient resource and skill, and inadequate accountability are factors that often lead to failure.

A sound business case and plans undertaken at the beginning of the project showing the resources, costs and returns should help overcome any resistance to releasing the resources required. This should then be monitored rigorously along with deliverables, benefits and time scales.

MAKING CRM STICK

Pitfalls to Avoid

In summary, any of the following pitfalls can result in failure:

- lack of top management commitment
- unclear scope and definition
- poorly mapped and documented processes and systems
- inaccurate and unclean data
- absence of baseline measures of performance
- unstructured project management methodology
- inadequate resources, skills and accountabilities
- poor communication of the project.

These and any other potential pitfalls should be identified at the beginning of the project and formalized in a risk mitigation plan that is agreed, monitored and remedied by senior management, usually in the forum of a project steering committee.

Given the complexity and cross organizational nature of most CRM projects, strong project management is essential and needs to be backed up by the commitment of senior management, and in particular, the CEO.

Realizing the Benefits

As a benchmark CEOs should aim to reduce costs and increase revenues by as much as 20% in the areas covered. This can have the effect of doubling profit.

Again if sufficient focus and attention is given to implementing quick wins and short-term benefits then often investment costs can be recouped in year with multiple returns delivered on a recurring annual basis thereafter.

CRM should be self-financing. If you think about it why shouldn't this be the case. It's only by treating our profitable and emerging customers that companies will be able to increase the value added to their business. Hence investment should be self-financing and should reap a significant return.

So although CRM may inject abject fear and paranoia amongst most CEOs, if planned and implemented correctly the benefits can be significant. Finance Directors and, in particular, CEOs should take note.

2004 © by Dave Rochford. All rights reserved.

MAKING CRM STICK

The Preemptive Turnaround: Renewing the Corporation: Body, Soul and Bottom Line – Tom FitzGerald

The Spontaneous Profit Surge

For 80 years it has been known that organizations that go right to the brink of disaster and then pull back - almost always under new management - experience a surge in profits, in performance, that can last two, three or even more years. Not only that, but by all measures, those turnaround companies revert to a younger, more competitive, more entrepreneurial stage of their corporate life cycle. A renewal and rebirth takes place. In the crisis of turnaround, something important within the organization is touched and changed.

What is not so well known is that, under the impetus of turnaround, units that never were in trouble - high performing, even world class units - also experience the same surge in performance, the same renewal, the same "turnaround". Just by being in the vicinity and sharing the same intense experience a renewal response is triggered. This response is derived from a place of strength rather than weakness, and from ambition rather than desperation.

Of course it is not feasible to revitalize a company by forcibly bringing it to the brink. But in the discovery that strong high performing organizations can measurably surge in performance and experience a spontaneous "turnaround" with the same management and at essentially no cost, we found a clue to a buried treasure that exists within every company: Its innate instinct to renew, to heal, to thrive.

MAKING CRM STICK

The Triggers of Renewal

During an actual crisis-driven turnaround a host of organizational drivers and behavioral triggers come into play, many of them unequivocally destructive. But from our research into the "spontaneous" turnarounds we found that in these cases much fewer drivers are involved. Of these drivers (seventeen in all) four overwhelmingly dominate the process. They are:

- A profound simplification of politics;
- A palpable discharge of emotional energy, corporate as well as personal - Catharsis;
- An investment, and a deep commitment, of this same energy into a simple, clear, picture of the future of the company - Cathexis; and
- Immediate action!

Finding a way to cause a company to create and to experience these drivers, especially the dominant four, became our challenge.

The Approach

It took a while, mostly of trial and error, but eventually we succeeded. We created a simple and predictable approach and process that triggers the renewal response within healthy companies. And it works for entire companies or units of companies.

The approach is based on truths that senior line managers know intuitively, but seldom talk about:

Every organization has an essential core, a corporate spirit. This spirit is not the CEO, though the CEO is and must be part of that core. Nor is it the corporate culture. It is something much, much greater.

When the essential core, the spirit, of a company is touched and changed, then the company changes.

When the core of the company changes, its people want to change, its units want to thrive and grow. If reengineering needs to happen, its people cause it to happen. If a fundamental new attitude to selling is needed, then its people will adjust, willingly, even eagerly. (Well 80% of them.) If quality needs to improve, they will see to that too. Whatever is hurting the company will be brought to the surface and there, in the bright light of day, dealt with. Whatever is needed for the survival and success of the company will be brought out also - and obtained.

MAKING CRM STICK

Under the right conditions, renewal happens very quickly and with almost no effort.

Renewal must be led by the managing officer. This need not involve a lot of time. At its simplest, the approach can be stated as:

- Identify the essential core (or what is to be the essential core) of the company
- Have it recognize and acknowledge itself as the essential core.
- Take this core through a process that will create within it the triggers/drivers of renewal: Simplification of Politics, Catharsis, Cathexis and Action!

This may sound too simple. But the reality turned out to be almost exactly that. The great complexity and expense of traditional corporate "improvement" programs from reengineering on back, often seems to be not really essential. They work from the outside in hoping that by changing the body the soul will change. Occasionally they work.

The Spirit of the Company

The spirit of the company - the essential core - resides primarily in the relationships between its senior managers. This is typically the CEO/managing officer, immediate reports and a few others, perhaps a dozen in all. The remainder resides in the subordinate teams. How they relate, how they view themselves as a group, and how they behave as an entity, shape the spirit of the company.

All it takes is that they see and acknowledge and empower themselves as that core, and - then behave as one. It may be easier when there is a charismatic and inspired leader, but it will happen anyway under the right set of circumstances.

Fortunately, under the right stimulus, individuals instinctively form themselves into such entities. If they are the senior managers of an organization, they become its spirit.

So how do you get the managers to become the spirit of the company?

Frankly, by just talking with them collectively, as if they were already an entity, expecting them to behave as an entity. Turning up the heat (more about that later) and having them/it face and battle and decide about the

MAKING CRM STICK

real GUT issues of the company. It is that simple.

As the individual managers work the issues of the company in concert with their peers - they become its core, its heart. Expecting it to act that way, and causing it to act that way, brings it into being.

And how do you get the core to change? That is relatively simple too. The same stimulus and the same conditions that cause the essential core to come into being, will change it. It does not happen instantly but it takes just hours.

For an individual to truly change is difficult, perhaps even impossible. Relationships however can change very easily. Small events can sometimes drastically change relationships. Usually it is for the worse. But under the right kind of stimulus, under the right conditions and controls, it is easy for relationships between managers to change positively. And as the spirit of the company resides primarily within the relationships of the senior managers, when their relationships change the core changes too. And then the company changes.

So how do we provide the right stimulus and create the right circumstances? How do we get the company to create the drivers of renewal?

A financial crisis of course, can provide the discharge of energy - catharsis. But in a real crisis, with real danger, a huge amount of energy is released and does a huge amount of damage. It traumatizes the entire company. True, turnaround management can use some residual part of that energy to break barriers and change direction. But in practice they can use only a tiny fraction. All the rest works its way destructively through the organization. The condition of everyone being in a survival mode can provide the other three drivers: Simplification; cathexis; action. But not all crises have a happy ending.

The Process

It took us a long time to create the process. Research provided insight and the four key drivers were identified early. But the process eventually required trial and error with scores of organizations.

The process turned out to be very straightforward. Only two people are needed to begin it. The first of course, is the CEO or the Managing Officer. It does not necessarily take a great deal of time but he must be involved as the initiator, periodically through the process, and as the final decision maker. Without his leadership and follow through nothing much happens. Charisma is optional.

The other is an outside Catalyst - unless the CEO is brand new and has the right experience. The process works so quickly that "facilitator" is inadequate as a descriptor. He works intimately with the CEO to identify the issues and drivers of the organization, to develop a plan of approach so that the managers can not slide off, to be seen as truly objective and acknowledged as the counterbalance to the CEO's authority and a fierce advocate of the company's success. The qualities needed in a catalyst are:

- Experience with many companies, our experience suggests more than 50;
- Broad expertise in hard consulting projects across all functions of business;
- Ability to handle group dynamics;
- An instinct for transmuting a negative issue to a positive thrust, to the bottom-line;
- Ability to fly with the corporate eagles – The management team.

There are Seven Steps:

Step 1: Put the senior managers in a room, those who are, or ought to be, the soul of the company. And create an emotionally safe place. Common sense will tell who the key players must be, the top 12 or so, usually. And a CEO who is committed to making a safe place for all his managers and all points of view will find he has done so. In our work we find it useful to have in the room no desks or tables behind which people may hide emotionally. An arc of chairs works best, facing very large computerized screens to display and record commitments. We use special software - MaxThink - for this.

Step 2: Cause them to identify as a group and individually, at the emotional level, the real issues and motivators of the organization, particularly the GUT issues that suck the life energies from the company. Intellectual identification alone is not enough. Cause them to see and accept the company as it really is, and themselves as they really are. The CEO is allowed to acknowledge some limitations here. In case of perfection he can lie.

Step 3: Allow them to feel and express revulsion at each issue that they do not like. They must do this individually and as a group. This is a lot easier than might be imagined. People do it instinctively, and it is never traumatic, though it might seem scary in anticipation.

Step 4: Create a catharsis on each issue. Cause the energies that have been bound up in these issues to be released. Again this is not difficult, people do it instinctively. If the issues are the real issues, if the group and the individuals do not slide off (so don't let them), the catharsis happens.

Step 5: Cause the energies to be transferred to, and invested in, an element of the CEO's and their vision of the future, immediately on the moment of catharsis - everyone will know it. In psychological terms the investment of energy and motivation into an idea is called cathexis. It happens in moments.

At first the elements will be just the antitheses of the issues, with the energies coming from revulsion and going into their opposites. But as the elements accumulate, as they begin to form a picture (blueprint) of the future, the managers begin to see and especially feel the possibilities for them and their company.

A real enthusiasm, excitement, builds. New energy becomes available and gets invested into new increasingly ambitious elements of the blueprint. As the managing officer is leading, as the senior managers are invested, each element will make business sense - that is the acid test. The catalyst will see to this. And the overall blueprint will have its feet in reality. Keeping the planning horizon down below three years helps too.

Without effort, intuitively, the business blue-print crystallizes around the vision of the CEO, even if it is unspoken, even if he is not there Each manager adds strategies, tactics, detail, color, flavor - whatever he needs. And without thinking about it the managers buy-in at the emotional level. Under other circumstances this buy-in is the most difficult thing to get. Here it is easy.

Step 6: Have the managers commit to, viscerally, specific action steps to achieve every element of the blueprint. Record these so all can see. We use a special system to record and display, in real time, these action steps. They become on-line action plans on the companies' LAN.

These action steps must convince everyone in the room that they can produce the results needed. And the drive and commitment of those who must perform the actions must be convincing too. Fortunately, very few people can lie convincingly under the close attention and interest of their boss (important), peers (more important) and subordinates (most important of all). So their commitment will be genuine. The catalyst, of course, wears the black hat.

Step 7: Begin implementation immediately - that day wherever possible. Monday at the latest. And follow up! Follow up! Follow up!

Of these seven, Step 2, identifying the true corporate issues is the only one that requires any preparation. There are a number of ways to achieve this from third party interviewing, to requests for suggestions, to open space planning, to round table discussion.

In our work, we use a special management questionnaire, The Corporate Profile®. This shortens the process greatly. This instrument is given to all managers and supervisors ahead of time. It is answered anonymously. It addresses more than 150 factors that we have found from our experience with hundreds of organizations to underlie, cause or predict organizational performance. The instrument also elicits suggestions.

It is never possible to predict which of these many factors will be issues for any given organization, though some are found more often than others. However, we have found that "good" companies - companies that are and have been consistently successful on the bottom line and in the marketplace - will find some thirty issues that the managers don't like, that are sucking up energy or causing serious distress. An organization that has been experiencing difficulties for some time may find perhaps sixty issues.

These issues absolutely have to be dealt with, not just intellectually, but viscerally, emotionally, in the very soul and belly of the company, before serious transformation can happen. This can be noisy but well worth while. It happens quickly and it's fun too.

Fred's Tale

Fred is president and founder. The firm makes small ticket leases - mostly automobile. He is a serious man, not prone to demonstrative behavior. Today he stands before his senior people - his direct reports and just a few others; twelve in all, thirteen with him. The number is unintentional but he is conscious of its symbolism. They form the essential core of the company. Their relationships with each other, the dynamic of their interplay, cooperation and conflict, he thinks of as the company's driving spirit.

MAKING CRM STICK

One year before, they had gone through a process that had left them strangely at peace. For the first time they - as a team, an entity - had seen and accepted the company exactly as it was - warts and all. They had seen themselves as they were too and accepted that. The process had been surprisingly easy and very quick. They had formed a safe place to do their work. And just did it!

They had gathered, consciously, as the core, the driving spirit of the company. And for the very first time, through them, the company had seen itself as it truly was. The facts, the figures, those it knew already. It lived with them day-in, day-out. But its inner drives, its hidden motivations, its unspoken, unacknowledged attitudes, policies and politics - they were a revelation. Every manager may have known but the company had not. The company had at last seen itself as it really was, and accepted that. It was at peace.

After that, it had to do something about what it had seen - about its problems, it potentials, its motivations - and it did. They - the managers, had said of themselves and of the company, in almost these words: "This is who we are. God help us!" Then they had taken the energy they had released and invested it deep in corporate and personal commitments to a clear and simple picture of their future.

Fred is now going through the numbers. He says that they are not important - that the transformation in the life of the company is more important. But the numbers also tell a tale: one year later, month over month, revenues are up 110%!

The Results

In steps 3 through 6, (revulsion, catharsis, cathexis, action!) which occur over and over until all the serious issues are dealt with, a great number of things happen and a great many benefits accrue. The most tangible is the creation of a business blueprint and action steps that are deeply committed to by the managers. These, of course, are valuable by themselves. And housing them on the corporate LAN makes them particularly useful. (You get an on-line strategic and operational plan through which you can drive and monitor every aspect of the business if you want it.)

The immediate surge in profits which we always find when the program has been undertaken fully, is also worth while. Greater than 20% in the first year is not uncommon. But the really important things happen within the spirit of the company. It is from these changes that the long term health

MAKING CRM STICK

and success of the company develops. The senior managers become a true team, the essential center of the company - its spirit. This spirit becomes aware and empowered. Centered on the CEO/managing officer, focused powerfully on the mission and blueprint of the organization which it has created and committed to, energized into action, this spirit empowers the individual managers including the CEO, and holds them accountable.

Unexpected things, seemingly contradictory and apparently mutually exclusive things, happen too. The CEO becomes more empowered as a leader and also as a delegator. At the same time his immediate reports become more adaptable, more responsive to the CEO and also more empowered to contribute and be heard as part of the essential core. All become more willingly accountable. Within their own areas, their power to lead and delegate grows as well. All this is not magic. When the right environment is created, that which is wise within the company and that which is instinctive within people comes to the surface and is enhanced.

In processing the gut issues of the company at the emotional level the politics of the organization become simplified and clean. Energy, that has been bound up in unresolved, unacknowledged, even previously unknown issues is released and reapplied.

The relationships between the individual managers change too. A changed set of relationships changes the spirit of the company. A changed spirit transforms performance. A changed performance changes the bottom line.

Over the last several years we have been fortunate to observe numbers of companies who have undertaken this process and been allowed to track their performance over the following two years. Those who have undertaken the full program have all significantly transformed corporate attitudes and performance. And the smallest first year profit increase we have recorded was 10%.

The only prerequisite for these companies to succeed was a CEO with the courage to look unflinchingly into the soul of his company and ask it to change - Body, Soul and Bottom Line.

Copyright © 2004 by Tom FitzGerald. All rights reserved. Contact FitzGerald Associates at www.managementconsultants.com.

MAKING CRM STICK

MAKING CRM STICK

The CEO and CRM – Glen S. Petersen

Current popular wisdom within the CRM industry places senior management support as one of the top ten success criteria. What is meant by support is never really defined but it is logical that the term embraces the notion of reasonable project funding, resources, and positive communication and backing from senior management. But is that adequate?

To answer this question, one needs to understand that the CRM industry identifies itself through the evolution and capabilities of technology. If the user community obligingly buys into that definition, senior management is likely to approach a CRM initiative as a systems project and charge middle management with the task of so make it so? Despite senior management support, this orientation and action represents abdication when perhaps in good faith, senior management thinks it is empowering the organization to act.

To better understand why this is true, one needs to go back to the definition of CRM. Based on a definition created by the Gartner Group several years ago, CRM can be segmented into two components:

1. CRM is a business strategy that commits the organization to being driven by the customer or otherwise being customer centric.

2. Technology is used as an enabler to deliver profitable value to customers through the understanding and anticipation of their needs.

This definition tends to turn current wisdom on its head because it positions CRM as first and foremost a business strategy. As a business strategy, senior management must be leading not merely supporting the initiative. Technology follows this lead by providing the infrastructure to deliver value and capabilities that enhance profitability. It is not about

MAKING CRM STICK

technology for technology's sake.

For there to be a radical shift in the reported success rate for CRM initiatives, there must be a fundamental shift in the end-user community's visibility and leadership of senior management. Without credible and meaningful input from the end user community, the industry will pursue differentiation through technology as opposed to practical solutions to end user requirements and profitability.

Who Is Really Customer Centric?

Few organizations would claim that they are not customer centric. Most would admit to needing improvement and that leads to the purchase of technology with the naive notion that the technology will somehow fix any perceived deficiencies. If being customer centric was that easy, then why the failure rates? Best practices relative to implementation have been widely publicized since the beginning of CRM, so perhaps 10 percent ignore these warnings; this still does not explain the failure rate phenomenon.

Most organizations remain structured in the traditional stove pipe functional configuration. In this definition of responsibilities, no one is really responsible for the customer, so how can the organization be customer centric? Want more proof? Consider the following:

The typical sales function is driven to achieve a revenue goal subject to maintaining expenses within budget levels.
Marketing is typically organized and driven by performance that relates to products, services, and programs.

Customer service has customer in its title but performance criteria tend to be driven by productivity measures. Further, by examining the business rules and policies that the function operates under, one often finds that the real objective is cost and risk containment.

At this point, you may say yes we have these characteristics but we measure customer satisfaction. This is certainly a good thing to do but what is really being measured and what actions does it enable? Further, to what degree can the organization link (more accurately correlate) customer satisfaction with customer behaviour metrics? It is customer behaviour that is the focus of CRM. Independent studies have shown that customer satisfaction is often not correlated with customer retention (a key customer behaviour).

MAKING CRM STICK

So the take-away here is that CRM is not a natural state for most organizations. No organization or function is trying to drive customers away, but the collective action of the organization often inadvertently achieves this result or otherwise dilutes its impact on the best or most profitable (includes potential) prospects and customers. This is what needs to be fixed.

The Profitable Acquisition of Customers and Delivery of Value

There is general agreement that customers perceive value as the total experience associated with the product or service. Delivery of the total experience occurs through horizontal processes that cross-functional boundaries. The focus of enterprise level CRM is to provide tools, data, and infrastructure to enable the profitable acquisition of customers and the development of their potential over the life cycle of the customer. The challenge of this endeavour (CRM) however, is that the organization is attempting to deploy a common set of tools and technology across functions that are basically operating to the beat of a different drum. It is a recipe for delays, miscues, cost over-runs, and resistance.

Enter the CEO

It should be very clear by now that the organizational issues are more likely to derail a CRM initiative than it is the technology. Organizations have lived with less than perfect technology since the discovery of the vacuum tube. However, when a system is introduced that changes the balance of how things are done, influences who wins and why, and has operational limitations, the prognosis is often terminal. CRM can represent fundamental change; therefore senior management cannot be on the sidelines they have to be on the field.

If CRM is a business strategy, then senior management must understand it, be committed to its success, and accurately assess its ramifications (consider the cost). The CEO is the person the organization looks toward for the direction of the company and its philosophy. In this regard, it is the responsibility of the CEO to sell this direction to board of directors, financial analysts, direct reports, and perhaps customers.

As indicated previously, the profitable acquisition of customers and the delivery of profitable customer value are achieved through processes that cross-functional lines. To the extent to which performance metrics and accountability issues get in the way of optimising these processes, the CEO

MAKING CRM STICK

(COO/President) is the person who must reconcile these issues and create an environment where everyone is pulling together relative to CRM.

The CEO must recognize CRM as a major organizational change initiative. The CRM project needs more than support; there must be commitment and leadership. The initiative must be firmly rooted with organizational goals and have specific success metrics and criteria. Without this foundation, the initiative will be like a sailboat without a rudder. Similarly, without a specific destination, a rudder is of small assistance.

The failure statistics speak to this issue loud and clear, a very high percentage of initiatives lack specific success metrics and goals. Selling an initiative on emotion may get the project to implementation but few if any reach success. CRM is all about business and only leaders need apply.

2004 © by Glen S. Petersen. All rights reserved.

Gaining Visibility and Commitment to Technology Projects (Part 1) – Douglas Arnstein

A project manager is called into his supervisor's office and told, "The SVP in Product Management just promised a new purchasing desktop application to the wholesale market, and she told them it would be delivered in four months. Go write requirements." Since project managers tend to have a Superman complex, the project manager immediately starts thinking of ways to make it happen.
In other words, he thinks, "The boss asked me to do this because he thinks I can handle the challenge." So he charges in, but with doubts about the ability to deliver anything realistic by the imposed deadline.

The above project is likely to jump into a premature solution and limp along while all parties hope that it will get straightened out before implementation. What results are delays, changes in direction, re-work, and cost increases. In today's world of corporate chaos, projects get lost in the 'noise' of too many projects, meetings, production problems, management fire drills, and hundreds of daily e-mails and voice messages.

By following four simple project planning practices, one can gain project visibility and obtain commitment from project stakeholders and participants to get the right project done right.

1. Project Sponsor & Project Charter

A project without a sponsor is doomed. The sponsor is the project champion; the senior business manager who benefits from the product or changes that are produced by the project.
The attributes of a good sponsor are she can make funding and resource decisions, she reports to executive management, she will shepherd the

project through issues and challenges, and she has a level of visible involvement that is recognized by project participants.

The first step toward gaining visibility and commitment is to interview the project sponsor and develop a Project Charter. Have her articulate the business drivers, project mission, project objectives, other internal organizations with a stake in the outcome, and her definition of what constitutes project completion.

The Project Charter document should be short, direct, and comprise the following sections; Introduction, Project Description and Justification, Business Drivers, Constraints, Stakeholders, Deliverables, Project Objectives for Time, Cost, Quality, and Scope, Project Resource Roles and Responsibilities, Preliminary Resource Identification, Assumptions, Dependencies, and Issues.

This information allows coordination with participating groups on the project. Use numbered lists for all sections except the Introduction and Project Description. These lists provide the relevant information in an easy-to-read manner that facilitates group review.

2. Stakeholders & Stakeholder Analysis

Project stakeholders are those who have a vested interest in project outcomes.

For technology projects, they would include managers who have to provide project resources, for example, from business end-users and marketing, application development, networking, and data center groups. Since projects are unique by definition, stakeholders are different for each project. After stakeholder identification, review the Project Charter with them and the project sponsor. It is their opportunity to hear project details, understand the impact to their respective areas, and provide feedback to the project sponsor.

Next, conduct a stakeholder analysis. It is important to understand what the stakeholders think about the project and how they define success. I have yet to conduct a stakeholder analysis without learning something unexpected that altered deliverables or affected project scope.

Ask each stakeholder:

- Does he/she agree with project objectives,
- What does he/she define as project scope,
- What does he/she view as project risks,

- How does he/she define project critical success factors,
- How would he/she define project quality,
- What, how, and how frequently does he/she want to hear about the project.

Interviewing stakeholders is just that. Do not use e-mail. If unable to sit face-to-face with a stakeholder, use the telephone. There are no rules other than to get their feedback. I have used directed and non-directed interviews successfully. For non-directed interviews, I merely ask the questions above. For directed interviews, I prompt the interviewee with lists of project objectives and scope from the Project Charter then solicit feedback. It is important to ask the same questions of all stakeholders.

3. Project Scope

After completing the stakeholder analysis, evaluate the data. The project sponsor sees the 'world' through her eyes. She may not realize that the requested application requires network upgrades and a general ledger system interface. This discovery now needs to be incorporated into the Project Charter.
Once revised, there should be a final document review with all stakeholders.

The rest of the stakeholder analysis information will be used to design the project and build the Project Plan. Specifically, stakeholder feedback will be used in the Risk Management Plan, Quality Management Plan, and Communication Plan sections of the Project Plan. By conducting the above activities, the project manager and planning team have engaged key participants, built early consensus, and given visibility to the project.

4. Project Plan

The Project Plan is the document used to manage project execution. It defines the project 'What, Why, Who, When, Where, and How'. It is a text document (not to be confused with a Microsoft Project Plan) which states how the project intends to achieve its objectives. It helps other internal and external organizations understand what they need to do and when in support of the project.

Although the project manager has primary responsibility for producing the Project Plan, it should be developed as a partnership between the business and technology organizations. A well-drafted Project Plan would include the following sections. Introduction, Project Charter, Milestones with

MAKING CRM STICK

Projected Dates, Resource Plan, Scope Management and Change Control, Quality Plan, Risk Management Plan, Communication Plan, Communication Matrix, Deliverables / Responsibility Matrix, and WBS.

Visibility and Commitment

These four proven project planning practices increase the chances for project success for one simple reason: inclusion. All stakeholders were included in the process, they understood the project needs and benefits, and they were given a chance to voice the matters that are important to their support of the project; a recipe for visibility, commitment, and success.

2004 © Douglas Arnstein, Absolute Consulting Group, Inc. All rights reserved.

Chapter 5: Making the Business Case for Change

Your client explained that they did not need a business case for a proposed CRM implementation because the key stakeholders were already "bought in". Despite your many efforts to help them understand that projects often lose their funding without compelling financial analysis, they explicitly excluded the business case from scope. After completing the Requirements phase of the project, creating a detailed implementation plan, and beginning to mobilize resources, the project team was put on hold when the project sponsor couldn't rally business support for the effort. Does this sound familiar?

How about this scenario: Your company would like to implement a new CRM solution that will integrate your Contact Centers worldwide. You have been engaged to make a plan, provide cost estimates and build a business case. Your team spent several weeks documenting the expected benefits of the solution using an industry-standard approach, and you created an excellent project plan. But the project is placed on hold because the steering committee didn't buy into the ROI documentation.

Decision-makers and budget-owners are frightened by the littered CRM landscape. Vendors, analysts and consultants are pitching different points of view on what CRM can do, and the promise of better things to come with the implementation of enterprise CRM systems. The press often reports that CRM projects are not delivering on projected returns. Thus, it is no surprise that organizations are skeptical that CRM can deliver a solid return on the effort.

Most everyone now agrees that a Value Case must tell the story of how a CRM program or initiative, whether it is process-based, organizational, or technology-based, will drive specific business value to the top and/or bottom line. The challenge is that there are a variety of opinions on how business value should be measured. How should we articulate the business benefit? How do we link our strategic initiatives to our company's strategic objectives? What impact will Siebel have on the bottom line? What should we expect for a revenue lift? How do we decide whether to buy or rent? How do we decide which piece of technology to install first?

The following white papers will help you think through some of these issues, and address the increasingly important success factor that we call Business Case, Value Case, or Case for Change.

The first paper, Dan Murphy's *Show Me The Money: Making the Value Case for Change*, addresses the question of whether a Value Case is a necessary component of a CRM project. The paper also describes the basic blocking and tackling of Value Case-building.

We felt that Richard Janezic's paper, *Information Technology (IT) and Return on Investment (ROI): Understanding Why, Where and How They Matter*, was a proper follow-on to Murphy's paper. The third paper in this chapter, also by Richard Janezic, entitled *ROI, Cost Benefit and Business Case Analysis: The ABC's of CBA*, was written as the first paper in a five-part series. We thought this paper would give the reader an appreciation that there are many different formulas for calculating the business value of a program or initiative. Janezic's paper introduces the ROI and DCF (Discounted Cash Flow) formulas. For those interested in digging deeper on the many other formulas (e.g., NPV, IRR, EVA, etc.), we encourage you to look for Janezic's articles at www.refresher.com, and in other journals.

Show Me The Money!: Making the Value Case for Change – Daniel T. Murphy

> "I will not rest until I have you holding a coke, wearing your own shoe, playing a Sega game featuring you, while singing your own song in a new commercial starring you, broadcast during a super bowl game you are winning." (Jerry Maguire)

The *philosophy* of CRM tells us that, if we become superb customer relationship managers – i.e., if we provide superb customer value – then the business benefits will follow. Jerry Maguire made the great leap of faith to true customer centricity. If you want to get your CRM program management team working in the spirit of CRM, rent a theatre and show them that movie.

The *reality* of CRM is another story. The idea that customer value will drive business benefit it is a great leap of faith that most budget owners will not make. The mantra is more typically "Show me the money!"

Yet, still we roll the dice. The business case is conveniently forgotten. How often have you heard such words as:

- We don't need a business case for this project. CRM is strategic for us.
- No need for any numbers to support this project. The stakeholders are already bought in.
- The CIO has said that CRM is our number one priority this year.
- Everybody already agrees that we'll get a revenue lift from this project.

MAKING CRM STICK

If your organization is already philosophically bought in to a CRM program or initiative, you should consider yourself lucky. Your path to success will be a little bit easier. You still need to face reality. A change in leadership in your organization may result in CRM becoming less *strategic*. What will happen if the CEO or CIO is replaced? What will happen (God help us) if the CFO is replaced? What if the Board of Directors asks the CEO "You're spending fifty million dollars on WHAT?"

IBM's recent *Doing CRM Right study (2004)* showed statistically and definitively that having a solid CRM Value Proposition is the top driver of CRM success. This argument has been made repeatedly by leading CRM practitioners. In late 2003-2004, IBM surveyed hundreds of executives across the world, and validated what the experts had been saying all along.

Without getting into the detail of whether the Value Case should be built around ROI, EVA, NPV, etc., or the recommended level of granularity around benefits, timeline (e.g., monthly, quarterly, etc.), I will list here some points that I would call Value Case imperatives – Things you absolutely must do in support of a large-scale (e.g., large enough for the CEO, CFO, or CIO to provide budget authorization) CRM program or initiative.

Strategic Linkage

The sponsor of a large CRM project or initiative should be able to describe how that project or initiative supports one or more key value drivers or strategic objectives. In other words, you should be able to say something like *"One of our strategic objectives for this fiscal year is to significantly reduce our customer attrition rate. This objective has been stated by our CEO and Vice-President of Sales in our Annual Report. Wall Street analysts say it is critical for our success during the next two years. The proposed project is wholly focused on customer retention. The technology that we are planning to implement as part of this initiative has been proven at other organizations to reduce customer attrition by up to . . ."*

Describing how a project or initiative supports one or more key business drivers is only the first step in the process of building a detailed Value Case. But for many of the stakeholders who do not have the stomach for the detailed quantitative details (e.g., Wall Street), it is a story that they will keep in their back pocket.

MAKING CRM STICK

Moving the Metrics

A key value driver (e.g., reduce customer attrition) will have one or more metrics (e.g., customer attrition rate) associated. The table below outlines some examples:

Value Driver	Associated Metrics
Increase Customer Loyalty	Increase Product/Service Penetration Per Increase Customer Tenure Increase Customer Referrals Reduce Attrition Rate Increase Product/Service Penetration Per Customer Improve Customer Satisfaction Score: Perceived Value of My Loyalty
Increase Customer Lifetime Value	Increase Average Customer Tenure Increase Average Customer Spend Decrease Average Cost to Serve a Customer Increase Number of Customer Referrals Decrease Average Cost to Acquire a Customer Decrease Time to Break Even

The second level of detail in a Value Case should describe how a proposed CRM program or initiative will move the metrics in the organization. You should be able to say something like *"The proposed initiative will increase average customer spend by six percent, and therefore increase customer lifetime value by 6-8 percent. The amount of movement of the metrics will be based on a set of assumptions (e.g., Historically, twelve percent of customers who purchase product A will agree to purchase accessory B, given . . .)."* The assumptions should be documented through collaboration, and in great detail. The goal should be to prevent a major stakeholder or budget owner from saying at the eleventh hour *"Hey, you obviously forgot to consider . . ."*

The metrics table becomes the basis for the next step in the Value Case-building process.

Financial Benefits

The next step is to document the financial benefits of moving each metric. You want to be able to tell the story *"Based on our customer base of six million, the expected six percent increase in average customer spend will result in an additional six percent of revenues per year."* Again, assumptions should be documented through collaboration, and in great detail. A best practice is to get the Finance department involved early in the process.

Total Cost of Ownership

You would think that defining total cost of ownership is a straight forward exercise. There are hardware costs, software costs, professional services costs, etc. Some costs are more difficult to discover and even more difficult to quantify without a collaborative effort. Include representatives from Finance, Human Resources, IT, Legal, etc. Start with the cost centers on your company's General Ledger.

Financial Pro Forma

No surprise here – The Financial Pro Forma for your proposed CRM program or initiative is built from the results of the Financial Benefits analysis and the Total Cost of Ownership analysis. Financial Benefits minus Total Cost of Ownership equals Return-on-Investment. Of course, it's not quite that easy – You will need to consider the rate at which your company borrows, other ongoing initiatives that may be impacting the same metrics (We don't want to double-count), the CFO's preferences for documentation of expected benefits (e.g., ROI, EVA, etc.), the company's cash flow (e.g., You may have effectively documented a billion dollar ROI, but if the company does not have the monthly cash flow to support the initiative, you will be dead in the water). At the risk of belaboring the point – Get the Finance department in on the effort early.

Conclusion

Sounds like a lot of extra work, doesn't it? In fact, you may be thinking "If we cut out the Value Case part of the project, we can trim costs by . . ."

In closing, I would like you to consider this scenario . . .

You are building a complex CRM solution with many integration points. You have built a strong business case that demonstrates a four-year return-on-investment of $40 million on a Total Cost of Ownership of $12 million. Problems occur in the integration testing phase of the project. Some of the system interfaces just don't work right, and will need to be redesigned and reconstructed. This will push your go-live date forward by six weeks, and the project will go over budget by $380,000. As the Project Sponsor, you

MAKING CRM STICK

will need to explain why this happened. When you sit down with the CIO, or perhaps with the CEO, or (God help you) with the CFO ("Jump right into my nightmare while the water is warm," said Jerry Maguire), you will have your Value Case to show the materiality of the cost overrun – one percent of ROI. The executives approve the additional $380,000 without question.

2004 © Daniel T. Murphy. All rights reserved.

MAKING CRM STICK

MAKING CRM STICK

Information Technology (IT) and Return on Investment (ROI): Understanding Why, Where and How They Matter – Richard D. Janezic

In the spring of 2003, Nicholas Carr, editor-at-large of Harvard Business Review, published an article titled "IT Doesn't Matter". The provocative title of Carr's article resulted in a firestorm of response, drawing comments from business and technology leaders, from well known CEO's including Bill Gates of Microsoft and John Chambers of Cisco, to executives and pundits within and beyond the technology arena.

The point in Carr's article (and subsequent book "Does IT Matter?") is that the empirical evidence to date suggests that the technology has not, by itself, demonstrated measurable economic value when compared with the vast sums that companies have invested. Carr's article caused a strong, but emotional, reaction. But once one reads beyond its provocative title, and grasps Carr's true message – that commodity computing does not add value – one would likely find agreement with many of his positions.

As with IT investment, Return On Investment (ROI) has also been viewed with skepticism as a reliable tool to measure the financial performance of technology investments. Post project reviews of expected v. realized ROI have lacked consistency. Is this cynicism toward IT and ROI warranted? Can IT truly provide significant business value, and can ROI accurately measure it? The answer to both questions is yes.

While many of Carr's ideas and arguments are valid, the title of the article was wrong or, at least, misleading. Information Technology (IT) does matter, when thoughtfully employed, skillfully deployed, and properly measured. Further, ROI matters as a tool to help improve decision making, and for conveying how and where IT matters in business.

MAKING CRM STICK

Technology investment has once again started increasing, albeit cautiously, following the last several years of anemic growth. But many senior executives express skepticism when thinking of technology's ability to create measurable value, provide a sustainable competitive advantage, and deliver improved business profitability.

Technology investment can make a business better, and the skillful use of ROI can help. But ROI has been overused as a term, and underused as a method. The casualness with which ROI is used is one of the root causes for IT and ROI skepticism. A necessary, but missing, element has been complete, specific, clearly understood, and compelling examples and guidelines of how to think about technology investments as a means to create significant, sustainable business value, and reliable methods to accurately predict and measure the success of these investments.

Value and Profits

Carr's article focused on discovering the effect of technology investments on creating the essence of value: profitability. His argument is that "commodity computing" creates minimal, if any, value. Carr made the analogy of relating commodity computing to electric service: you need it to operate a business, but, in and of itself, it does not create a competitive advantage.

What does commodity computing mean? Simply stated, it means using computing technology to automate, but not fundamentally change, the manner and cost structure of a business. Conversely, business value can be created when automation – meaning the use of computing technology – is combined with, and is used to deliver, process changes, improvements, and innovation in such a way that it does change the cost structure of a business, relative to competitors methods and practices. This process is typically referred to as business process reengineering, or BPR.

Installing new automation tools alone, however, is not BPR, rather, it is a component of BPR, or an enabler of it. To be considered financially successful, process reengineering, and any accompanying investments in technology, must improve operational effectiveness by reducing operational cost structures. Let's use a brief example:

Much has been invested in Enterprise Resource Planning (ERP) and Client Relationship Management (CRM) systems over the past several years. Businesses that invested in ERP and CRM, but changed few processes, may have seen some economies of scale benefits, but often, not enough to offset the total AIM (Acquire/Install/Manage) costs of the systems. Studies indicate that where ERP and CRM have delivered value is in those situations in which business processes were changed in concert with systems that enabled and supported those streamlined processes, such that the business produced more output with fewer resources. Fewer resources – resulting in lower cost structures – means fewer people (increased productivity), faster cycle times (increased productivity), and less cost for an equal or greater service level (increased profitability).

How does this all relate to ROI?

The "R" part of ROI (Return On Investment) stands for Return. Return means profits, and profits are the foundation of business value. Recurring higher profits are the engine for sustainable business value, increased stock price, improved cash flow, and many other benefits. Stated financially, when profitability increases because of sustainable improvements in operational effectiveness, the result is an improvement in "Quality of Earnings". Improvements in Quality of Earnings are what industry analysts and investors desire, as they translate into increased business value and higher stock prices.

ROI in Brief

ROI is a tool that is used to compute the benefits (returns) of an investment, relative to its costs. (For the purpose of this article, the term "ROI" will be used, but the method could be IRR, NPV, DCF, TCO, or other more elaborate methods. Each of these terms and methods will be briefly defined and compared later, but for more detailed examination, try CEO Refresher. Moreover, not all CFO's and organizations prefer ROI. For convenience, the term ROI will signify either ROI, or your company's preferential method.)

Cost-benefit analysis (CBA) methods, as ROI and other such methods are known, are a class of financial calculations that measure the financial consequences of making an investment. Please note that these methods can be used to both predict future performance, as well as measure past performance of an investment to test and validate prior assumptions.

One of the most important thoughts about technology investment is perhaps the most simple. To paraphrase a quote from former President John F. Kennedy, "Ask not what the technology will do for you. Ask what you will do with the technology." What does this mean? It means that the value from technology results not from owning it. Instead, it results from how well it is used – in your particular environment. Not "could be" used. Not "is possible to be" used. Not "may be" used. Those are capabilities, and unemployed capabilities don't count. It is only when capabilities become realities – capabilities that truly help the business lower costs and improve quality and productivity – do the benefits from investing in and using them create value.

It is important to understand that while ROI is an evaluative tool, its greater and more meaningful value is that it is used as a comparative metric. Computing ROI for a new investment or purchase may yield a seemingly impressive figure, but, in isolation of other options, its computational result can lack both comprehensive coverage and business specific relevance. For example, a 325% ROI may sound exceptional, that is, until you know that the existing method yielded 295% return.

For more clarity about the specifics of ROI, we'll review it, and the various CBA alternatives later in this article. For the moment, let's concentrate on how to think about ROI and something called a business case.

A Financial View of ROI, the Business Case, and Technology Projects

ROI values are used in many technology conversations. The promise of value and ROI from an investment in technology is easy to suggest, but, in reality, is not as easy to measure. When one understands the effective value and use of ROI, one understands that without intimate knowledge of the business, a reliable ROI cannot reasonably be predicted. But, you may be wondering, who needs, and really uses ROI? The short answer is the CFO, but the true answer should be everyone involved in decision process.

The CFO, or Chief Financial Officer, is most likely the final stop in the approval process of a Capital Request. (While Capital Request, Capital Expenditure, or CapEx are common terms, your company may refer to this process by another term. What these terms refer to is the process by which your company decides how to spend large amounts of money.) A Capital Request asks the company to fund – that is, to make an investment into – a project, with the expectation that the result will produce a value greater than its cost to the company. Let's briefly examine some of the factors that confront the CFO to better understand what leads them to approve or deny a Capital Request.

Your CFO has among the most challenging jobs in an organization. He or she must work with CEO and executive team to make the business better

MAKING CRM STICK

(better means more valuable, which means more profitable). The CFO must tell shareholders and investors how the business has performed, and what is being done to improve its performance. CFO's must ensure that the business is sustainable, and has "capital adequacy" – that is, enough money to spend to cover how it generates and consumes cash. There exists a fiduciary responsibility to invest responsibly, and, in light of a new and more stringent regulatory environment from regulations like Sarbanes-Oxley, the CFO must also assure that the business maintains regulatory compliance.

Your CFO has a significant role in determining in those areas in which the business should invest for future success. The CFO, in concert with the CEO, set the strategy that the business will use to compete. The two fundamental choices of strategy are to compete on price ("price-led"), or to compete on difference ("differential value").

This choice of a price-led or differential value strategy is influenced by the business itself, with its own unique capabilities and philosophies. Strategy is also strongly influenced by the industry in which the business competes. Dr. Michael Porter developed the concept of Industry Analysis through a model referred to as Porter's Five Forces Analysis. The Five Forces concept states there are 5 unique, but interrelated, pressures that govern the size, health, growth prospects, and direction of an industry. These forces are Buyer Power, Supplier Power, Threat of New Entrants, Threat of Substitutes, and Competitive Rivalry.

Using both Industry Analysis and the pricing strategy, the CFO and CEO make decisions about how best to use the time, talent and treasury of the business to help it grow and succeed. The decisions about how to compete lead to decisions about in what to invest to fulfill the strategy. This means the choices in strategy form the basis of though about in which areas the company will deploy capital. Another way to state that is that the strategy drives the tactics, and these actions combine to determine which Capital Requests get funded. How are these decisions made? It is a simple, yet complex and computation intensive process.

The simple answer: invest in those things that make the business better, meaning more profitable. As mentioned earlier, profits are the basis for determining how valuable the business is, and if it is publicly traded, current and future profits have a significant impact on stock price.

The complex answer: invest in those things that make the business more profitable, adjusted for risk, adjusted for current operations, adjusted for what the business can spend, adjusted for the company's strategy, adjusted for what competitors are doing and how they will likely respond to changes in your company, adjusted for company priorities, adjusted for those things that the company can and will best leverage for advantage, etc.

An investment results in one of two conditions: it either creates value, or it consumes it. Creating value means that the company received more back in benefit than it invested (a positive return). Some investments will not, by necessity, create value. Examples of this might include risk reduction investments and regulatory compliance investments. These types of investments will not help a company create higher earnings, but will help it preserve value. Most investments, however, are expected to be accretive, that is additive, to the company's earnings.

Another consideration for the CFO is the overhang of prior investment performance. Executives are skeptical of the because of prior claims that technology investment would make the business more financially successful. As Carr and others state, the evidence indicates quite the contrary. Much of the investment in technology has not produced tangible value. As mentioned in Carr's works, and consistent with many other studies like ones by Standish Group, an estimated 70% of investments in technology are "not successful".

"Not successful" in this context does not mean a technical failure; rather, it means a lack of financial success. While technical success (meaning it operates as expected) may have been achieved, if the investment underperforms its expected financial result, it is not considered to be successful. An important way to think about such a circumstance is that the business, in essence, "lost" the profit that could have been created by investing in a different project that would have created a positive return (an equal or better ROI). Technical successes are indeed important. What is more important, however, is to achieve a business (financial) success that results from a technical success.

Realize further that your request is but one of many requests under consideration. CFO's receive numerous requests, more than what the business can spend or effectively manage. So how does the CFO decide which projects/investments should receive funding approval? By using tools like the business case and ROI.

The Business Case

To make informed investment decisions, an exercise called a business case is a prudent place to start. Business case analysis (BCA) tells a story, a story about the business: its history, products, services, clients, competitors, operations, results, successes and challenges. BCA is a favored method in business schools, as it helps convey a more complete picture of the business, its drivers, business investment challenges and choices. This framework provides better rationale for improved decision making.

BCA tells readers about conditions of the business. It combines financial, operational, and strategic insight to help the reader understand challenges, imperatives, and available options worth considering, and why they merit consideration. The author(s) of the business case often includes a SWOT (Strength Weakness Opportunity Threat) analysis as part of the strategic review, as well as selected financial details. But the core of the business case is focused on the operational aspects of the business, as it is the operational aspects – in fulfillment of the strategy of the business – that produce the financial results.

The ultimate purpose of the business case is to convey a situation, or plea, for change. Similar to a legal proceeding, the business case uses evidence to product a "fact based" case, or approach, to support its "claims" (the need for change).

In its use as a decision making tool, the business case discusses the basis and need for change, recommendations for what to change, and importantly, the results expected from the proposed change. Further, a well-constructed and well-reasoned business case analysis correctly identifies and measures the problem, and provides validation of the significance, sources, and solutions.

In short, the business case tells a detailed, fact-based story about the business – how its problems and challenges are affecting the business, what needs to be fixed/changed/ improved, and how business performance is expected to improve from these proposed changes.

How ROI relates to the Business Case

The last component of the business case is how the business' performance is expected to improve from proposed changes. This is where and how ROI is used. ROI is not the business case; rather, it is a supporting piece of data, or evidence, which exists within the business case. ROI provides a future picture of the financial results that are created by the proposed investment.

ROI give a measurement of how well the business problem will be solved by the recommended course of action. Accordingly, it should be a factual, non-fiction document. The combination of the business case and ROI gives the reader a future view the aspects of the business that will be improved, and the value or magnitude of these changes. These changes are referred to in both qualitative (example: better inventory levels) and quantitative (example: lowering inventory levels by 28% by the 3rd quarter of next fiscal year) measures. While the business case discusses both qualitative and quantitative changes, ROI is quantitative, that is, it yields a specific value.

Note that ROI, as with the business case, are a "snapshot", or picture of business conditions at a specific moment in time. Just as the Income Statement can change significantly from quarter to quarter, so too can operations, the business case, and any recommendation(s).

When developing the business case and ROI, it is prudent to consider the audience to whom it is directed. Often this is the CFO, but may include the senior executive team (typically including the CEO, CFO, COO, CIO, Presidents, and Vice Presidents).

While many executives have "worked their way up" through the organization, some executives may possess a more intimate understanding of the operational specifics that are solved by the proposed investment. The operational and technology implications, and ranges of solutions, may not be apparent to all audiences, particularly with rapidly changing technology markets, products, and techniques. For example, high cost, high risk and long duration technology investments may also require the review and approval of other decision makers, such as the Board of Directors. Accordingly, the business case should be composed and written to meet the needs and expectations of all audiences involved in the decision process.

Further, recent regulatory changes for publicly held firms, including Sarbanes-Oxley (affectionately referred to as "SarbOx"), require new levels of diligence and rigor in decision making. The business case (including ROI analyses), therefore, has an even stronger requirement to be detailed, complete, and defensible. SarbOx requires that executives certify financial statements and operational controls, and the penalties and publicity for non-compliance are significant. This means that for an executive to approve an investment, they must have an appreciation and understanding for why this proposed investment makes financial and operational sense, and how the investment contributes to performance.

A Brief ROI and Cost Benefit Portfolio Review

For the purpose of simplicity, we've been referring to ROI as a generic term. As stated earlier, ROI is one of many methods for calculating and measuring the financial benefits of an investment. We refer to these methods as Cost Benefit Analysis (CBA) tools. We'll briefly look at the more popular methods to help explain each method, as well as compare and contrast them. For a more detailed examination, refer to the article titled "ROI, Cost Benefit and Business Case

Analysis: The ABC's of CBA"

Method	Meaning	Measure	Benefits	Disadvantages
ROI	Return on Investment	% or $	Comprehensive, well known, related to DCF and EVA	Requires detailed calculations
IRR	Internal Rate of Return	%	Useful for comparing with hurdle rates, competing choices	Less indicative of risks, costs
NPV	Net Present Value	$	Less intensive and easier to compute than DCF	Not as accurate as DCF
DCF	Discounted Cash Flow	$	Very accurate; favored method of many CFO's	Requires detailed calculations
EVA	Economic Value Added	$	Provides value created, less financing costs	Requires Activity Based Costing to get full benefit
TCO	Total Cost of Ownership	$	Focuses on operational costs of investment	Focuses on costs rather than benefits
Payback	Payback Period	Time	Provides time when benefits exceed costs	Less sensitive to risks, costs
Real Options	Real Options (also known as Black-Scholes)	$	Best insight for changing and volatile conditions; considers external factors	Involves many, very complex calculations

Is any one method better than all the rest? It depends upon whom you ask. ROI has become the most discussed method, as it offers a broad range of advantages. As stated previously, the "best" method is the one that 1) provides a reliable answer, and 2) is acceptable to the CFO and decision team.

MAKING CRM STICK

Lies, Damn Lies and ROI Lies

Critics of technology, and its value as expressed by ROI, have a plethora of studies that corroborate that technology, as a financial investment, has significantly underperformed against expectations. Supporters and advocates of technology point to numerous examples in which technology has enabled significant change and advantage. Which position is correct?

Actually, both stories are correct. Numerous studies have recounted stories of woe and stories of wow. One study of particular note was produced by consulting firm McKinsey & Company, who commissioned an exhaustive study that measured the impact of IT on productivity. The study, which examined the effects of technology on an industry-by-industry basis, was quite revealing: only 6 of the 53 industry sectors examined showed a positive correlation between investment and results. This study illustrates that on the average, technology investments have underperformed expectations, but in specific cases, technology investments have created definable and measurable economic value.

A value that ROI – and all of the CBA tools – provides is the ability to perform a pre and post project review, and to compare the projected results with the realized results. This allows the team, and the company, to learn lessons by comparing those projects that over-perform with those that under-perform. Borrowing a technique used by the military, called an After Action Report (AAR), this method provides constructive insights that can be used to improve the company's processes. AAR can help improve all aspects, from business case analysis and development, to how the selected proposal is delivered.

Building a Better Business Case and ROI

Much has been written about ROI. Books, trade publications, websites, and entire companies are dedicated to discussing ROI. There are loud cries of support for, and equally loud cries of criticism against, the use and effectiveness of ROI. What seems to be ignored is that, like any tool, ROI is subject to misapplication and misuse.

The effectiveness of the tool is dependent on technique, the thoroughness of the analysis, and the skills of the practitioner. Just as a scalpel can help a surgeon remove a problem, so too can its misuse cost the doctor a patient. ROI, like the scalpel, does not come with explicit instructions. Its value, therefore, is highly dependent on how skillfully it is used.

MAKING CRM STICK

While there are a great many companies that claim they have a "ROI model", most do not provide comprehensive treatment to the many factors that affect "realizable" ROI. What is "Realizable ROI"? Simply, it is, within a narrow range, what the proposed investment will produce in your environment. Compare this with what level of ROI that a proposed project could produce. The difference is significant – it is the difference between a highly successfully and earnings enriching investment, and one that is a miserable failure. Realizable ROI means using more detailed methods that consider your company's unique abilities, culture, and probabilities to enjoy the maximum benefits from the proposed investment.

There are two chief defects with most "average" ROI calculations. First, they assume best outcome scenarios, and second, most average calculations lack comprehensive treatment needed to accurately predict ROI.

The problem with best outcome scenarios is that they predict a financial return which will be realized only under the most favorable of circumstances. The probability of a best outcome scenario is indeed possible, but it is low. There are risks inherent in every project, and it is neither realistic nor prudent to give casual treatment to such risks. Risk exists, and it is incumbent on all members of the project team to surface, analyze, and develop risk reduction strategies that improve the probability of financial and technical success.

Comprehensive treatment means that the manifold factors that affect performance in the company are well understood, and are computed into the expected results. Among these factors are the thoroughness and quality with which the business case was analyzed and considered, selection of the proposed solution v. other choices, and the quality and thoroughness with which the deployment strategy and tactics were considered.

Most CFO's will quickly discount – or outright reject – business cases and ROI calculations that do not reflect realistic projections. The greater the complexity, in terms of size and values of time duration, talent requirements, technical change, and treasury (cost) the project, the more likely the CFO will significantly discount the returns and inflate the costs. Unless these items are properly discussed, the CFO's adjustment process may result in the project not being approved.

Conversely, the more detailed and explicit the calculations include company specific and project specific factors and risks, the more believable the projections will be to the CFO and approval team. This increases the credibility of the projections, and thereby, the probability that the investment in the project will be approved.

So what should be included in this "Realizable ROI" (or perhaps "Risk Adjusted ROI") set of calculations? The short answer is every factor that could prevent the project from being successful. The combination of a business case that discusses factors – risks – that could affect the performance of the investments, along with how those risk factors relate and change the ROI calculations significantly improve the accuracy of projected ROI. This builds credibility into the case, the ROI, and its sponsors with the CFO and approval team.

This host of factors, and some of the factors to follow, gets at the heart of the difference between the capacity of the project to deliver results (the results it could deliver) v. the probability and likelihood of the results it will deliver. While the following list is not all encompassing, it provides factors worthy of consideration:

Use More Than One CBA Method

Because each of the CBA methods provides different insight, many organizations have opted to use more than one method as a second comparison to corroborate results, such as combining ROI and Payback Period. The first method provides the primary metric, with the second calculation used to corroborate or validate the results. When investment options appear to deliver similar value, the second calculation can serve as a "tiebreaker". For example, Payback Period can be used as the tiebreaker to indicate which investment delivers value first. A Portfolio Management approach (discussed later), particularly one that uses a risk-, time- or value-based scoring method, can be a worthwhile tool.

Existing Situation v. Proposal v. Alternate Options

For greater credibility and relevance, the body of the business case should compare both existing and proposed operational costs and benefits, as well as alternate options that were considered, but not selected. This analysis helps the author to explain in explicit detail the objective consideration of a broader range of options, and it further informs the reader – the decision team – that competing choices were given due consideration, and the rationale for why they were not the recommended course of action.

MAKING CRM STICK

Project Management

As discussed earlier, managing a project for financial and technical performance is critical. Technology project management, as a technique, has significantly improved in recent years, but the integration of managing for technical and for financial performance – financial results, not simply the cost of the project – is not strongly linked.

A wealth of project management tools and techniques exist. The Project Management Institute provides training, education, certification, and support in the standards and practices of professional project management. Project management tools include PERT, GANTT, and numerous other methods, and a broad range of software tools.

Progress Measurement

Closely related to project management is the need to have timely and high quality feedback and measurement systems. These systems inform project team member and sponsors of actual results v expected results at any point in time.

Such systems can help identify successes and challenges as the project matures, and can provide valuable feedback to make adjustment to team strength and support as required to ensure success. Like a compass, measurement systems tell us if, and where, we are still on course.

Risk Management

An important element of understanding the ability of a technology project to deliver value to the organization is the concept of risk. Risk defines the likelihood of success.

As projects increase in complexity, the complexity of risk increases as well. New risks may be added, which might range from having a team that understands all technical and business aspects, risk of cultural acceptance of new changes, risk of delays, risk of unintended and unexpected outcomes, and so forth.

Technical risks include failure of the technology to perform as expected. This can include outright technology failures, or an ineffective fit of the technology with the application requirements, or overly complex business practices. Changes in the boundary condition of what the technology project was proposed to address, otherwise referred to as project scope, can also affect the projects ability to meet expectations. Terms are used to describe the extent of the change range from minor - "scope creep" - to major - "scope leap".

As is true in other business situations, adjustments to changing circumstances are often required. Changing project scope to allow flexibility as a response to changing business and/or technical situations is important, but the implications and risks must be clearly understood so as not to jeopardize success.

Having a sufficient technical staff, with the skills to properly understand and deploy the project, are of obvious importance. In this case, "technical" can refer to technology, as well as business and process specific skills. Integration, or the ability to make systems work together with no or minimal manual intervention, is similarly important, from both a business and technical perspective.

Before a technology investment is approved, a thorough risk analysis should be performed to fully examine and plan for risks that could cause the project to fail, or under-perform against expectations, from a technical, operational, financial, and cultural perspective.

Sensitivity testing should be performed to understand how changes in assumptions affect the resulting calculations. Sometimes, company or project specific financial models can include unique variables or calculations. Slight changes in some variables can, in some cases, cause large changes in calculated results, and be inaccurate or misleading. Sensitivity testing helps identify and avoid such problems, thereby improving decisions.

Cultural Acceptance

As stated in the risk section, consideration should be given to organizational readiness and commitment of the new project. A technical success will not deliver financial success if the new product or system is not used, or is underused. While this is not a problem of the technology, it is, nonetheless, a risk to the organization which must be considered. In his book Why Decisions Fail, Ohio State professor Dr. Paul Nutt examines cases in which organization factors caused such failures.

Cultural factors can include resisting change, as well as an inability to understand how to successfully transition to a new style of operations. Whether deliberate or unintentional, complete or partial failures cost the organization time and money, and can be significant contributors to technology project failures.

Portfolio Management

A Portfolio Management approach which considers factors such as projected value, projected cost, estimated risk, and expected duration can help management teams apply focus and attention to a smaller, but better quality group of investments.

Portfolio Management considers the value and status of each project on its individual merits. Interestingly, the portfolio management model and approach borrows its philosophy from none other than...finance.

Evaluation Approaches

Numerous tools and techniques exist to evaluate investments and projects in general. Managing technology projects have a variety of specialized tools as well, but many are focused on the aspects that ensure technical successes. Rather than discuss the many types of evaluation methods, we'll focus on two techniques worth noting.

An After Action Report (AAR) is an exercise, borrowed from the US Military, which reviews the actual performance and results of a project with those that were expected. Positive and negative differences are used as learning experiences to improve future performance, such that the organization changes its institutional practices. AAR's are intended to be used as a training and developmental tool, and not punitive, unless required.

Real Options is a quantitative technique that relies on calculation model called Black-Scholes, named after the two Nobel laureates who developed it. Real Options calculates the expected future value of a project or investment with currently known information and expected future trends. Most CBA techniques are "inside-out" weighted, that is, they consider the internal project and company factors first, and the external results created by them. Real Options is "outside-in" in that it considers factors and trends external to the company to calculate future returns, and evaluate which investment commitments a company should maintain.

Real Options, using the Black-Scholes model, offers a very dynamic and highly quantitative method of evaluating projects during execution. Where most methods wait to fully evaluate a project until it is complete, the Real

MAKING CRM STICK

Options approach asks a different question: should the company still be committed to completing a project investment?

Real Options is mathematically intensive, and factors risks, changes in technology, changes in competitive situations, project status and currently expected benefits, relative to other project investment choices. As with the Portfolio Management philosophy, Real Options has its foundations in finance.

Real Options focuses on what is in the best financial interest of the company, instead of using assuming that once a commitment has been made that the company must maintain that commitment to complete the project.

Conclusion

Nobel-laureate economist Robert Solow, when asked for his thoughts about the effects of technology on economic performance, once remarked, "You can see the computer age everywhere but in the productivity statistics." Such observations, added with the evidence of failed and underperforming projects, has lead to a cynical and defensive posture toward technology investment by many CFO's.

The economic shocks of Year 2000, 9-11 attacks, stock market bubbles, accounting reform, and globalization have contributed to CFO's being more cautious. An IT investment philosophy that once accepted "spending more to keep up with the competition" has abruptly changed to one of "doing more and spending less". This cautious approach has led to downward bias on technology pricing and the perceived value of technology investment. In lieu of proof otherwise, the skeptical posture will continue. Hence, there is more pressure – and value – to develop strong business cases which correctly and accurately prescribe technology investments, and which contain defensible and realistic ROI metrics.

IT does matter, and can make significant contributions to the health, competitiveness, and profitability of a company. Whiles numerous successful examples exist, four standout companies where an IT enabled strategy has made a profound difference are now household names: Amazon, Dell, eBay, and FedEx. These companies that have dramatically changed the way we work, think, and purchase in both our professional and personal lives. All four have, and continue to, use IT to create value, advance their lead against competitors, and to enrich the companies and their shareholders with profits.

MAKING CRM STICK

But rarely are business successes realized without accompanying changes in business processes. Moreover, a high quality IT investment that delivers superior ROI is achieved only when the business diagnosis is correct, clearly understood, skillfully deployed, and properly measured.

IT and ROI require an intimate understanding of the business, its challenges and opportunities, and its likelihood to fully use the capabilities of IT for business benefit. When these points are carefully considered and prudently followed, the investment in technology will likely be one that adds significant, measurable, and sustainable value.

2004 © Richard D. Janezic. All rights reserved.

MAKING CRM STICK

MAKING CRM STICK

ROI, Cost Benefit and Business Case Analysis: The ABC's of CBA – Understanding and comparing ROI, NPV, IRR, DCF, EVA, TCO and Real Options (Part 1 of a 5 part series) – Richard D. Janezic

Scenario: It's your responsibility to choose whether to make a $2M investment for the company. An existing system fails often, at a cost of thousands per hour. A proposed new system, expected to take 1 year to install, is from a small, unknown vendor. Should you fix what you have or opt for a new system? Your choice carries "career consequences". How do you choose?

Competition and shareholder pressure are causing the value of effective, prudent decisions to be increasingly vital to survival and success. New expenditures are exposed to more stringent evaluation. While investments may provide substantial business benefit, improper choices can be more than just embarrassing; they can be devastating. Example: A 22-hour outage in 1999 caused auctioneer eBay an estimated $4M in fees, and $5B in market value.

Given such risks, executives are exceedingly cautious about making sound decisions. The result often means more thoughtful analysis, and longer decision cycles. With some projects' costs in the millions, it's crucial to be able to clearly "step through" the future effects of decisions, as undoing them may not be an option. A variety of decision tools exist, but is there a best choice?

ROI has become a hot business term in recent years. Recent studies found that 80% of companies require some form of formal justification for new technology related projects, with a strong preference toward using ROI.

MAKING CRM STICK

Interestingly, the same study found that 1 in 5 companies have a formal policy to measure actual performance against the ROI projections.

Whether you're involved in selecting or selling technology products or services, chances are you've been asked about ROI, or to help construct the business case. But, you ask, precisely what is ROI? Isn't ROI the same as a business case? How does ROI differ from other methods? Is there a preferred method, or best choice to use? How is the analysis performed?

Collectively, these terms refer to evaluations called Cost Benefit Analysis, or CBA. This article will help demystify CBA by reviewing and comparing some of the popular methods. We'll examine the value that each method reveals, as well as where each may be more suitable.

What is CBA, what does it do, and why does it matter?

As the name suggests, cost benefit analysis compares what a new item will cost with how it's expected to benefit a business. CBA is a decision support method used to help answer "should we" and "what if" questions, such as, "should we fund this project?", and "what happens if we do?".

In its essence, CBA is a mathematical method to measure, or quantify, the benefits of a course of action. More importantly, CBA tells a story which is rich in detail, about why a course of action (usually involving an expenditure) should be followed. CBA simulates (sometimes referred to as "modeling)" how the proposed action is expected to change the economics of creating and/or delivering products and/or services.

CBA is a commonly used method for evaluating "make/buy" decisions, that is, should a company do a project internally or outsource it. CBA is attractive because it allows for foresight in testing the merits of a decision prior to committing any significant amounts of capital. Some tools are broad in application (ROI for example, can be used to evaluate entire companies), but most often, they are used to evaluate the merits and value of specific projects. While CBA is primarily a tactical tool, it can provide some illuminating strategic insight.

Why is ROI so popular now in IT? During the 1990's, US companies spent over $1 trillion on IT. That fact, combined with lower economic growth rates, increasing global competition, and numerous reports of minimal gains from the investments are among the factors that are pressuring business leaders to more carefully think through the value and payoff of new projects.

MAKING CRM STICK

Who started this cost benefit analysis stuff anyway?

Economic accounting is not new. The Frenchman Dupuit, followed by the Englishman Marshall, gave us the concepts over 100 years ago. In the 1920's, the US Army Corps of Engineers (for years, West Point was one of the few engineering schools in the US) developed a process for economically evaluating which public projects to pursue. Economists adopted the Army's process, and have been formalizing and standardizing CBA since the 1950's.

Today, competitive pressures have created a keen focus on improving quality, speed, and cost structures. CBA provides a repeatable, objective method for measuring if, and by how much, the economics of a business change by pursuing investment options. Interestingly, some Federal level technology projects actually require – by law – the use of CBA in justifying projects.

Cost benefit analysis and business case analysis: Are they the same? How do they differ?

ROI, CBA, and business case are often used interchangeably. Each of these methods explores the expected consequence of an action. To be technically correct, ROI and CBA are quantitative, economic components of Business Case Analysis (BCA).

Business case analysis is a more encompassing discussion of the business reasons that a change is being considered. The business case analyzes the current situation, metrics to indicate what's wrong or what needs to be improved, and the underlying reasons why. BCA often includes relevant background information about the problem, and may discuss history, competitive strategy, risk factors, and external market and other factors. The purpose is to provide a more comprehensive discussion of the reasons that a proposed action is being considered. An important element of business case analysis is that of risk analysis; the risks of both the status quo and the risks of pursuing change. Risk is an important theme which will be discussed later.

It's important to note that there is not a rigid, precise format for the business case or some of the cost benefit tools (such as ROI). Companies, and even departments within the same company, may have differing standards for formats, and which items should be included in the analysis.

MAKING CRM STICK

So ROI is not the best choice?

It depends. Each CBA method yields a different answer, with each giving a slightly different perspective of the same situation. A business case analysis may include ROI and one or more alternative CBA methods. For example, in a well-documented business case analysis, you may find ROI, NPV and payback period analysis of several different scenarios. The advantage is that each of the scenarios are compared and contrasted, thereby defining which course of action offers the greater advantage. Using ROI in isolation of a business case may give an incomplete picture of whether a decision is prudent or not.

It can be beneficial to use CBA methods that compliment one another, rather than relying upon only one. Each provides a deeper and somewhat different analytical insight, so that risks, timing, and rewards are better understood and quantified. When used in concert, CBA methods reveal more detail about how much an action will really cost, what its true benefits are, and why.

Before we proceed, it is important to underscore that the methods are quite related. While they each have their unique differences, they do share some key commonalities:

- At their essence, each method helps to calculate the value that results from selecting an action. In some financial circles, the terms refer to the value that is either "created" (inferring that it is "cash positive" - it produces more value than it costs) or "consumed" by selecting the option (meaning that its costs exceed the value it creates).

- Each method includes time and money in its calculations. Benjamin Franklin warned that, "Time is money". Most, but not all methods use the "time value of money" concept, which states that $1 today is worth more than $1 in the future. The time value of money is an important topic that we'll discuss in a moment.

- "Sunk" costs (previously incurred expenses) are not included in CBA calculations, however, actual salvage value of equipment that will be retired and sold can be included. The business case may discuss what was spent; CBA looks ahead to what will be spent.

MAKING CRM STICK

Much has been written and said about the value of analysis. Two favorites are:

"Torture numbers, and they will confess to anything." and "Statistics are like a bikini. What they reveal is suggestive; what they conceal is vital."

Humor aside, the methods are not infallible, and can be misapplied. When used correctly, each method is reliable, so it's important to have a clear, consistent process for how and when they're used. The value is in allowing the numbers to tell the story.

A key concept: The Time value of money

The time value of money is a central concept in all of the methods. As mentioned earlier, the reason is that an amount of money received today has greater value than getting that same amount of money next week, quarter, or year. Two important terms are present value and future value. This section is deliberately brief. It assumes you have had previous exposure to the material, and is included only as a quick refresher. Please note that it is critical to understand these concepts before proceeding.

The time value of money is affected by 2 primary factors: the time between now and a date in the future, and the interest rate. In finance terms, the time element is measured in the number of time "periods", which can be set in days, months, quarters, or years. The interest rate is the percentage increase of the speed, or rate, at which money or "capital" grows in value over time.

Present value (PV) is the currency value of what capital, received at a future date, is equivalent to in today's dollars. Future value (FV) is the currency value of what capital, at this moment, will be equal to at a future date. Both use time and interest rate in their calculations. When performing the calculations for PV and FV, it is critical to be consistent with the measures of time and interest. (We'll use formulas later; for this section, it's the concept that is important.)

Another related term to the interest rate is the discount rate. The interest rate is forward looking: how capital increases in value over time (think future value). But because the value of capital increases over time, capital that we will receive in the future will be worth less than it is in today's terms. Why? Because we did not have it to invest. How much less is it worth? The value by which it will be decreased in value, relative to today's terms, is its discounted value. The discount rate is the rate by which we diminish the value of capital which will be received in the future.

Let's illustrate using a brief example. $10,000 in 1 year at an interest rate of 10% is worth $11,000, otherwise called its future value. The present value of $11,000 to be received 1 year from now is equal to $10,000, assuming a discount rate of 10%.

Before proceeding, make sure that you are comfortable in understanding PV, FV, interest rate, and discount rate, as we'll be using the terms in discussions and calculations.

With that brief background, let's look at the competing methods. We'll begin with ROI or return on investment, given its current popularity, and then discuss and compare some of the other popular competing methods. Each method will be defined and described, followed by a strength and weakness analysis. Later, we'll do side-by-side comparisons using a consistent example to review the answers that each method provides, and the facts which each method uses.

In the interest of brevity, the discussion will be limited to the most common points and concepts, rather than attempting to go into exhaustive detail. With than intro, let's begin...

ROI: Return on Investment

ROI was originally developed by an engineer in E.I. Dupont's treasury department named F. Donaldson Brown circa 1913. It is currently in vogue, as when well detailed, it is among the more comprehensive and practical of the methods. (Note: The strict definition is Return on Invested Capital, which is typically used to measure overall corporate performance. ROIC is rumored to be one of the favored measures of legendary investor Warren Buffet). ROI is used to evaluate individual projects or decisions.

One reason for the appeal of ROI is that it appears simple: divide the return, or incremental gains that will be received from an investment, by the costs that were required to achieve that gain. While simple in concept, obtaining accurate measurements of the returns and of the costs can be difficult and complex.

How expressed: ROI can be expressed as a ratio, or as a percentage where the benefit-to-cost ratio is multiplied by 100. Example: a 3.5, or 3.5:1, or 350% ROI are numerically equivalent.

MAKING CRM STICK

How to evaluate: Larger ROI values are better, as they indicate greater economic "return".

Strength: When well detailed, ROI provides a comprehensive evaluation.

Weakness: ROI can be complex and time consuming to accurately construct, and unless discretely calculated by time period, it indicates if, not when benefits are realized. Because costs usually occur in the early stages of an investment and returns occur in the later stages, how the analysis is performed can have a dramatic impact. Assessing "true" costs and returns, and properly matching costs (especially if "allocations" are involved) can also be a complex and potentially misleading process when not performed correctly or consistently.

DCF: Discounted Cash Flow

DCF is a newer technique, about 50 years old, and is a favored method with finance and investment professionals. DCF is, as its name implies, a sum of the cash flows from an investment/purchase, adjusted for the diminished or discounted value of dollars received in the future. DCF is closely related to net cash flow (NCF), internal rate of return (IRR), and net present value (NPV), but it adjusts and compensates for the time value of money.

Example: You've decided to purchase new software or a piece of machinery. You are expecting that it will both save money and help generate greater revenues, but it will take three years to begin seeing the cost advantages and revenues. DCF tells us what the monetary value of those dollars in will be in three years, less the cost of obtaining

A strength of DCF is its usefulness for comparison, that is, when comparing two or more different scenarios, each with differing cash flow streams. Note that it can be used to compare different alternatives for the use of capital, not just for comparing projects. Also, managers specifically trained in finance may prefer the analysis using both discounted and non discounted methods.

How expressed: DCF is a series of dollar values over the time period(s) indicated, expressed in positive (cash is generated or created) or negative (cash is used or consumed) terms.

How to evaluate: Higher positive DCF values are better, as they indicate greater cash flows.

MAKING CRM STICK

Strength: Discretely illustrates cash flows on a period by period basis, adjusted for the time value of money, and is a preferable method for comparing multiple scenarios or choices.

Weakness: Similar to ROI, DCF can be complex and time consuming to accurately construct

2004 © Demand Econometrics, Inc. All rights reserved.

Chapter 6: Beyond Requirements: Architecting the Future-State Customer Experience

First made famous by Steven Covey, "begin with the end in mind" has become a mantra. In the CRM world, this means having a clear and compelling vision of the future-state Customer Experience. It goes beyond simply collecting requirements from the customer point of view.

We believe there is a creative exercise that must be done to architect a CRM solution with impact. The exercise is a painting of the picture of what it will be like to be a customer or employee of the company after the CRM solution has been deployed. Together, the qualitative future-state Customer Experience and the quantitative business case should tell the story of the value of a CRM program or initiative, with the ultimate goal of having nobody say, "Why are we doing this?"

Think about the competing needs and wants of the three stakeholder groups in an enterprise – the *customers*, the *employees*, and the *stewards* who include or represent the owners or shareholders in an organization (e.g., C-level executives, governing board members, P&L owners). A successful CRM program or initiative should ideally deliver value to all three stakeholder groups. When it doesn't, we see the risk of failure increase.

"Business case! Business case! Business case!" seems to be the chant of the year. Having a compelling ROI business case, which describes the bottom line dollar benefit of a proposed program or initiative is certainly a success factor for CRM success. The studies by IBM, Accenture and others have certainly shown this to be the case. But the ROI business case

MAKING CRM STICK

is really only targeted towards the stewards in the organization – the leaders who are entrusted to deliver value to the owners or shareholders of the business – typically in the form of earnings-per-share and dividends.

Customers and *employees* don't really care very much about the ROI business case. Even employees with stock options or salaries tied to company performance will have a very limited interest in the business case behind a CRM solution. But they are two very important constituencies who can cause a CRM implementation to fail, if they have not bought into the benefits behind the solution. They are interested in knowing how the proposed CRM program or initiative will make their lives better. They want to know "How will the proposed CRM program or initiative make it better for me to be a customer of the organization or an employee in the organization in the future?" As the CRM sponsor or project manager, if you can create a compelling vision of how the *future* will be a *better place* for customers and employees, then you will derive the benefit of the buy-in of these two stakeholder groups. The question is . . . How do you make the vision *compelling*?

This chapter begins with Helen Mazur's *Strategic Visioning*. We have included three additional white papers in this chapter to present points-of-view on how to articulate the future-state Customer Experience with sufficient rigor. The second white paper is entitled *A Quantitative Business Case Is Not Enough: Document the qualitative benefits of integrated CRM technology in a future-state customer experience scenario*. It describes a two-year period in the future life of a fictional character who is the customer of a financial services company that deploys new CRM technology. This is an example of how we believe the future-state Customer Experience should be articulated and communicated to customers, employees, and other stakeholders in a compelling way. Two additional white papers, originally part of a series of white papers called *Focus on Late Adopters*, is included as follow-on readings.

Strategic Visioning – Helene Mazur

Imagine That

The process of developing a vivid picture of the future is an important step in creating a future that is better than today. A clear, motivating image can inspire us to reach higher and overcome challenges. Once created, a vision will begin to impact today as a foundation for new decisions.

While all that sounds great, crafting a meaningful vision of the future isn't always that simple! A blank piece of paper can be daunting whether you are an artist, a writer, a programmer, or a CEO. If your natural inclination is to skip 'the vision' and get right down to business, read on. Everyone can be a creative visionary!

Art and Science

It is not a surprise that visual thinking plays an important role in the creative process; what many people don't realize is the role that creative thinking plays in the strategic thinking and planning process.

Henry Mintzberg in "The Rise And Fall Of Strategic Planning" makes a clear distinction between the skills necessary for strategic thinking and the skills needed for planning. He explains that planning involves the left side of the brain with a need for logic, reasoning, linear and rational thinking. Strategic thinking, on the other hand, requires the ability to examine new possibilities involving the right brain. Strategic thinking entails tasks such as dealing with large chunks of information, and the ability to pull pieces together into a big picture. Planning involves words and numbers and strategic thinking requires patterns and visual images.

MAKING CRM STICK

Links

In "Strategic Thinking And The New Science," T. Irene Sanders tells us that "strategic thinking has two major components: insight about the present and foresight about the future." Visual thinking can help us link our intuitive sense of events in the world with our intellectual understanding.

Although there are different viewpoints, most current scientific research shows that while no one is totally left-brained or right-brained, most people have a distinct dominance on one side or the other.

In tasks such as the development of a long-range strategy, where thinking needs to come from both sides of the brain, it is important to find ways to draw out both our imagination and our analytic abilities. Visual based techniques can help us link possibility thinking, intuition, and current realities.

Visualization

A vision can be a mental picture of an "ideal" organization, relationship or life. Studies have shown that we are more likely to reach an objective if we can see it and can imagine the steps to reach it. Visioning is a common strategy in sports. Olympic skaters imagine themselves going through the steps and landing a perfect jump.

Visual thinkers create pictures or models of a problem in their mind, play with the visual, move it around, refine it, and use it to raise more questions. A drawing or model helps push thinking further. Albert Einstein imagined himself traveling through the universe as a "man in a box" on a ray of light. This vision helped him develop the theory of general relativity.

Tools and Techniques

In a strategic planning process, there are four fundamental questions: "Where are you now?" Where are you going?" Where do you want to be?" and "How are you going to get there?"

Visual ways of addressing these types of questions help the mind "to see." Seeing can help identify issues and opportunities, organize information, prioritize, clarify thinking, and set goals on a personal and/or organizational level. Try out one of the following exercises:

Envision an article written in the future about you or your company.

MAKING CRM STICK

Record your desired future in a diagram, sketch, model, or in a photographic montage. In "The Artist's Way," Julia Cameron suggests creating collages or journals to help develop ideas.
Imagine yourself receiving an award for a major accomplishment. What is the award for? What has been accomplished?

More complex visual diagramming techniques can reveal patterns, interrelationships and interdependencies, stimulate creative thinking and enable new ideas and innovations. When working with groups of people, visual tools can help to foster creative dialogue, create perspective shifts and help to record ideas.

Mind Mapping

Mind Mapping is a powerful technique that can help in developing a strategy, or expand thinking on a subject. The 'Map' uses words, lines, logic, colors, images, and links to draw out associations and stimulate thinking. The technique works as well in large group brainstorming sessions, as it does one-on-one with a coach.

While there are many different "mind mapping" systems, the basic process involves expanding on ideas using key words and branches. The objective is to make a complex or thorny topic easier to understand, explore, or remember.

Create a simple mind map:

- Draw a circle in the middle of a blank sheet of paper and write a project, goal, dream or idea in the center of the circle.
- Draw lines (spokes or branches) radiating out from the central circle.
- Write down thoughts/ideas that relate to the central circle at the end of each spoke and circle them.
- From each of the new circles repeat steps B-C, continuing out as far as you feel comfortable.

Next, translate the ideas to an outline form and try to create some action steps based on your thinking.

Scenario Planning/Future Mapping

Scenario planning tools have been around for decades and are useful to help anticipate change, predict the elements of different scenarios and develop strategies to be able to shape each possible future.

Today there are many models that take scenario planning to the next level. Dr. Canton's "Future Mapping" tool makes the distinction between forecasting (getting advance information about the future based on analysis of existing conditions and trends) and foresight (the ability to see what is emerging). The tool creates scenarios based on key change drivers, trends and "forces that can shape the future of an enterprise, market, industry, society or civilization." Read more about Future Mapping at: http://www.technofutures.com/article31.shtml.

Support

Visual tools and techniques are the most effective when they are set in the right framework. One of the keys to good visioning is asking good questions. The combination of questioning and visual techniques can bring out the "creative thinker" in even the most task-oriented person.

Are you focused on the right questions?

Copyright 2004 by Helene Mazur. All rights reserved. Helene Mazur is the President of Princeton Performance Dynamics, a business coaching company.

A Quantitative Business Case is Not Enough: Document the qualitative benefits of integrated CRM technology in a future-state customer experience scenario – Daniel T. Murphy and Andres A. Salinas

The CRM Practitioner Perspective:

As CRM practitioners, we are all able to explain why CRM is important – Customer expectations are still significantly on the rise. Customers care less about brand and more about choice. They have come to expect frequent flyer miles and other rewards every time they shop. Loyalty continues to diminish. Customers expect consistency across multiple channels or "touchpoints" and accessibility 24 by 7. They expect to be able to touch the seller when they want, where they want, and how they want. In the new multi-channel world, customers will increasingly expect to self-manage their relationship with sellers. Expectations are high and getting higher. And the competition is only a click away.

Nearly all CRM practitioners can eloquently describe the spirit and objectives of CRM – Collecting, analysing and utilizing customer knowledge to provide higher quality and more personalized service. It is about better managing the customer touchpoints and maximizing the lifetime value of customer relationships.

Many CRM practitioners can eloquently describe the features and benefits of the various technologies that make CRM happen – From the touchpoint technologies (e.g., telephony, web, PDA, web chat, email Response, etc.), to the true customer management applications (e.g., Siebel, Peoplesoft CRM, Oracle CRM, Pivotal, etc.), to the database technologies and architectures (e.g., Oracle, Sun, Microsoft, etc.) that make it all possible.

MAKING CRM STICK

As CRM practitioners, we have also become adept in the building of the Business Case behind a CRM implementation. We have refined our approaches for articulating and documenting the business benefits of a CRM implementation - the documentation of the sales and service strategy, the strategic "levers" (e.g., increase cross-selling) that will be "pulled", and the associated performance measures (e.g., percentage of sales per quarter which included cross-sells) that will describe the quantitative benefit of a specific CRM technology.

The CRM Practitioner's Challenge:

Yet, there is one area where we often struggle. It is in bringing to life the future-state business vision in living color. Helping the client and their customers truly picture in their mind the future-state CRM-enabled business is indeed a challenge. Helping the client to be able to articulate that future themselves is perhaps the greatest challenge for a CRM practitioner.

Two years ago, we were implementing a complex CRM solution at a large financial services organization. We were discussing options for communicating the new CRM capabilities to several thousand sales and service representatives as well to as customers. Our client said "Listen, my customers don't want to hear all that mumbo jumbo about customer knowledge, personalization, and customer lifetime value. They really only want to know one simple thing - What will the customer interaction of the future feel like, look like, taste like, etc.?" A good analogy would be, "Do I need to stop buying VHS movies, and start building my DVD library?"

To help answer these critical questions, we now develop a detailed "Two-Years-in-the-Life" scenario that can be published whole or in part for sales and service functions within the organization, or externally for customers. To build the Two-Years-in-the-Life scenario, we typically:

- Bring together a small group of forward-thinking sales and/or service representatives from the current-state touchpoints (e.g., sales reps, CSRs, etc.);
- Select a point of time in the future, say five years from now;
- Select a customer segment (e.g., "family builders");
- Begin storyboarding on a whiteboard or with flipcharts;
- Tell the story of multiple customer interactions, across (a) multiple touchpoints, (b) an agreed period of time (typically two years), (c) multiple product purchases, and (d) multiple existing technologies,

MAKING CRM STICK

new technologies, and perhaps some yet-to-be invented technologies.
- Work through the two-year timeline discussing possible interactions or "acts" across a customer lifecycle, from the Attract phase of the customer relationship through the Evaluate, Purchase, Service and Retain phases;
- Develop a scenario for each customer segment.

> In the storyboarding exercise we document the experiences of customers across the entire Customer Lifecycle. We typically emphasize the service delivery phase in order to "bring to life" the service experience of the future. Using whiteboards or flipcharts, we document a series of customer interactions or "acts" in which we weave in multiple product and media interactions to "paint the picture" of what it will be like to be a customer x years in the future.

The benefits of this approach are several:

It provides a qualitative business case for CRM expenditures. When coupled with a quantitative business case, it creates a powerful cost justification. This helps all business executives rally around the cause, and specifically helps to bring into the conversation, executives who are focused on things other than the dollars and the IT architecture.

Our experience shows us that, once the future-state customer experience has been articulated, executives will use it as a tool to champion the cause - at board meetings, shareholder meetings, and Marketing communications.

It provides sales and service representatives with a vision of the desired future-state customer experience. It presents an expected outcome and a light at the end of a potentially long tunnel of complex point solution implementations, stop-gap solutions, and disruptions in day-to-day business.

It provides Human Resources and sales and service management with a blueprint for recruiting, selecting, training, evaluating, retaining, and rewarding the employee skill sets and personalities who will make the future-state business a success.

Customers will greatly appreciate knowing what it will be like to do business with the company in the future. In fact, customers who are on the verge of defecting to a competitor who offers the latest whizbang

MAKING CRM STICK

touchpoint technology may decide to change their mind if they see that their existing service provider is, in fact, planning to deliver the same technology eventually.

The following is an example of a customer scenario that we developed with a financial services client. It features a customer named Rolando.

Two Years in the Life of Rolando

The year is 2006...

My name is Rolando. I'm 30 years old, married with 3 children. I guess FINCO would say that I am in their "family-builder" customer segment. I work for a medium-sized company and have an annual income of $120,000. Some day, I would like to start my own company. But in the meantime, I climb mountains, windsurf, and ride motocross. I'm a real extreme sports guy!

This past January (2006) I decided I wanted to purchase a life insurance annuity. Since I already had a small life insurance policy with FINCO through my employer, I went out to the FINCO web site to get some information. I saw that FINCO has a link for corporate members like me, so I clicked on it and logged on with my company id. I saw my existing policy information, and a place to provide updated personal information (e.g., income, household information, ages, interests, education, etc.). So, I updated my personal information. Based on my updated input, I saw very targeted advertisements based on my personal profile. I was also able to see all of my accounts with other financial institutions as well (including my whole life policy with Prudential). All my accounts! Checking account, credit card accounts, investment accounts, frequent flyer accounts, all on one page. Alongside several of my account summaries, I saw advertisements for similar FINCO products. Cool.

I clicked on the whole life insurance link because I was initially interested in increasing my coverage. A screen pop-up told me that FINCO's whole life coverage is cheaper and has more features than my current whole life provider (a policy my parents opened for me 20 years ago). Very interesting. I decided to revisit the whole life option later though, because the web site also gave me a screen pop-up product recommendation for a Variable Annuity contract based on my customer profile. The screen pop gave me the following options: Email me, call me, chat with me, search the FAQs, or call FINCO's 800 toll free number.

MAKING CRM STICK

Rolando doesn't know this, but...

- When he interacted with the FINCO web site, Rolando was assigned a FINCO broker, and an automatic activity notification was sent to the Assigned Broker's inbox. The notification provided the FINCO Broker with information on the time and nature of Rolando's interaction.
- In addition, a tickler was automatically sent to the Customer Care Center for a "Did you get the information you needed?" follow-up call.
- An Email will automatically be sent to Rolando in a few days (if he hasn't made a purchase) with a specific offer.
- Rolando's click stream activity on the web site was recorded in his customer profile. For the next year, his activity will be visible by any Customer Care Rep or FINCO Broker that he speaks with on the phone.
- A notification will automatically be sent to Marketing, informing them that a customer is considering migrating to FINCO from a competitor provider, in this case Prudential.

Now, Back to Rolando...

I clicked on the FAQs link and browsed a bit, but then I didn't do anything with the information for a week. I received a call from a FINCO Customer Service Rep asking me if I had found the information I had needed on the FINCO web site. I told her I had found some information but was interested in additional information on the Variable Annuity product. She told me that she would have someone call me. I then received a call from my "Assigned" FINCO Broker, Claudia Ng. Wow! I didn't even know that I had an Assigned FINCO Broker. She gave me the additional information I needed, and after some discussion about the product, I bought a Variable Annuity contract.

I completed the entire transaction online:
- I filled out the application, approved it with E-signature;
- I downloaded the prospectus;
- I downloaded the policy pages;
- I chose to receive electronic statements over paper statements;
- I chose a consolidated statement instead of several separate statements;
- I chose my payment option of checking debit;
- And I chose to receive new product update alerts.

It was great - I didn't have to leave the comfort of my own home to get a new policy.

MAKING CRM STICK

Six months later...

In June 2006, I wanted to re-allocate my portfolio, so I went to the FINCO web site to do the re-allocation from growth funds to bond funds. It was easy as pie! When the web self-service feature asked for my "reason" for the transfer, I clicked "other".

Rolando doesn't know this but...

- The Customer Service Center received a tickler to call Rolando to confirm his satisfaction with the transaction and ask for a reason for the transfer.
- Rolando's Assigned Broker, Claudia Ng also received a tickler with a recommendation to check in with Rolando and simply ask "What's up Rolando?"

The next day...

I received a call from a FINCO Customer Care Rep asking how the transaction went. They also asked for a reason for my re-allocation. I laughed to myself because I guess they wanted to know why I clicked "other" on the web-self-service page. I told them that I was applying for a small business loan. My Loan Officer wanted me to reduce my risk ratio. Hence, my transfer from growth funds to bond funds. The smart Customer Care Rep asked me if I had established benefits (life, 401K, etc) for my employees or set up an IRA for myself. I told the Rep that I was setting up my own ten person company and needed "the whole shebang". The Rep used web collaboration technology to click with me through the Small Business Owner sub-site, and then electronically created a sales lead that was sent to my Assigned Broker.

My Broker Claudia called me the next day and told me she had received a notification from the Customer Care Rep that I was interested in the whole shebang. Like the Service Rep, Claudia had a record on her screen with every interaction I have had with FINCO. She had a history of all the calls I had made, emails I had sent and received, web pages I had hit (I think they call it "click stream"), and my online purchases. I figured wow, these guys really know who I am. And I really trust them. So I purchased the whole shebang with FINCO.

MAKING CRM STICK

Fast Forward to June 2008...

My company now has 7,000 employees and $1 billion in revenues.

Last week I had a question about my individual Variable Annuity and called FINCO. I was surprised to get the same Customer Care Representative that I have been talking with during my last three calls to FINCO. Her name is Julie McCoy (yep, like the Cruise Director on the Love Boat).

Rolando doesn't know this, but...

- He has been assigned a permanent Customer Care Representative (Julie McCoy) because he is now considered a high lifetime value customer.
- He has also been transferred from having an Assigned Broker to a Top-Tier Assigned Broker (Mark Baker). A Broker receives Top-Tier status when they have been recognized by FINCO for their excellence in customer retention, and that excellence has been tracked and proven by numbers.

Back to Rolando...

And now my new Top-Tier Broker, Mark Baker is sending me birthday cards and tickets to the Lakers games. Needless to say, I am now a loyal customer.

In the last few years I have revisited my homepage many times. I have converted most of my accounts with non-FINCO institutions to FINCO accounts. I have used FINCO's slick financial calculators that recommended several additional products that I have purchased. I've interacted with my Top-Tier Broker (Mark Baker) and my own personal Customer Care Rep (Julie McCoy) via every media touch point available. I have executed transactions, asked questions, and I've even answered surveys. In fact, last week I gave feedback on a web survey, regarding my service experiences and my service professionals (Mark and Julie), and I received an email from a FINCO Senior Vice-President thanking me and promising to take the lead on an improvement that I recommended. And I'm sure he'll follow thorough on his promise. They always do.

MAKING CRM STICK

Conclusion

Rolando's story illustrates the power of proactively recognizing customer needs, and in having the ability to build on an existing customer relationship with affective CRM capabilities. Indeed, his case is one in many where various players (in this case Brokers, CSRs, etc.) working for the service provider (FINCO) were able to recognize, or were alerted to opportunities in which Rolando was already interested (e.g. Whole Life upgrade, Variable Annuities, etc.).

Rolando's story also illustrates the power of going beyond simply defining the right portfolio of service offerings. His customer experience is compelling because Rolando had the opportunity to choose from several touchpoints and channels when dealing with FINCO and in researching his options. Rolando could have gone to several competing providers for the services he needed. Yet he remained loyal to FINCO because he recognized the relationship was founded on a keen understanding of his service and channel needs. He also recognized that as his own business grew, so did the exit costs associated with seeking another competing service provider. As with any successful partnership, the Rolando's relationship with FINCO grew in strength, just as it evolved in breadth.

Copyright © 2004 by Daniel T. Murphy and Andres A. Salinas. All rights reserved.

Focus on Late Adopters Series: CRM Technology and the Marina of the *Near* Future – Daniel T. Murphy and Andres A. Salinas

The following is the first in a series of narrow industry-focused articles that we are writing to illustrate how CRM will eventually revolutionize even the most stodgy change-resistant "late adopter" industries. As additional CRM technologies continue to trickle down to the middle market and below, and late-adopters begin to catch-on to the spirit of CRM, we should expect to see some exciting changes in some of those industries which are near-and-dear to our hearts.

This first article is for those recreational boaters out there who just can't wait until their local marina discovers the principles and technologies of CRM.

Introduction

We were excited about writing this article because it was an opportunity to combine our experiences as sailors and consumers of marine products and services, and also as management consultants who focus on the principles and technologies of Customer Relationship Management (CRM). Simply put, we help our clients develop sales and service strategies and plan and implement the technologies that make those strategies come true.

Our customers are facing challenges like never before. Customer expectations are still significantly on the rise. They care less about brand and more about choice. Customers have come to expect frequent flyer miles and other rewards every time they shop. Loyalty continues to diminish. Customers expect consistency across multiple channels or "touchpoints" and accessibility 24 by 7. They expect to be able to touch

MAKING CRM STICK

the seller when they want, where they want, and how they want. In the new world, customers will self-manage their relationship with sellers. Additionally, competition is only a click away.

Now, we realize what you are all thinking right now. You're thinking "Ya, right. That may be the case for Amazon.com, but it will never happen in the marine industry, and certainly not at my marina." In fact, unless you own a megayacht, you probably don't want your marina to act like Amazon.com. You want your marina to continue to operate as a "mom-and-pop" operation, right?

But let's face it folks. Everyone wants very high quality service. And there are relatively few people who are truly satisfied with today's marina experience. We love the idea of mom-and-pop marina, but we are often disappointed in the laissez-faire attitude, the service managers who never call back, the floats that are in disrepair, the security guards who fail to notice that one of your fenders floated away in a storm, etc. Even our federal government agencies are realizing that, in the new customer-centric world of sales and service, they eventually must give the customer what they want when they want, where they want, and how they want. The marine industry will as usual be late adopters. But they will adopt these practices and technologies. There is no doubt about it.

Ironically, the marina consolidation we have seen in recent years may not be so bad. It will likely provide some unexpected benefits to the customer, especially since larger operations will have greater available resources for integrated CRM technology. In our experience, we say adamantly that when CRM is implemented well, the customer is always better served. A professional Customer Care representative who has your customer profile, your account information, and your entire call history does, in fact, provide service that is superior to mom-and-pop.

As consultants, there is one area where we often struggle. It is in bringing to life the future-state business environment. Helping the client and their customers truly picture in their mind the future-state CRM-enabled business is indeed a challenge. Helping the client to be able to articulate that future themselves is perhaps the greatest challenge for a CRM practitioner.

Two years ago, we were implementing a complex CRM solution at a large financial services organization. We were discussing options for communicating the new CRM capabilities to several thousand sales and service representatives as well to as customers. Our client said "Listen, my customers don't want to hear all that mumbo jumbo about customer knowledge, personalization, and customer lifetime value. They really only want to know one simple thing – What will the customer interaction of the future feel like, look like, taste like, etc.?"

To help answer these critical questions, we now develop a detailed "Year-in-the-Life" scenario that can be published whole or in part for sales and service functions within the organization, or externally for customers. To build the Year-in-the-Life scenario, we typically:

- Bring together a small group of forward-thinking sales and/or service representatives from the customer "touchpoints" (e.g., sales reps, customer service representatives, service managers);
- Select a point of time in the future, say five years from now;
- Select a customer segment (e.g., "Under 30-years-old, single professionals");
- Begin storyboarding on a whiteboard or with flipcharts;
- Write the story of multiple customer interactions, across (a) multiple touchpoints, (b) an agreed period of time (typically 1-2 years), (c) multiple product purchases, and (d) multiple existing technologies, new technologies, and perhaps some yet-to-be invented technologies.
- Work through the two-year timeline discussing likely customer interactions across a customer lifecycle, from the Attract phase of the customer relationship through the Evaluate, Purchase, Service and Retain phases.

The benefits of this approach are several:

- It provides a qualitative business case for technology expenditures. When coupled with a quantitative business case, it creates a powerful cost justification. This helps all members of the organization rally around the cause.

- Our experience shows us that, once the future-state customer experience has been articulated clearly, executives will use it as a tool to champion the cause – at board meetings, shareholder meetings, in marketing communications, etc.

- It provides sales and service representatives with a vision of the desired future-state customer experience. It presents an expected outcome and a light at the end of a potentially long tunnel of complex point solution implementations, stop-gap solutions, and disruptions in day-to-day business.

MAKING CRM STICK

- It provides Human Resources and sales and service management with a blueprint for recruiting, selecting, training, evaluating, retaining, and rewarding the employee skill sets and personalities who will make the future-state business a success.

- Customers will greatly appreciate knowing what it will be like to do business with the company in the future. In fact, customers who are on the verge of defecting to a competitor who offers the latest whizbang touchpoint technology may decide to change their mind if they see that their existing service provider is, in fact, planning to deliver the same technology eventually.

Many of our clients are stodgy financial services companies, utilities and government agencies who wouldn't be able to envision the future if they watched the Sci Fi Channel for a year. For these clients, we take them through a "test drive" of the Year-in-the-Life approach using an industry that they find fun. We usually do "A Year-in-the-Life of a Golf Course Customer in the Year 2005". We recently had a client where most of the management team were sailors. Here is the scenario we developed. It describes a year in the life of a marina customer named Rolando.

The year is 2000

My name is Rolando. I am 40-years-old, married and have a wife and two children. Last year I purchased a new 2006 45-foot Beneteau cruising yacht. I started looking around for a marina that would fit my needs. My expectations were very high. I wanted a very high level of personalized service, all the amenities, and lots of things to keep my kids busy. In other words, I wanted everything that a large marina would offer, combined with a level of service that is typically available at the best family-operated marinas.

Several friends recommended that I check out Starfish Marina. So I logged on to www.starfishmarina.com. Very cool. Starfish Marina has 600+ slips, two restaurants, a beach for the kids, service center, marine supply store, and a bunch of other amenities.

Shopping For a Slip

So, I created a username and password on the Starfish Marina web site and was given my own Starfish Marina home page. And this was one of the most useful web pages I have ever seen. As I was signing up, it asked me a bunch of questions about myself and created a personalized page that

MAKING CRM STICK

directly reflected my preferences and lifestyle. Just like my bank. For example, I was asked to enter the zip codes for my favorite cruising locations, and it automatically showed the current and forecast for each location, the tides and currents, race calendars, and a www.Mapquest.com link to view an online chart for those locations. I also learned that if I kept my boat at Starfish Marina, I could use my own personal Starfish Marina home page to:

- check on my boat every day via webcam (at night too, because the video camera is infrared);
- check out of my slip for extended periods of time (for a long weekend, for example) and share in any revenues that the marina would receive for "sub-letting" my slip while I was away;
- sign up for Friday night races out in the bay;
- sign my kids up for the summer sailing program;
- send an email inquiry to the Starfish Marina Customer Service department with a guaranteed response within one hour via the media channel (e.g., email, phone call, fax, etc.) of my choice;
- create a service request for my slip for a telephone hookup, cable TV hookup, electrical hookup, holding tank pumpout, boat wash and wax, oil change, in-water bottom cleaning, etc.
- join a biannual web chat with the Starfish Marina CEO;
- create a cruising calendar with my probable summer cruise locations and dates;
- send an invitation for an onboard cocktail party to several friends, receive their online RSVP, and have the system automatically send them directions to the marina and a reminder on the day prior to the party;
- easily send emails to other Harbor Island Marina customers.

Very cool website. But the dockage fees seemed a bit high, and I wasn't quite sure that I wanted to keep my boat there.

Rolando doesn't know this, but Starfish Marina has placed him in their "family builders" customer segment based on the information in his customer profile, and intends to spend the next few years presenting him with advertisements for products and services that specifically fit his needs and lifestyle. Read on.

A week later, I received an email from Starfish Marina offering me an online coupon with a ten percent discount if I signed up for dockage before 11/6/06. The email included a "select your slip" link. I clicked on the link, and it took me to a graphic map of the marina. Unavailable slips were coded red. Available slips were coded green. Several slips that were

MAKING CRM STICK

intended for 35-45 footers were highlighted. Two slips were flagged as "easy to manoeuvre for sailboats", and two slips way down at the end of the marina were flagged as "additional ten percent discount". When I clicked on various slips, I was able to see the slip "options" (e.g., electrical, telephone, etc.) as well as panoramic photos of the views from the slip. I thought – Wow, this is like purchasing concert tickets online. But it's even better.

Rolando's Purchase

So I added slip number B33 to my "shopping basket". I entered my credit card number, opted for monthly payments, confirmation via email, and created a service request for an electrical hookup. Two days later, I logged onto mystarfishmarina.com and used the web cam to zoom in on my boat located in slip number B3. I clicked on the link called "my account" and saw that the first payment had been debited to my credit card, and that another was scheduled for the following month, and that my balance had been adjusted accordingly. I also noticed that there was a banner advertisement to sign my kids up for KidSail, the children's sailing program. I clicked on the banner ad and checked out the prices, but decided to check out the KidSail program at a later date.

The Marina Cross-Sells

The next day I received an email from my "assigned" Customer Care person at the marina. His name was Kevin McCarthy. Kevin's email confirmed my order and also provided additional information on the children's sailing program with a phone number to call. I called Kevin a few days later to sign my kids up. Here's where things got very interesting. Kevin asked me to bring up myhorbourislandmarina.com on my computer. Kevin also brought it up on his computer. He coached me through the entire process of signing my kids up for the KidSail program. I entered my children's names, ages, etc., and I made the payment online with my credit card. Kevin explained to me that when I clicked on the banner add for KidSail, it sent a "tickler" to the KidSail Program Director and my assigned Customer Care rep that I was a potential customer for this service. I usually hate getting junk mail and phone calls from telemarketers. But in this case I didn't mind at all because it was something I was already shopping for.

Starfish Marina's CRM software automatically suggests additional products and services that Rolando may need based on the Customer Profile information that he entered when creating his home page, and on

MAKING CRM STICK

clickstream analysis (the links he clicks on throughout the harborislandmarine.com web site.

Rolando Makes a Service Request

Starfish Marina turned out to be a great choice. I moved my boat into slip number B33 and spent several weeks enjoying the easy access in and out of the marina. The friendly and helpful staff, the clean facilities, the fitness center and the restaurant. In fact, I ended up spending many more weekdays at the marina than I expected. I started actually working several days per week from the boat. So, I decided I needed a broadband connection for my laptop. I entered myhourbourislandmarina.com and used an online form to create a Service Request. Within an hour I received a phone call from my assigned Customer Care Rep. We scheduled the installation on the phone. I received an email confirmation of the expected installation date. I received another email notification when the installation had been completed and the Service Request officially closed. And I received another email with a customer satisfaction survey. And along with the email notifications I also noticed on myharbourisland.com home page that my service request was continuously updated by the Customer Care rep and by the Dock Manager.

Starfish Marina's CRM software allows all service representatives, sales representative, and managers to have a 360-degree view of the customer – account information, customer profile and preferences, contact information, Service Requests, etc. Rolando will never need to repeat his request to multiple service representatives. He won't have to worry that his request is lost. He will not have to worry about miscommunications between the dock master and the Customer Care Rep. And he can rest assured that the person is emailing or speaking to on the phone can view the history of his emails, phone calls, web clicks, etc.

Managing Capacity

One day I received an email advertisement from the marina with a special offer for an oil change on my boat. I needed an oil change, so I clicked on the link and was taken to a calendar page where I clicked on my preferred date. Then my request automatically appeared as a Service Request on myharbourisland.com home page.

Starfish Marina's CRM software looks for excess capacity and automatically sends out suggestions for Service Requests to fill capacity gaps, based on a customer's profile. It works well for the customer

MAKING CRM STICK

because they received targeted and discounted offers. And it works well for the marina because they fill excess capacity so that the marina mechanics and other service personnel don't sit around un-billable.

Fast Forward Another Few Years

In the last few years I have revisited my Starfish homepage many times. I have added weather links, travel links, an email account for my sailboat, etc. Everything that is remotely related to my sailing hobby can be accessed via my Starfish home page – which is nice because I can access everything from any computer anywhere, especially from the kiosks on the dock. I've interacted with the Starfish staff via every media touch point available. I have executed transactions, asked questions, and I've even answered surveys. In fact, last week I gave feedback on a web survey, regarding my service experiences and my service professionals, and I received an email from the Starfish CEO thanking me and promising to take the lead on an improvement that I recommended. And I'm sure he'll follow thorough on his promise. Starfish always follows through.

Conclusion

Rolando's story illustrates the power of proactively recognizing customer needs, and in having the ability to build on an existing customer relationship with affective CRM capabilities. Indeed, his case is one in many where various employees working for the service provider (Starfish) were able to recognize, or were alerted to opportunities in which Rolando was already interested (e.g. the children's sailing program, etc.). Rolando's customer experience is compelling because he had the opportunity to choose from several touch points and channels when dealing with Starfish and in researching his options. Rolando could have gone to several competing providers for the services he needed. Yet he remained loyal to Starfish because he recognized the relationship was founded on a keen understanding of his service and channel needs. As with any successful partnership, Rolando's relationship with Starfish grew in strength, just as it evolved in breadth.

Copyright © 2004 by Daniel T. Murphy and Andres A. Salinas. All rights reserved.

MAKING CRM STICK

Focus on Late Adopters Series: And Would You Like A New Bath Tub With That? The CRM-Focused Plumbing Company – Daniel T. Murphy and Andres A. Salinas

This is the second in a series of narrow industry-focused articles that we are writing to illustrate how CRM will eventually revolutionize even the most stodgy change-resistant "late adopter" industries. As additional CRM technologies continue to trickle down to the middle market and below, and late-adopters begin to catch-on to the spirit of CRM, we should expect to see some exciting changes in some of those industries that we deal with every day in our own neighborhoods.

I saw an interesting article the other day. It said "If there's one thing Welch (Jack) and savvy execs like him understand, it's that a good idea is where you find it. And good ideas don't limit themselves to the corner offices of gleaming corporate skyscrapers. In fact, many of them may be hiding in plain sight – at the neighborhood hair salon, with your kids' swim coach, or in the gallery behind the dugout at your local ballpark." (S. McGregor, "Lessons from the Small Business Front", *Profit: Oracle's E-Business Magazine*, February 2002.).

One place where McGregor's viewpoint doesn't hold water (no pun intended) is in the plumbing industry.

The plumbing industry is one of those industries that just doesn't get it when comes to customer service. There are certainly a few exceptions out there (e.g., Demar Plumbing, which was featured as one of Tom Peters' "Service with Soul" providers in the early nineties). But for the most part, plumbing companies pay zero attention to collecting customer information, customer history, segmentation, lifetime value, direct marketing, etc. Most

MAKING CRM STICK

plumbing companies simply wait for the phone to ring, and then answer with mediocre service.

I always have the worst luck with plumbers – especially with the plumbers who I call to fix the boiler that heats my house. I can never get them to answer the phone, arrive at my house at an agreed time, and fix things correctly on the first try.

Here is one of my typical experiences with the plumber:

- I own an old two-family house with old boilers, old plumbing fixtures, and old pipes. I went out of town on a business trip. My tenant called to tell me the heat didn't work. So I called a plumber to go fix it.

- The first plumber I called just didn't show up. The second plumber showed up and supposedly fixed the boiler. But then the next day, my tenant called me to say that the heat still didn't work. I called the plumber again and again and left multiple messages on their answering service. No call back. And the temperature continued to drop.

- I called a third plumbing company and left a message at their answering service. No call back. When all else failed, I called my brother-in-law (not a plumber). My brother-in-law bypassed the safety control valve (with duct tape) to start the boiler. This started a fire and nearly burned the house down.

- When I returned home from my business trip, I found in my mailbox (a) a newspaper with an article entitled "Homeowner's Boiler Repair Starts Fire"; (b) invoices from two plumbers for a boiler that still wasn't fixed; (c) a building code violation from the Fire Department; and (d) a hotel bill from my tenant.

So, if there is a plumbing company out there who would like to attract and retain many new customers, please consider doing the following seven things:

1. Improve Your Touchpoints – Let me interact with you 24 by 7 using my desired media. Build a website that allows me to complete a personal home page where I tell you the equipment that I have in my house (e.g., 1974 Sears gas-fired water heater, 1978 HB Smith oil-fired steam boiler, etc.). Then, you will know exactly which types of services that I may be interested in purchasing (e.g., an annual cleanout for my oil burner). Allow me to set up services on your website (e.g., sign up for oil delivery service) and tell you which hours are best to call me or deliver service (e.g., weekends, after 5:00 PM weekdays, etc.).

2. Know Who I Am – When one of your service people comes to my house and fixes something, or when I call your office with a question regarding my bill, capture the customer "touch" somewhere. Next time I call you, I want you to know who I am and the history of our interactions. My phone company does this. I expect the same from my plumber. Also, when we interact, know that I spend $5,000+ with you every year and should be considered a "Gold" customer, unlike my neighbor who spends $50 with you per year and makes multiple service complaints. Also know that I referred four customers to you last year, and they spent a total of $14,360.40. You at least owe me some Red Sox tickets for that.

3. Manage Your Business Capacity – You can use the customer information that you collect to manage capacity. For example, next time one of your technicians cleans my oil burner, have him jot down the type and age of my hot water heater. You will notice that my hot water heater is 15 years old and very inefficient. During the summer, when your business slows down, send me an email (you collected my email address on my personal home page) and let me know that you are running a special on hot water heater replacements. Keep your plumbers busy in the off-season and you won't have to lay them off. Lower attrition means better service for the customer and increased profitability for the plumbing company.

4. Sell to Me – Along with the broken boiler, there are probably ten other things around the house that I am thinking about eventually replacing. After your plumber fixes my boiler, they should ask me about these things and be able (either with a price book or Palm PDA) to give me a typical range-of-fees for this service. I may decide to purchase on the spot. And if I don't purchase right away, you should make a record in my customer profile and call me back in the spring, after I have received my tax refund check.

5. Call Me – Although I don't like getting phone calls from obscure telemarketers trying to sell me credit cards, phone service and magazines, I will welcome an occasional phone call from one of my trusted service providers who I know by name (e.g., my plumber, my auto mechanic, etc.).

6. Follow-Up – Call me one day after you fixed my boiler to ensure that I am satisfied. Call me two weeks later to double check. If I am one of your "Gold" customers, please have the plumbing company president call me. And if I visit your web site and create an email inquiry, please answer it the same business day or the next business day.

7. Hire Nice People – Plumbing companies should send their grumpy plumbers to the commercial jobs and send nice plumbers to the residential jobs. It ain't about the pipes. It's about the people.

Use your creativity! There are dozens of additional things that you could do to provide me with better service, to better understand my preferences as a customer, to tailor products and services to better meet my needs, and to reward me for being one of your high-value customers.

Copyright © 2004 by Daniel T. Murphy and Andres A. Salinas. All rights reserved.

Chapter 7: The Old New World of Learning and Development

We spend millions of dollars on installing new CRM technology and redesigning business processes, and then we assign the most junior members of the project team to throw together a slide deck to teach the end users how they should do their new jobs. Or, worse still, we buy ten million dollars worth of learning technology, and load it up with content that misses the mark. Then, we don't bother marketing the training or following up to ensure that everyone has attended, and that they have understood and agreed to do what they were taught. Big surprise that nobody is using the new SFA application!

If you read the horror stories of failed CRM implementations, you hear things like "It was a great system, but nobody knew how to use it!" After all these years, many people still don't seem to understand the basic principles of adult learning, and do not practice the fundamentals of instructional design.

Trainers are supposed to be the experts at 'lessons learned' and applied. Jim Clemmer's paper, *Why Most Training Fails*, talks about how, even after many years of hard lessons learned, training programs continue to fail.

Managing Training-Related Risks in a CRM Deployment, by Dan Murphy, Andres Salinas and Michael Scruggs describes the basics of planning a CRM training program. In *End-User Training: Lessons Learned from Recent Enterprise-Wide CRM Deployments*, Dan Murphy and Joe Grady reflect on some of the newest challenges and opportunities faced by those charged with the learning and development activities on a large, complex CRM engagement.

MAKING CRM STICK

We liked Frank Troha's paper entitled *A Bulletproof Model for the Design of Blended Learning* for its timelessness. In the new world of emerging training technologies, distance learning, blended programs, offshore audiences, etc., Troha's advice is poignant – Read this paper and apply the principles, and you will improve end-user acceptance and adoption.

A recent Gartner article said the following:

> One indicator of mainstream adoption is that many enterprises have discovered the key obstacles to e-learning success: The successful deployment of e-learning requires much more than simply putting content up on the Web; getting people to use e-learning entails more work than making content available; and designing e-learning requires more complexity than building textual instruction in a sequential flow. ("Hype Cycle of Corporate E-Learning, 2004", W. Arevolo, J. Lundy, G. Phifer, K. Shegda, S. Hayward, F. Caldwell, L. Latham, *Gartner*, June 25, 2004)

A recent Forrester article similarly stated:

> The way we learn is changing. Users become the center of the process and identify the appropriate material and way they want to learn. The time period for online learning is shorter and employees apply the learning directly to their work situation to drive innovation and remain competitive.
>
> The opportunities for learning are expanding. Technology provides access to new ways to learn both formally and informally. The younger generation of workers grew up with technology — and demands online access to information, research, processes, and new skills. Expect great changes in the way workers are educated and interact through the learning process. Knowledge management, performance support, collaboration, and embedded learning are all ways of gaining knowledge in this expanded learning environment. ("The Future Of Learning: Putting Users In Charge", Claire Schooley, *Forrester*, June 28, 2004)

The world of training is changing at a rapid pace. If you have been charged to lead a large, complex CRM implementation, you will be challenged by an unprecedented need for speed, multiple overlapping

MAKING CRM STICK

deployments, global barriers (e.g., the English-speaking instructor teams will be useless in Beijing), insufficient training budgets, etc. You will have no choice but to rely on distance learning technologies. We have included two papers that will help you begin to think through some key learning technology considerations. Dr. Terrell Perry addresses a key question that every CRM project manager will ask: *When Should Your Organization Use Technology-Based Training?* Christina Morfeld's *Are Your Virtual Classes as Successful as They Could Be?* underscores the idea that some of those new learning technologies come with their own set of risks. These technologies must be used as enhancers, rather than elixirs.

You may be wondering why this chapter is more comprehensive than the others in the book. The reason is, frankly, that we are biased. We believe that training done wrong will destroy a CRM initiative, even if you have done everything else superbly. Botch-up the business case and you still may get lucky and deliver a successful CRM implementation. Do a shoddy job on project management, miss a few milestones, blow your budget, and your CRM implementation may still be a success. Miss the mark on training, and you are destined for failure.

MAKING CRM STICK

Why Most Training Fails – Jim Clemmer

Most organizations use their training investments about as strategically as they deploy their office supplies spending. And the impact on customer satisfaction, cost containment or quality improvement is just as useless.

One of the biggest causes of wasted training dollars is ineffective methods. Too often, companies rely on lectures ("spray and pray"), inspirational speeches or videos, discussion groups and simulation exercises.

While these methods may get high marks from participants, research (ignored by many training professionals) shows they rarely change behavior on the job. Knowing isn't the same as doing; good intentions are too easily crushed by old habits. Theoretical or inspirational training approaches are where the rubber meets the sky.

Another way of wasting dollars is failing to link training with organizational strategies and day-to-day management behavior. What happens in the classroom and what happens back on the job are often worlds apart.

Trainees learn which hoops to jump through, pledge allegiance to the current management fad, give their enthusiastic "commitment" to building "the new culture," get their diploma - and then go back to work.

Here are a few steps to using training as a key strategic tool:

Use training technologies that build how-to skills that are highly relevant and immediately applicable. Research clearly shows far more people act themselves into a new way of thinking than think themselves into a new way of acting.

Training that produces tangible results starts by changing behavior - which ultimately changes attitudes. Most executives and many professional trainers (who should know better) get this backward.

Follow up on training sessions with on-the-job coaching and support from managers. A Motorola Inc. study has found that those plants where quality improvement training was reinforced by senior management got a $33 return on every dollar invested. Plants providing the same training with no top management follow-up produced a negative return on investment.

An earlier Xerox Inc. study showed a paltry 13 percent of skills were retained by trainees six months after training if managers failed to provide coaching and support as the new skills were being applied.

And Western Gas Marketing Ltd. of Calgary uses its performance appraisal system to hold managers accountable for applying the principles that have been taught to them.

Build training around organizational objectives and strategies. Trainees should immediately see the connection between their new skills and where the organization is going. This makes training more relevant - and gets everyone focused on applying their new skills to the organization's key priorities and goals.

Another key principle is practiced by Vancouver-based Finning Ltd., the world's largest Caterpillar dealer. Chief Executive James Shepard and his executives are not only first in line for service and quality training, but they are also the trainers delivering sessions to their people.

This trend to "cascade" training down from senior management snaps everyone to attention. Training attendance problems disappear. Results-oriented executives jettison all the nice-to-do but irrelevant training. Trainees don't cross their arms and ask, "Is the organization really serious about this stuff?" In addition, managers achieve a deeper level of skill development when they teach others and are put on the spot to practice what they are now preaching.

Naturalist William Henry Hudson once observed, "You cannot fly like an eagle with the wings of a wren." Most training efforts never get off the ground because the methods don't change behaviour or the training is poorly delivered and integrated by the organization.

The waste of money is tragic for such a vital investment in competitiveness - and ultimately Canada's standard of living.

MAKING CRM STICK

Originally appeared in Jim's column in The Globe & Mail. Jim Clemmer is a bestselling author and internationally acclaimed keynote speaker, workshop/retreat leader, and management team developer on leadership, change, customer focus, culture, teams, and personal growth. During the last 25 years he has delivered over two thousand customized keynote presentations, workshops, and retreats. Jim's five international bestselling books include The VIP Strategy, Firing on All Cylinders, Pathways to Performance, Growing the Distance, and The Leader's Digest. His web site is www.clemmer.net.

Copyright © 2004 by Jim Clemmer. All rights reserved.

MAKING CRM STICK

Managing Training-Related Risks in a CRM Deployment – Daniel Murphy, Andres A. Salinas, and Michael Scruggs

I. Meeting Customers' Rising Expectations

To be competitive in the global marketplace and maintain economic health, customer-focused businesses must improve the skills of their workforce and invest in technology that transforms their businesses into customer-centric operations. All areas of a customer-focused organization:
- recognize the customer from the point of contact
- appear to operate seamlessly in the customer's view, and
- are easy to do business with from a the sales or service perspective

The root-cause of most service or sales organizations' problems results from a combination of misaligned process and under-prepared people (Performance in Practice). In today's service-focused economy, the failure to satisfy customers can generally be attributed to employees' lack of system or procedural knowledge to effectively anticipate and address customers' changing issues.

The bottom line is the cost of retaining a customer is far less than the cost of replacing a customer. Customer loyalty is a source of continuing revenue.

Yet the gap between your customers' demands and your ability to meet them is only getting worse. Skill requirements in the front office are rising, at the same time employers report difficulty finding qualified workers. Inadequate training investment is one factor leading to:
- poor worker performance,
- lower productivity (among workers who lack specific job knowledge),

- reduced effectiveness of Customer Relationship Management (CRM) technology and ultimately,
- business objectives are not achieved.

While CRM training is not the only answer to the skills crisis, it should be a large part of the solution.

II. Becoming Customer-Centric

So how do you begin a CRM implementation that will improve your sales and service organization? First you must understand the culture of your organization. Is your business customer-focused or product-focused? When your business is customer-focused, it is prepared for every contact with the customer. When customers contact your service or sales representatives they want to be recognized. They want you to know their name, the products and services they buy, how long they've been a customer, how valuable a customer they are, their latest order, and who handled their last call. If your organization is prepared with this information your CRM investment pays off in the improvement and in the value of service your business provides.

To shift your organization to become customer focused you need to optimize customer relationships by properly tracking customer information and measuring return on investment of individual customers. CRM technology is the key to being able to understand customers' preferences, dislikes, and purchasing habits which is essential to establishing a winning relationship between you and your customers.

Once a business knows its customers, to create the maximum value from CRM technology and best service its customers, the company must reevaluate the role and shape of the front-office operation. The foundation of this reorganization is to structure the organization and its processes around the customer. This will be predominately evident in sales and service, where the process and the customer come into contact. A single point of contact, with the right technology, can gather information about the customer and share that data across all areas of the organization, enabling the entire company to work toward the same goal.

The effectiveness of the CRM technology in allowing a company to manage and share information across the business is dependent on the ability of the front-office workforce. This group of sales and service representatives will be both the company's voice to the customer, and the customer's voice to the company. They will drive changes that deliver outstanding value to the organization and the customer. Leading companies are realizing that CRM is fast becoming a competitive necessity, and providing their employees with the processes, tools, and training they need to build strong relationships with customers. As a result, these leading organizations are seeing the connection between a well-trained workforce, customer satisfaction, and top-line revenue growth.

Implementing a new technology for these critical areas of your business means your organization must:
- Redefine sales and customer management processes that will seamlessly integrate with the new technology.
- Teach sales and customer relationship personnel how to use the new technology as a competitive advantage and to support relationship building.
- Instill in your sales force the need to be disciplined technology users – "Once reps start working outside the bounds of the product...it is very difficult to get them back on track." (*Sales & Field Force Automation*, June 1999).

III. Understanding CRM Training Needs

Before training can begin, companies should methodically address the risks of an under-prepared end-user community to fully understand what type of training and support needs to be implemented. The focus should be on four areas:

- **Audience Assessment** – Do we know who needs to learn?
- **Content Assessment** – Have we correctly determined what they will learn?
- **Delivery Assessment** – Have we correctly planned how, where, and when they will learn?
- **Infrastructure Assessment** – Are the necessary methods, procedures, and supporting infrastructure in place?

Audience Assessment - Who Needs to Learn?

Without a clearly defined Audience Assessment process, there is a risk that some end-user segments may fall through the cracks and not be trained or provided sufficient performance support. Sounds simple right? We need to identify very specifically who needs to learn. Occasionally entire end-user groups are overlooked. More typically, the training requirements of peripheral users are under-emphasized.

MAKING CRM STICK

There are several ways to reduce these risks. First, all user groups should be identified and documented. Second, the document should be communicated throughout the organization so that end-user groups who have been overlooked have the opportunity to speak up. Finally, the unique performance support needs of each discrete user segment with similar requirements need to be grouped for efficient delivery of training and performance support. This entire Audience Assessment process, along with the Content, Delivery, and Infrastructure Assessments should be clearly defined on the system implementation work plan at the beginning of the project.

Case Company: A large telecommunications company effectively identified and carefully segmented the sales and customer service end-user groups for their new CRM application. Upon conducting a more formal risk assessment, they discovered that they initially failed to appreciate the criticality of training several "peripheral" end-user groups, including the Marketing Department team that would be responsible for feeding up-to-date product and service information into the CRM application. In the end, several additional end-user groups were identified and deployment resources needed to be reallocated.

Some other areas to consider in the Audience Assessment:
- Identify any groups with higher turnover so that training design may include more comprehensive programs and/or delivery methods better suited for use on a regular, more frequent basis.
- Assess the level of detail needed in materials, identify the lowest reading level at which written materials intended for distribution should be written, and make assumptions about attention span, level of variety, and course length.
- Determine the need to translate materials and allow time for translation.
- Identify the need for shift training and/or adjusting work hours to meet time requirements and facility constraints.
- Identify the need to accommodate any trainees with special requirements and maintain compliance with the Americans with Disabilities Act.

Content Assessment - What Will They Learn?

The risk here is not that the learning objectives are not achieved. Rather, the risk is that although the learning objectives are achieved, the

MAKING CRM STICK

participants still don't know how to carry out the mission or use the system. This is a scary prospect because it means that the training content was off the mark. The performance objectives must be revisited. It is typically not a matter of tweaking the existing materials of finding a better instructor. Mitigating this risk requires a very comprehensive combined top-down approach to instructional design.

By top-down we mean that there should be clear linkage between the company's overall business strategy and the CRM training program. For example, a CRM solution is being implemented to increase cross-selling of products and services across strategic business units, then the CRM training program should be based on performance objectives related to cross-selling. At the same time, there should be a bottom up emphasis.

There should be rigorous analysis to determine what content under each performance objective should be trained versus what should be delivered via another medium (e.g., knowledge support system). Training is only one of the ways to deliver knowledge to end-users to help them perform on the job. As a thumb rule, employees should only be trained on the content that must be committed to memory. Other content (e.g., content that they use infrequently, but must still be readily available) can be delivered via a job aid or knowledge support system.

The final component of the Content Analysis is to determine the proper sequence to ensure that the right content is delivered via the right medium (e.g., instructor-led, computer-based, etc.) to the right people at the right time. It is important to group and sequence the training so that it addresses the unique needs of each user group identified in the Audience Assessment. The content can be grouped by job title (e.g., Customer Service Representative, Sales Representative, Sales Managers, etc.), by system functionality or module (e.g., Contact Management, Activities, Pricing, etc.), or by business objectives or themes (e.g., Cross-Selling Cellular Services and Products). There are advantages and disadvantages to each. For example, organizing the training program by theme may make the content more strategy-aligned. Yet it may also result in less effective transfer and retention of skills and knowledge related to the system functionality.

Case Company: A leading media and entertainment company had a very challenging training situation. Customer Service Representatives in a new Human Resources Center (HRC) needed training on several different CRM technologies as well as process training and soft-skill training. The easiest

> approach would have been to have the CRM vendors teach the technology, and then have the process design team teach the process, and finally have specialists teach the soft skills. Instead, the technology, process and soft-skill topics were interwoven into one program with a supporting case study. In other words, the participants learned a little technology. Then they learned portions of the processes and soft skills. Then they learned some more technology. And so on. Participants described the event as much more "real world" than most training programs.

Delivery Assessment - How, Where, and When Will They Learn?

With the Content Assessment, we are seeking to ensure that the learning objectives and delivery mechanism(s) are sound. With the Delivery Assessment, we are seeking to ensure that the learning objectives are achieved and that the delivery mechanism(s) are effective. Even when the content is correct, there is a risk that the skills and knowledge are not effectively transferred and the learning objectives will not be met. It may be because the materials were not well developed, or the instructor did not perform well.

To mitigate risk in CRM training delivery, consider:
- *Class Size* – the optimum number of learners per class and ratio of instructors to learners (Bigger or smaller is not necessarily better. The optimum class size will vary, depending on the CRM technologies and processes being taught – e.g., Campaign Management training sessions should be smaller than Customer Service training sessions.)
- Instructors – hiring the right instructor(s) for the delivery (For example, depending on the situation, the best scenario may be to have a CRM vendor and solutions-selling specialist co-instruct.)
- Lead Time – minimizing the length of time between the training and application on the job
- Certification – whether the training will be mandatory and whether participants will become certified upon completion
- Materials – the need for reusable or "shrinkwrapped" training materials (It is especially critical to discuss whether the training will be delivered by experienced presenters who often require nothing more than an outline to teach, a call center supervisor who has never presented before, a combination of both, etc.)
- Travel – the extent to which the staff and instructors will travel for training and the inherent logistic requirements
- Facilities – the extent to which facilities and equipment requirements should be met by existing, rented, contract, or to-be-built resources

MAKING CRM STICK

- Training Technology Environment – the availability and stability of a technology environment (both the CRM application and the underlying database) to support the training

> **Case Company:** Selection and preparation of instructors is an often-overlooked critical success factor. A pitfall for many large companies is to invest a great deal of time and resources in the training materials, but not in the selection of the instructors. Yet, in our experience, training effectiveness is directly linked to the skills and insights of the instructors. The instructors must have the right mix of subject matter expertise and presentation skills.

A large media and entertainment company had great expectations that their call center staff could "rise to the occasion" to deliver the company's new CRM training program – despite the fact that they were relatively new users of the system (In fact, their only experience was in user acceptance testing), and they had no formal training as presenters or facilitators. The bad news: New hires received a less than professional introduction to the company and the new CRM tool. The good news: It was only a pilot, and the company quickly reassigned professional trainers to deliver the remainder of the training.

> **Case Company:** The training environment is another area often overlooked. A large telecommunications company was expanding the deployment of their custom CRM application by several thousand users. Their size of their ongoing CRM training effort was being increased significantly – more trainees, more instructors, more training locations. The bottom line – More users than ever before were accessing the server than ever before. The CRM application server and the training database could not handle the increased load.
>
> There was also a version control problem. Because the IT department used nearly all of their resources to support the deployment of the additional CRM application and database "instances" across the US, they did not have sufficient resources to keep the training instances of the system up-to-date. So, not only was the training environment overloaded and unstable, it did not contain the most up-to-date system functionalities. The instructors were frustrated and the trainees' (most of them new hires) first experience with the new CRM application was not positive.

MAKING CRM STICK

Infrastructure Assessment - Methods, Procedures, Supporting Infrastructure, and Assimilation

Establishing an integrated training support infrastructure is critical to the success of the CRM training effort. Activities required to develop effective training (e.g., analysis activities, design, development, delivery and assessment activities) should be formally integrated into the system development lifecycle. Training activities, milestones and deliverables should be placed on the release calendar alongside the application development and delivery activities, milestones and deliverables. And over time, these activities should have associated templates so that the training lifecycle becomes more repeatable and accelerated over time.

> **Case Company:** To effectively execute a highly complex CRM training program at a large telecommunications company, we recently recommended steps to create a Training Management Office (TMO). This should be considered a best practice for all large and/or complex CRM implementations, especially those that cross business units. If no such organization exists, a director, or "internal champion" of training should be identified to lead its creation. Developing a TMO should not be a collateral responsibility. Rather, the creation, execution, and continued management of the TMO should be the sole or primary role of a dedicated training professional. The TMO should be staffed with training professionals with expertise in conducting audience, content, and delivery assessments. The TMO staff should also be proficient in developing detailed curricula and training material in support of the CRM (or other) learning event. Finally, the TMO should be responsible for creating learning metrics to track the effectiveness of each learning event from the perspective of content, delivery, and audience retention. The importance of this role can not be overstated considering the investment in time and money the organization will have made on the CRM deployment.

An effective Infrastructure Assessment must also include a dedicated assimilation and change management assessment and plan. This plan becomes critical to the long-term success of the CRM training, and more importantly, to attaining the strategic objectives to which the training is linked (i.e. increased customer satisfaction and loyalty, increase share-of-wallet, etc.). The most well executed audience, content, and delivery assessments alone do not ensure the staying power of the new CRM system, processes, and procedures.

MAKING CRM STICK

An effective assimilation plan will:

- Define the new work processes
- Define the new roles and responsibilities (and expectations)
- Define the change incentives for users at the CSR level to the executive suite
- Link the organization's performance evaluations to specific CRM metrics
- Address the "What's in it for me"? question for each impacted user community
- Define new reward systems for the CRM environment
- Ensure accurate, timely, and effective communications in support of the CRM initiative

As new processes are mapped, roles and responsibilities change, so too should the requirements for recruiting, retention, and accession planning. In the case of the new CRM environment for example, the organization should strive to attain (and promote) more technically proficient and customer-focused people. Similarly, the organization should ensure the proper incentives are in place to keep them around long enough to glean the benefits of the initial and subsequent CRM training investments.

This often ignored assimilation planning will ensure that CRM does not become yet another fad, but the way of doing business, and will accelerate and maximize the effects of those first steps toward becoming a customer-focused organization.

IV. Summary

These are the four areas of analysis and infrastructure development that will influence the success your CRM training solution. The bottom line – CRM training professionals must work with your organization to establish the training requirements of your sales force and customer relationship managers, assess existing competencies, identify and then close gaps by deploying a comprehensive learning and knowledge transfer strategy. A sound strategy will result in a training solution that meets the needs of your organization and produces bottom line results.

2004 © Daniel T. Murphy, Andres A. Salinas and Michael Scruggs, Inc. All rights reserved.

MAKING CRM STICK

MAKING CRM STICK

End User Training: Lessons Learned from Recent Enterprise-Wide CRM Deployments – Joseph B. Grady and Daniel T. Murphy

Finally, there seems to be some light at the end of the tunnel. As 2003 progresses, we are beginning to see companies reinvest in the enterprise IT projects that they had put on hold in recent years. This time, rather than a trickling of investments in CRM point solutions that will be stitched together later, we are seeing a great many companies building CRM blueprints that are truly enterprise-wide, extending across multiple business units, multiple geographies, with execution planned across multiple years.

Many of the enterprise-wide projects that are being contemplated today have complex integration points that would not have been considered three years ago. The trend toward larger, more complex, and longer term CRM projects is likely to continue, as the economy continues to recover, and as more companies begin to spend again. The ripple effect of this trend is profound. Everything seems to be changing. We are seeing changes in the way we organize projects, changes in the way we do design, development and testing, and especially in the way we train end users. This white paper is intended to describe some of the changes we are starting to see in the area of CRM end-user training.

CRM and Learning Transformations in Parallel

We were recently working on an enterprise-wide, global CRM deployment for a large manufacturing organization. The company needed to develop and deliver over 75 hours of training across dozens of audiences scattered throughout the world. For reasons of logistics and budget, it was agreed

MAKING CRM STICK

that we would rely almost exclusively on web-based training (WBT). We developed over twenty self-paced web-delivered courses.

In the months before we began this CRM transformation effort, the company constructed an online corporate university. Using a well-known learning management system (LMS) platform, the company put in place a solid backbone technology that would provide a robust set of learning capabilities. This company intended that, eventually, all company courses, both instructor-led and self-paced, would be contained in one location. The company's course material library and all job aids would be available online. Employees would have the ability to enroll and complete web-based courses online, while management would have the ability to track employee course completion and satisfaction.

There are many large companies out there who have invested in LMS technology, but the LMS has yet to be institutionalized within the organization. These companies have built the learning backbone, but their employees haven't had a real reason to immerse themselves in the new learning technology. Our client decided early in the project that all of their new CRM end-user courses would be delivered using the company's new LMS. This was a huge challenge for this large, high-tech manufacturing organization. Delivering an entire training program via the online medium was something that had not yet been done successfully at this company.

We watched the sales and service representatives go through an experience that was wholly transformational. They were given new CRM technologies. They were given new processes. And they were given a new learning platform to learn about those new technologies and processes. Our client carefully considered the costs and logistics of a traditional training program to support a worldwide CRM implementation, and they opted for a distributed learning program, leveraging the LMS that they already had in place. They made their LMS the "only show in town" for learning about the new processes and technologies – and they truly created a learning transformation in their organization. Our recommendation to companies on the verge of a large enterprise-wide CRM deployment – If you do not already have an LMS to lean on, strongly consider implementing an LMS before or in-concert with CRM.

Simulation Software

The coming of age of simulation software is perhaps the biggest change in IT training in the last two years. This is the coolest stuff since sliced bread. There are several products out there. IBM's Simulation Producer, in our objective opinion, is the most advanced. Gone are the days when an instructional developer builds course content, and then revises it again, and again, and again, every time the application or process changes, all the way through user-acceptance testing. Gone are the online courses with static screen bitmaps and callout box instructions. The new simulation tools provide a rich 'picking' and 'clicking' experience that makes the learner feel like they are using the real application. Simulation software allows the instructional developers to create the courses faster. The learner experience is highly realistic, and we have found that we can actually deploy without a training environment or sandbox. The best simulation software uses low-bandwidth applets that allow end-users to complete training across ordinary phone lines.

On our most recent enterprise-wide CRM training deployment, we used the new generation IBM Simulation Producer software to build our entire suite of courses. We worked faster than ever before. We were able to wait until very late in the development lifecycle before we began training development. We delivered courses that set a new standard for realism. Web-based courses with simulation applets, deployed on learning management systems are the wave of the future, period. Our advice – Make the investment, and reap the benefits in speed of execution and cost reduction.

To Train or Not-to-Train

Again, technology deployment is getting faster all the time. An enterprise-wide CRM deployment that would have taken two years in 1999 is now being forced into six months. Even government projects are getting quicker, and along the way, many corners are being cut. Requirements definition is done more quickly, and is sometimes only cursory effort. Development is done on a nearly round the clock basis with cheap labor imported from overseas. There is less unit testing, less integration testing, less user acceptance testing, and less end-user training. To keep up with the hectic pace of change, we have seen a trend toward accelerated and less rigorous training analysis. This is not a trend that we need to follow in the training space.

Now, more than ever, instructional developers should rigorously apply a number of analysis tools to ensure first, that all the new business processes affected are being addressed; and second, that the training program will sufficiently prepare the organization for the post-transformation world. One of the most useful tools in the kitbag should be a 'train or not-to-train' filter. This filter will help instructional designers to make the decision on a process-by-process basis, as well as point them in the direction of the proper instructional media.

On a recent project, we looked at every activity in every future-state business process. We passed each activity through a rigorous set of filters. We estimated the level of complexity of each activity. We discussed how often the activity would be done in the post-transformation business. And we looked carefully at the risk of an end-user not doing the activity correctly. We consulted with subject-matter-experts and asked ourselves some tough questions, like "With the new web-interface, is this activity really that difficult?" and "Will the sales representative really look unprofessional if they whip out a job aid to complete this activity in front of the customer?" On this project, we applied a bit more analytical rigor than we had typically used in the past.

In the end, we felt we had a training program that was truly the right size. Activities that didn't require training weren't trained. For activities that were complex and not done very often, we produced job aids, rather than courses, since it was not necessary for the end-users to commit these activities to memory. There were a few activities that only needed to be learned by a small handful of back office people. These people didn't need a formal course with formal course materials and job aids. They just needed a business analyst or a developer to spend some time with them and show them how to do the new work. Simple!

To be like everyone else in the new speed-focused world of IT, we could have arbitrarily reduced our time spent on analysis and training development. Instead, we increased our level of rigor on analysis, and in the end, reduced our training development time significantly and in the right areas.

We Build It, You Make Them Come

The best training program in the world, whether it is a planned instructor-led event with Britney Spears singing at the opening night party, or whether it has the coolest web-based courses that have ever been developed on the planet, is useless if nobody shows up to learn. Just getting the word out that the courses are available isn't enough. Sending out emails to the business unit leadership isn't enough either. Let's face facts. Let's be brave and not use the word "incentivize". In most organizations, sales representatives must be harassed to complete training.

On a project we completed in early 2003, we required that somebody's

MAKING CRM STICK

performance evaluation be tied to course completion. In the end, we had an aspiring junior executive step up to this challenge. He did send email advertisements for the training program. But he also followed up with hundreds of phone calls to the end-users and their managers telling them which courses they needed to take and when they should take them. Ninety percent of the sales representatives completed their training on time!

In years past, nobody got in trouble when end-users didn't show up for training, mostly because it was very hard to track who took the training. These days, things are different. If you build it, and nobody shows up, everyone will know that nobody showed up, and somebody will have some explaining to do. Be smart! Get a senior business owner to take responsibility for end-user training completion.

All Executives Onboard

Again, we believe, in this new world of speedy worldwide deployments of new process and technology, that web-based training is the way to go. Yet, the ripple effect of just one or two executive naysayers can cripple an enterprise-wide web-based training deployment.

On one recent project we had a handful of executives who said, right from the start, that "Web-based training will never work here." Instead, they had a vision that they would rehire as subcontractors, dozens of trainers who had been laid off in previous years while the training department had been downsized nearly to nonexistence.

We worked hard with these executives from day one. We talked to them about their previous experiences to find out what went wrong. We talked to them to find out what they thought web-based training was. In some cases, we found that their understanding of computer-based training was based on their experiences from several years ago. We showed these executives how the new simulation software products provide a very realistic picking and clicking experience, and we showed them how they could track course completion and satisfaction for their employees. Most importantly, we showed them the cost savings in not deploying instructors around the world, the cost savings of not needing a training environment, and the risk that was mitigated by not relying on dozens of human instructors who would deliver the training differently from location-to-location and from day-to-day.

In the end, we had a handful of executive stakeholders demonstrate their

MAKING CRM STICK

strong support for the new way of learning. We drafted emails for them to cascade through their organizations, and we drafted talking points for them to use in their weekly staff meetings.

Think Waves and Habitual Learning!

The CRM technology that you are deploying today is most likely the first of many waves that you will be deploying to your sales and service employees and to your business partners and customers. The functionality that is deployed in each successive wave builds on the previous wave. If you aren't thinking in terms of waves already, you better start now. With the accelerated rate at which CRM technology is being deployed, the end user community must be brought into a learning rhythm. Learning must become habitual.

On every new project, the first thing we emphasize to end-users is that their world will be changing. We emphasize that they will now be seeing new technology emerging all the time. We emphasize that the technology will be released in waves, every few months. We explain that some of the technology will improve their sales productivity. Some of the technology waves will improve management's view into their activities. Some waves will deliver technology that will help them improve the service they deliver. Most importantly, we emphasize that each technology wave will have an associated training wave. With each wave, they will be expected to learn something new: a new process in November; a new software and process in December; new business controls in February; etc. We emphasize that, to be a high performer in the in the future organization, it will also be necessary to be a proactive and habitual learner.

In Summary

As the future of learning comes into a clearer focus, we expect to see Learning Management Systems become the focal point for learning, and the emphasis upon self-paced will continue to increase exponentially. Simulation software is the wave of the near future – Organizations cannot afford not to not make the investment in simulation software. Executives must get onboard and take ownership in a new world of learning, where training comes in waves, and end-users must yell "Surfs up!"

Copyright © 2004 by Joseph B. Grady and Daniel T. Murphy. All rights reserved.

A Bulletproof Model for the Design of Blended Learning – Frank J. Troha

"Why is it there is never enough time to do a job right, but always time enough to do it over?" - Anon.

If Time and Money Matter, So Does Instructional Design

I hope you'll never hear an outside consultant tell you that it will take another $250,000 and an additional six months to complete your e-learning or blended learning project. By blended learning I simply mean e-learning (or online learning) combined with another venue, typically classroom training.

Blended learning is hot and understandably so, combining the best features of online learning (e.g., 24/7 accessibility) with the best features of classroom instruction (e.g., live, face-to-face interaction). No doubt it's here to stay. But why do so many blended learning initiatives turn into frustrating boondoggles, consuming far more time and money than anyone anticipated? The answer – just as with most troubled initiatives – can be found in poor planning (i.e., instructional design), the bitter fruits of which often appear during the implementation of training, or long after substantial amounts of time, money and enthusiasm have been expended.

Whether you and your staff have experienced designing e-learning or blended learning, it's critical that you at least attempt to define the major aspects of your project before consulting with any outside service providers. The rationale is simple. By deliberately thinking through, specifying in writing and confirming – with all internal parties involved – who your audience is, their learning objectives, the exact content to be covered, constraints, etc., you'll be better positioned to:

- understand the true scope and nature of your project;
- gain the support of all internal stakeholders early in the process;
- efficiently and accurately communicate project scope and requirements to potential providers;
- hire the best provider for the job; and
- confidently manage and monitor project tasks to ensure success.

The First of Its Kind Model for the Design of Blended Learning

The Bulletproof Model for the Design of Blended Learning is intended to help guide you and your team through the process of blended learning design. By virtue of its checks and balances, you are essentially assured of a successful outcome.

Accompanying the model is a list of sections for an instructional design document (Figure 1), which – as it's developed and fine-tuned – provides a vital discussion document and focal point for all parties involved in the project.

Note: The following design model presumes a performance analysis has indicated the need for training, as opposed to another type of performance improvement intervention.

Design Steps:

1. Gather standard background information on the training need, just as you would if designing a course for classroom delivery. Consider: the title/function of audience members, their location, total number to be trained and the time frame for doing so, their level of interest in the subject matter, likes/dislikes concerning learning activities experienced in the past, what they need to come away with as a result of the training (i.e., specified knowledge, skills and attitude), known and potential constraints affecting any aspect of the classroom training from design to development to delivery, etc.

2. Answer, in writing: "What exactly do we want our audience to know, do and feel as a result of the training?" The list of specific, carefully worded outcomes or learning objectives should be prefaced by: "As a result of completing the training, participants should:". Before proceeding to the next step in the process, *be sure to confirm the list of learning objectives with project decision makers, influencers, all design team members (including any subject matter experts) and any other parties involved.* If the objectives are inaccurate, there surely will be inaccuracies committed in the steps that follow.

3. Based on the confirmed learning objectives, outline the topics and subtopics that must be addressed by the training. Essentially, you and your team (including any subject matter experts) should answer this question for each learning objective: *"If the audience is to be able to accomplish this objective, what exactly do we need to cover?"* The output of this step should look like the table of contents in a textbook, i.e., highly detailed, comprehensive and logically sequenced.

4. Next to each item listed in the content outline, note the type of learning activity that is best able to convey the item of content to your audience in a traditional classroom setting. The premise for noting only in-class learning activities at this point in the design process – instead of both classroom activities and online activities – is two-fold: 1) By working within the context of the classroom – a venue with which you're probably very familiar – you're establishing on paper the "ideal" learning experience: *live, face-to-face, instructor led and peer-collaborative.* 2) By virtue of having designed the "ideal" learning experience, you have a tangible blueprint ("Content / Learning Activities Outline") that you can – later in the process – pare back as much or as little as your particular circumstances indicate.

5. Develop a transfer of learning strategy, outlining what can be done before, during and after training to make it "stick". At this point, having produced a "Content / Learning Activities Outline", you and your team would have a sense as to how the manager of a participant might encourage his/her on-the-job application of the content specified. This step is crucial, yet often neglected. *If learning is not transferred from the place of learning to the place of work, there can be no return on investment.* Prior to training, the manager could, for example, review the course's learning objectives with the participant and discuss their relevance to his/her particular developmental needs. After training, the manager and participant might discuss, fine tune and commit to implementing an action plan drafted by the participant during training. Additionally, a second look at the "Content / Learning Activities Outline" – from the standpoint of ensuring learning transfer – might reveal additional opportunities for skills practice and the distribution of quick reference tools (e.g., checklists, templates and memory joggers) for on-the-job use. The transfer of learning strategy, which can include methods beyond those referred to above (e.g., linkage to performance review criteria), is captured in writing before proceeding.

6. Develop an evaluation strategy, outlining how the effectiveness of the training can be determined. A look back at the learning objectives and the "Content / Learning Activities Outline" can help answer these types of evaluation questions: After confirming the accuracy of course materials with subject matter experts and other reviewers, will you test the relevance, value and appeal of course materials (in the final draft stage) by conducting "walk-throughs" with a sampling of your target audience? Will you conduct a dry run so decision makers, influencers, training personnel and others can assess the course prior to rollout? How will you measure the target audience's degree of learning and behavioral change? Given the nature of the training, can its impact on the organization be determined? If so, which metrics will you use? How long after the delivery of training should you wait before measuring its impact on the organization? Answers to these types of evaluation questions are documented.

7. Identify and catalogue any existing documentation that may later be used to facilitate course development (and thereby avoid reinventing the wheel). In addition to detailing all topics and subtopics to be addressed, the "Content / Learning Activities Outline" represents a sort of shopping list for directly relevant materials that may already exist in your organization or elsewhere. Do your best to locate pertinent reports, articles, books, videos, CDs and training programs that can potentially save time, money and effort by eliminating the need to create your entire course from scratch. Pre-packaged e-learning lessons related to a number of your training's topics/subtopics may also be available and can be searched via the Internet. Any subject matter experts working with you and your staff should prove especially helpful in locating and assessing the potential value of existing materials. Certainly, by virtue of their own expertise, subject matter experts should be able to close any informational gaps left un-addressed by your search for existing documentation. However, this should not occur until after approval of a blended learning design has been received and the go-ahead for development of courseware has been given. Here, in this step of the design process, *only a detailed listing of what is available and what is lacking needs to be prepared.*

8. Organize all outputs of the process thus far into an instructional design document (i.e., discussion document) that will be used later (in Step 10) to communicate your preliminary design. See Figure 1.

9. Using the instructional design document, identify elements within the "Content / Learning Activities Outline" for potential online delivery. Since the intent is to combine the best of both worlds – the 24/7 availability and efficient global delivery provided by online with the live, face-to-face human interaction of the classroom – elements of the outline that appear to lend themselves to effective online delivery should be highlighted by you and your staff. *Such elements tend to include content / learning activities that are easily understood, straightforward or basic, e.g., key terms, process overviews, guiding principles, self-assessments, etc.*

10. Brief all internal people involved in the project on your design, elicit their feedback and gain approval to proceed. Getting buy-in from project sponsors, decision makers, content experts and others at this point in the process is crucial. First, this meeting should confirm whether you're on track in terms of what the target audience needs and what management wants. Second, by virtue of providing the opportunity for all involved to weigh in on the design, their continued support is better ensured. And, third, *you (and they) can feel confident that you're ready to begin talking with blended learning experts who – after being thoroughly briefed by you – can offer their views on how they would take your design to the "next level".*

Note: Because technical questions may arise about the eventual delivery of proposed online learning, it's recommended that your organization's IT function be represented at this meeting.

11. Meet with blended learning providers with an eye toward: increasing learning efficiency through 24/7 accessibility, fully optimizing precious classroom time and ensuring optimal return on investment. Using the design document as a roadmap for your meetings with providers, your intentions and questions can be systematically addressed. Key outputs of your meetings should include: 1) a clearer understanding on your part as to what should be delivered online versus offline and why 2) a decision as to which provider seems most appropriate for the job 3) which aspects of the project can be accomplished using internal resources and 4) a revised instructional design document ("Blended Learning Design Document"), specifying in the "Content / Learning Activities" section how each element of content would be addressed, including the venue to be used and estimated time required. Other sections of the design document (e.g., Duration [total online time vs. total classroom time], Constraints, Evaluation Strategy, Transfer of Learning Strategy, etc.) should also be adjusted, depending on decisions reached.

Note: At these meetings it's critical that your organization's IT function be represented. Many of the outside experts' recommendations are likely to require a clear understanding of your organization's current technological capabilities and limitations.

12. With your outside provider, present the blended learning design to all in-house stakeholders (as in Step 10), elicit their feedback, gain approval and identify next steps. A key part of this briefing is comparing and contrasting the first approved design document (based on the live, instructor-led classroom venue, but including the highlighting of certain elements for possible online delivery) with the second design document (based on the optimal blending of online and classroom venues within the context of your organization's unique circumstances). *By doing so, the full extent of paring back (or extraction) of certain content / learning activities (deemed suitable for online delivery) from the classroom-based design document can be clearly seen, explained and discussed. In the end, the potential benefits to be derived from a blended approach should be made apparent to all.* Typical benefits include: reaching large numbers of learners "anywhere, anytime" and usually much faster (and cheaper) than multiple classroom deliveries alone could; reducing yet optimizing in-classroom time by limiting its use to instances where the presence of a live instructor and face-to-face interaction among participants is truly needed; automating training administration via a proven Learning Content Management System; and reducing training costs overall. Once the blended learning design is approved, next steps are discussed and agreed upon before adjourning the meeting.

An Ounce of Prevention

A review of the recommended model for the design of blended learning reveals a number of checks and balances that are especially apparent within steps 2, 10 and 12. Consequently, this model – *when diligently applied* – virtually ensures a successful outcome; hence, the name, *Bulletproof Model for the Design of Blended Learning.*

Too often, corporate learning and development professionals simply delegate the design of blended learning to their chosen outside provider. Perhaps they believe they lack the time, instructional design skills or knowledge of the latest learning technologies needed to effectively orchestrate and lead the planning effort. The design model explained here is worth the time, requires only basic instructional design skills to implement and even includes learning firsthand about relevant, leading-edge technologies.

With so many e-learning and blended learning initiatives, ranging from hundreds of thousands of dollars into the millions, aren't the stakes too high to do anything less than take control from the very beginning?

MAKING CRM STICK

Major Sections of an Instructional Design Document (Figure 1)

I.	Course Title
II.	Purpose Statement
III.	Audience Description
IV.	Duration
V.	Prerequisites (if any)
VI.	Learning Objectives
VII.	Constraints
VIII.	Content / Learning Activities Outline (For each item of content to be addressed, indicate how it would be conveyed to audience members and the estimated time required.)
IX.	Transfer of Learning Strategy
X.	Evaluation Strategy
XI.	Content Sourcing (What We Have vs. What We Need)
XII.	Add any other sections that are needed to clearly and comprehensively communicate your design, including project management documentation.

Copyright © 2004 by Frank J. Troha. All rights reserved.

MAKING CRM STICK

When Should Your Organization Use Technology-Based Training? – Terrell L. Perry, Ed. D.

Many companies are feeling the pressure to employ technology-based training solutions instead of continuing their reliance on traditional classroom training. Some have even taken the plunge with pilot projects, producing both favorable and unfavorable results. But before you go wading into the pricey waters of technology-based training, take the time to look at why many professionals feel it will vastly improve and enhance your training efforts. Instructional multimedia, the kind of training delivered over the computer, has some major differences and some powerful benefits over classroom training. The two current front-runners, CD-ROM and Web-based training (WBT) have many similarities, but some vastly different capabilities that may require some trade-offs on your part.

Comparison of Multimedia to Classroom Training

When you begin to compare multimedia to classroom instruction, several differences emerge. I have broken these differences into three categories: Cost, Instruction, and Administration. Cost refers to the impact of training on the bottom line, or the cost of doing training. Instruction in this case refers to how the instruction is accomplished. Administration refers to those tasks related to managing the instruction. The scheduling of training, making training accessible, tracking student progress and the posting of successes or deficiencies all fall into this category. Table 1 is a comparison of multimedia and classroom training using these delineations.

Cost

One of the biggest reasons why companies adopt multimedia training is the cost savings it brings. Under the right conditions, multimedia can far surpass classroom instruction relative to the cost of doing training. Studies have shown that training costs can be reduced from 25 percent to as much as 75 percent over classroom instruction (Multimedia Training Newsletter Study, 1996). Two examples of cost savings attributed to the use of multimedia attest to this. The first is a report by the U.S. Coast Guard, where the HH60J helicopter CBT flight simulator training program saved over $11 million over a three year period (Janson, 1992). The other is a report by Federal Express, where the company estimated a savings of over $100 million on employee training (Miller, 1990).

The types of savings typically found when multimedia is used include fewer dollars spent on instructors, renting facilities, and the travel and lodging of students. Fewer dollars are spent because training takes less time, productivity is not lost to travel time, and administrative activities (like grading tests by hand) are not necessary

In addition, using CBT simulations instead of scarce or expensive equipment saves dollars by not taking the equipment out of service or risking damage. CBT scenarios also save money by replacing hazardous environments where the student can be injured while training. See Table 1 – Comparison of Multimedia versus Classroom Training.

Custom multimedia courseware, the kind developed for a specific company, is cost effective beginning at about 1,000 students. Off-the-shelf multimedia courseware (not customized) can have a much lower break-even point depending on the initial outlay for the product(s) and computer systems on which the product(s) runs.

Instruction

The application of instruction, or how the course content is dispensed to and manipulated by the student, varies widely between multimedia and classroom delivery. In typical classrooms, students spend many hours listening to one-way broadcast, perform some workbook or other exercises, ask some questions, and then take quizzes and a final test. Course content can vary drastically and is heavily dependent upon the skill of the instructor; the monitoring of student progress is relegated to the students' attendance and how they do on go/no go tests.

MAKING CRM STICK

Table 1. Comparison of Multimedia versus Classroom Training

RATED FACTORS	CLASSROOM	MULTIMEDIA (INCLUDES CBT, CD-ROM, INTERNET/WBT)
Cost		
Cost Per Student	Initially lower at startup, but increases over time. Cost remains constant for each student, each time course is taught.	Has higher development cost, which declines as the number of students increases.
Cost of Training Resources	Equipment simulators and the associated classroom instruction have higher life cycle cost.	Multimedia simulations have comparable development cost, but much lower life-cycle cost.
Safety/Accident Prevention	Use of costly, dangerous, or scarce equipment in actual environment increases cost and number of accidents.	Use of computer simulations reduces accidents and reaches training goal through successive approximations to actual equipment and conditions.
Instruction		
Application of Instruction	Learning scheduled in discrete blocks, applied at later time after instruction.	Learning takes place in context, at the moment knowledge is required.
Consistency of Content and Instruction (Delivery Variance)	Depends largely on instructor's skill.	Consistently high, no variability in content or way course is taught.
Student Interaction – Sharing of Past Experiences	Extremely effective at sharing personal experience.	Ineffective for sharing spontaneous anecdotal experience.
Instruction/ Assessment of Higher Order Cognitive Skills	Better accomplished by classroom instructors.	Difficult to create applicable interactive methods on computer.
Monitoring of Student Performance	Can record attendance, not actual learning, during instruction. Record performance on quizzes and tests.	Automated systems track usage, capture student progress, correct poor performance, reinforce successes, and record a variety of statistics related to performance.
Administration		
Scheduling Flexibility and Access to Training	Student must adjust to the training schedule and instructor's availability.	Training can be adapted to student's schedule.
Tracking of Student Performance	Can record attendance and scores on quizzes and tests.	Automated systems track usage and a variety of statistics during instruction.

Self-paced multimedia instruction engages students at the same time as they encounter new content. It allows students to learn at their own speed, skipping or skimming areas where they are strong and investing more time in areas of weakness. This new-found control enables them to take more responsibility for their own learning and become more efficient and effective learners.

The use of multiple sensory modes, combining visual presentation with audio and text explanations, delivers information in a format that is easily personalized and understood by those with differing learning styles. Immediate interaction and feedback provides constant, highly effective reinforcement of concepts and content. The course content and its delivery remain the same each time it is taught. Student progress is monitored and assessed with a multitude of statistics that can be used to do anything from correcting inappropriate student behavior to modifying faulty course content.

Two areas where classroom instruction is considered superior to multimedia delivery are in the teaching of higher order cognitive skills, and the application of past learner experiences in the learning process (See Table 1 - Comparison of Multimedia versus Classroom Training). The instruction of cognitive skills with multimedia is highly dependent upon the skill of the developer. The sharing of anecdotal student experiences is becoming less and less a problem in multimedia with the advent of electronic conversations via the Internet.

Administration

When it comes to administering training, flexibility is a key concern. In classroom instruction, the administrator must wait till there are enough students to form a class so that training is cost effective. With multimedia training, the more students that take it, from across the hall or across the nation, the more cost effective it becomes. Deploying multimedia training on CD-ROM or over the Internet or Intranet makes training immediately available to workers. So there are no real "class" schedules to maintain. Multimedia training allows students to make use of courseware whenever it is needed, promoting the benefits of just-in-time learning.

The tracking and reporting features of multimedia training can help companies certify that employees have been trained on required safety, regulatory, and other job specific issues. Unlike the classroom where much of this is done by a person, multimedia courseware has built-in tracking and reporting and automates the process.

MAKING CRM STICK

What are the Benefits of Multimedia?

There is a substantial body of research supporting the prowess of multimedia training as one of the more effective ways to deliver training. There are also some commonly accepted facts about the value of WBT and CD-ROM training.

Benefits According to the Research

Over the last 15 years, a number of research studies have shown the effectiveness of multimedia to deliver training. Adams explored six studies conducted by the U.S. Army, IBM, Xerox, United Technologies, WICAT, and Federal Express that compared multimedia to classroom instruction (Adams, 1992). Miller analyzed over 30 evaluative studies that conducted the same comparison (Miller, 1990). And, Wright examined approximately 25 studies comparing multimedia to classroom instruction on a number of variables (Wright, 1993). Their research findings can be broken down into the five categories shown below.

Less time needed to train. Training compression, the amount of time it takes students to complete an interactive course compared to classroom, was reported between 25-75% for interactive. The learning curve relative to the amount of time it takes learners to reach mastery of their course content was 60% faster for multimedia learners compared to classroom learners.

Higher student achievement/job proficiency. Learning gains of how well students performed on final tests or comparisons between pre- and post-test were analyzed for multimedia and classroom subjects. Gains for multimedia students were found to be between 38-56% greater than their classroom counterparts. Three other studies found a significant difference in gains for multimedia students. Concerning how consistent the interactive learners' understanding of content was compared to the classroom learner (consistency of learning), the interactive learners' understanding of the content was 50-60% more consistent.

Higher content retention. Students receiving multimedia instruction had a 25-50% higher retention rate compared to those receiving the same content through classroom instruction. Content retention refers to the learner's ability to recall content days, weeks, or months after the initial training is completed. It is a measure of how much content reached long-term memory.

MAKING CRM STICK

More consistency in delivery of content. Multimedia learners had a delivery variance of between 20-40% less than their instructor led counterparts. The slight variance for the multimedia learners can be attributed to the different paths available to the students as they progressed through the interactive courseware.

More student/course satisfaction and motivation. Several studies reported high student satisfaction with multimedia training because they felt they could move at their own pace, were more involved in their own learning process, received individualized responses, and had privacy.

Benefits of WBT Compared to CD-ROM Training

The following advantages favor WBT over CD-ROM training:

- Lowers development and distribution costs;
- Allows immediate updates and revisions to courseware;
- Makes courseware available to a wider range of platforms (Windows, Mac, O/S 2, and Unix);
- Makes assessment and certification easier;
- Harnesses the use of electronic conversations to expand the learning environment;
- Improves access to a wealth of knowledge on the Web (Linking to numerous sites);
- Makes courseware more accessible as a resource and reference.

Benefits of CD-ROM Training Compared to WBT

The following advantages favor CD-ROM training over WBT:

- Allows for a wider range of sophisticated teaching designs;
- Has fewer restrictions on media like video and audio due to lack of bandwidth;
- Allows for more types of interactivity – a greater number of test question and exercise types.

When is Multimedia Appropriate?

Taking the leap into multimedia is best accomplished in small increments. Conducting pilot projects, building momentum and support within the organization, and proving the technology is the best way to start. The use of off-the-shelf courseware is usually preferable to developing your own custom courseware in house. Developing your own multimedia requires

MAKING CRM STICK

more stringent criteria because of the greater cost involved. The criteria for when multimedia is right for you and what kind is best for your situation is outlined below.

Consider whether Multimedia is specifically desired or currently exists. Consider whether classroom training is specifically required. Then, consider whether:

- You want to reduce your training time, increase achievement and job proficiency, increase retention, increase the consistency of your content and content delivery, and increase course satisfaction.
- Your training population is large, widely scattered, has diverse skills, varied proficiency levels, or wide ranging learning styles.
- Your content is stable or can be changed in predictable, manageable amounts.
- Your content is dangerous to perform or requires equipment that is costly to take out of service, scarce, or sensitive.
- You want to reduce the number of resources required by instructor-led training.
- You have workers that find it hard to take time away from work for training.
- You want to reduce the number of full-time trainers or your trainers are hard to schedule, recruit, train, or expensive to employ.
- You want to maintain more accurate and consistent student performance data.
- You want to reduce the amount of time and money spent on employee certification.

Next, determine whether CD-ROM training or WBT is the training of choice:

"CD-ROM vs. WBT Training" Questionnaire

Very Important		Less Important
	1. You want to keep your development and distribution costs as low as possible.	
	2. You want to update, revise, and implement courseware as quickly as possible.	
	3. You want to reach the widest range of platforms possible.	
	4. You want to use electronic conversations as an integral part of your training.	

	5. You want to reference and search the Web, using it as a knowledge base.	
	6. You want maximum accessibility to your courseware as a resource or reference.	
	7. You want a wide range of teaching designs.	
	8. You want the highest video and audio quality and responsiveness.	
	9. You want the highest level of interactive techniques (questions/exercises).	

If you answered "Very Important" for items 1-6 and "Less Important" for items 6-9, then WBT would be your choice. On the other hand if you answered "Less Important" for items 1-6 and "Very Important" for items 6-9, then CD-ROM is best for you. If your answers fall in between these two choices, then you probably need to weight the importance of the various factors.

References

Adams, Gregory L., "Why Interactive?," Multimedia & Videodisc Monitor, March 1992, pp. 20-25.

Bunderson, C. V. and Olsen, J. B., "Instructional Effectiveness of an Intelligent Videodisc in Biology," Machine Mediated Learning, 1.2, 1984.

Janson, Jennifer L., "Computer-Based Training Helps Firms Trim Budgets," PC Week (PC Week Special), January 27, 1992.

Janson, Jennifer L., "Interactive Video Expedites Training At Federal Express," PC Week (PC Week Special), January 27, 1992.

Janson, Jennifer L., "Simulation Program Helps Coast Guard Sink Training Costs," PC Week (PC Week Special), January 27, 1992.

Miller, Rockley L., "Learning Benefits of Interactive Technologies," The Videodisc Monitor, February 1990, pp. 15-17.

Wright, Elizabeth E., "Making the Multimedia Decision: Strategies for Success," Journal of Instructional Delivery Systems, Winter, 1993, pp. 15-22.

Copyright © 2004 by Terrell L. Perry, Ed. D. All rights reserved.

Are Your Virtual Classes as Successful as They Could Be? – Christina Morfeld

"Blended learning" is the carefully-managed integration of formal training programs and informal knowledge-enhancing opportunities. It is becoming an increasingly popular business strategy for two primary reasons:

- As opposed to traditional training, which tends to be a series of isolated or unrelated events, a blended approach is self-reinforcing. Additionally, as an important first step in communicating learning as a core corporate value, it has the power to improve performance at both the individual and organizational level.

- Thanks to the Web's robust collaborative capabilities, face-to-face gatherings are no longer a prerequisite for knowledge transfer, brainstorming, and teamwork. This translates into significant cost savings for employers, particularly those with geographically-dispersed workgroups.

There are many Web-based applications on the market that support synchronous ("virtual") meetings and classes. These include Centra, HorizonLive, and PlaceWare, to name just a few. While several noteworthy differences exist between them, most of their features and functions are quite similar – and specifically designed to mirror the activities of a traditional classroom.

That being the case, why is learner engagement such a tough challenge for synchronous trainers? It's not that the necessary tools and utilities aren't available; in fact, they're built right into the software we're using! Instead, it seems that we're simply not leveraging them to their fullest extent.

MAKING CRM STICK

PrimeLearning, a leading provider of business and professional skills eLearning, utilizes Centra for its synchronous events, and has graciously allowed me to share information included in a virtual class I designed for them. Its goal was to demonstrate "best practices" for developing and delivering training via Centra, but the advice – which focuses on strategy rather than mechanics – applies equally well to other platforms.

Strategy #1: Vary the "look and feel" of the presentation

Synchronous classrooms contain a "content window" in which information is displayed. Slides uploaded from a presentation application such as Microsoft PowerPoint are commonly used, just as "overheads" might be employed in a traditional setting.

During the Development Phase:

While your slide set should be consistent in terms of background color, placement of company logo, etc., diversify the way the subject matter itself is presented as much as possible. Bulleted lists are certainly preferable over paragraphs, but also be creative in your use of tables, single-item screens (for impact), and simple graphics in lieu of text when appropriate.

Limit text to key concepts, phrases, and questions that you will verbally expand upon. (Hint: Use the presentation software's "notes" feature to document what you plan to say in support of the text, then print out a hard copy to serve as a "cheat sheet" during delivery.) And while colored text should not be used excessively, it is a helpful way to indicate "action items" such as activities and questions.

Finally, avoid the use of animations, slide transitions, build slides, and other special effects, as they will not "carry over" into the classroom environment. (Note: It's possible that the other platforms – as well as newer releases of Centra – do, in fact, support these.)

During the Delivery Phase:

As you discuss each slide, use the application's whiteboard tools to draw attention to important items. But don't just settle for one! Instead, alternate between the standard pointer and using a variety of colors to underline, highlight, and enclose text within rectangles, ellipses. etc. Doing so probably won't have much of an effect from an instructional perspective, but adding a bit of visual interest certainly doesn't hurt.

MAKING CRM STICK

Strategy #2: Capitalize on the power of questions

While this issue may seem applicable only to the delivery phase of a virtual class, it is strongly recommended that you pre-determine when and how you will employ questioning techniques. Be sure to keep the following methods in mind:

ASKING Questions
- Use open-ended questions.
- Give learners up to 5 seconds to respond.
- If no volunteers, give a hint or example rather than immediately providing the answer.
- Frequently ask learners of they have questions.
- Instead of asking whether learners understand something, pose a question that allows them to demonstrate their understanding.

ANSWERING Questions
- Repeat/paraphrase to ensure that entire class has heard and to confirm your understanding
- In general, provide direct answers only if you alone possess the knowledge to respond appropriately
- Redirect the question to the group
- Help the questioner come to his or her own conclusion
- Admit when you don't know the answer (but commit to quickly finding out and getting back to the learners with the information

In short, don't tell your learners something if you can get them to tell you instead!

Strategy #3: Take advantage of the system's interactive capabilities

Most platforms offer sophisticated functionality such as application sharing and breakout rooms, and you should use them as appropriate. However, each also supports a variety of simple techniques for increasing participation and appealing to a wide range of learning styles and preferences. For example, you can:

- Ask learners to respond "Yes" or "No" (by clicking the appropriate button) to a closed-ended question.
- Pose a question to the group and ask those who wish to respond to raise their hands. You may alternately ask one or more learners to type their own responses on the screen.

MAKING CRM STICK

- Ask learners to brainstorm about a specific issue or topic using the "chat" feature. This tool lends itself especially well to discussions about personal feelings and experiences, such as "what XYZ (e.g., customer service, effective communication, etc.) means to me."
- Ask learners to "vote" by placing a gold star (or some other whiteboard indicator) next to the item of their choice.
- Create a two-column matching exercise in which a volunteer draws lines between the corresponding items in Column A and Column B.
- Poll learners with a single multiple-choice question.
- Quiz learners with a series of multiple-choice or fill-in-the-blank questions.
- Consider using "pre-work" – such as an article, case study, etc. – as a means of stimulating discussion at the very start of your presentation.

Bottom line: With advance planning that gives special consideration to the online environment – and a bit of practice – your virtual training sessions can be just as effective (and enjoyable) as those that take place in a traditional classroom setting!

Copyright © 2002-2004 by Christina Morfeld and Affinity Business Communications, LLC. Originally published by Suite101.com. All rights reserved. Christina Morfeld is president of Affinity Business Communications, a provider of high-quality Instructional design, technical writing, and content development solutions. Whether writing to instruct, inform, or persuade, our work is reader-focused, benefits-oriented, and results-driven. Visit our website at http://www.affinitybizcomm.com or call 203-595-9418 to learn how we can increase your firm's sales and effectiveness!

MAKING CRM STICK

Chapter 8: Project Management and Governance

In IBM's *Doing CRM Right study (2004)*, effective Project Management and Governance is a huge contributor to CRM project success. According to the companies polled, *Budget Process Management* has a 12 percent impact on project success, and Governance has an 8.2 percent impact.

Certainly, of all the success factor groups described in this book, *Project Management and Governance* is the one we don't need to worry about very much, right? We've been doing project management and governance for years, and the expertise is certainly not in short supply, right?

Clearly, some projects are failing because of poor project management and governance. This is happening because the rules of the game are changing. Sometime in the near future, you will probably hear somebody say "Hey, I can manage this project in my sleep. I have a hundred CRM projects under my belt." Yikes. *Beware* the CRM Project Manager who has a *hundred projects* under their belt. Here's why:

First of all, companies are now embarking on more multi-phased, multi-dimensional, cross-border CRM implementations. Large, multi-phased, multi-country projects are becoming the norm. Finite point-solution implementations that serve single workgroups or individual business units are becoming less common. Complexity is at an all-time high. In size, modern CRM implementations are beginning to resemble ERP implementations. However, in *complexity*, the CRM implementations are significantly *more difficult* to implement than ERP – because they typically include a mix of technologies (e.g., Siebel on top of Oracle with Avaya, Microstrategy, SAS, Kana, etc., plugged in).

MAKING CRM STICK

Second, if things aren't complex enough already, we are now moving into a more advanced phase of IT outsourcing and utilization of overseas assets. Project teams, tools and assets are spread out across the globe. Project team members are often hourly workers who are making a few dollars an hour in a 'coding factory' in a developing country. This situation makes a project even more difficult to manage.

Third, let's face it, companies lost large numbers of talented and experienced IT professionals during the recent years of economic recession. Consulting companies suffered the worst. Internal IT organizations have suffered almost as much. A reshuffling of resources will likely continue to occur as business and IT professionals make career moves in an improving economy. For the time being, at least, projects will be less *repeatable* than they were before the economic recession.

Back in 2001, do you remember hearing things like "Our Siebel Workflow Team has done ten projects together!"? This is not the case anymore. More likely, you will hear things like "Our guys haven't really done Siebel Workflow before, but they're scheduled to attend Siebel training when the project starts . . . as soon as they arrive from Bangalore, India." Bottom line – During this next growth period, project teams will not have the same collaborative history together. They will be strangers to the firm, strangers to the culture, strangers to each other, and they may never have the opportunity to interact in person.

In this new highly-complex post-recession environment, the bar has been raised higher, and it should not come as any surprise that we are seeing highly complex schedules and budgets mismanaged, stakeholder groups forgotten; communication breakdowns, staffing breakdowns, and business cases that collapse under their own weight. Complexity is our new enemy.

The papers in this section focus on some of the controllable interventions CRM practitioners can exercise to prevent the preventable. We've all practiced these to some extent, but we challenge our readers to read on and ask:

- How disciplined am I about following fundamental project management principles and establishing and executing governance practices? For example, we hypothesize that most CRM practitioners build communications plans, but later fail to fully execute them. How does this impact stakeholders' understanding of the CRM goals and their buy-in?
- What happens to most of our work plans after we've developed them, obtained signoff on them, and documented them in our project

charter? Are they managed, updated, and communicated? Or do they collect dust in some project repository?
- How well do we proactively manage risk?
- Do we have measures to determine the success of our CRM project? Are we tracking them in a disciplined manner?

Sometimes a little bit of truth, even if painful, can serve as a healthy reminder as to why we may need to return to the fundamentals of good project management practices.

In his white paper entitled *How the CEO Should Move the Monkey for Major IT Projects*, Walter Adamson calls attention to what he believes to be the global project-killers and provides insights on how CRM success requires careful management of the *white space* between project streams.

Douglas Arnstein's *Gaining Visibility and Commitment to Technology Projects - Part 2* emphasizes some of the blocking and tackling fundamentals that a CRM project manager should consider in the development of a project plan, whether it is for a CRM project or any other project. Sounds like straightforward stuff – But if you read it closely, you may be surprised at the gaps you will discover in your project planning approach and documentation.

In our experiences, we have found a frequent correlation between superb CRM project management and the presence of a Project Management Organization (PMO). Organizations are clearly realizing the benefit of having a PMO provide oversight to the multitude of IT projects that are concurrently underway in any large company. We believe that a PMO is a governance best practice and a key enabler for many of the other success factors in this book (e.g., aligning the organization, building commitment, building the business case, etc.). *Effective Use of a Program Management Office in CRM and Other IT Projects* by James Butler and Andres Salinas teaches the basic benefits and characteristics of a PMO. This paper is a must-read for Project Managers and staff who have oversight of a multi-phased or multiple work stream CRM project.

At first glance, you may wonder why Walter Adamson's paper *Why Planning Fails in Middle-Sized Enterprises*, is included in this book – It isn't focused on CRM per se. But we believe it describes the strategic mindset and context in which a CRM program should reside. Adamson explains how executives can greatly increase the chance of success of strategic change initiatives (including CRM initiatives), even those induced by anxiety or shock, by appointing Change Leadership Teams, and

MAKING CRM STICK

concurrently paying serious attention to using vision, mission and values statements as implementation tools. The key message . . . your CRM program, and the key requirements, features and functionalities of that program should have clear linkage to your vision, mission and values statements.

Finally, a paper by Javad Maftoon and Dan Murphy addresses an area that may become the CRM project manager's greatest pain-in-the-neck – It is entitled *The Challenge of Knowledge Transfer in the New World of Outsourcing and Offshore CRM.*

How the CEO Should Move the Monkey for Major IT Projects – Walter Adamson

Achieving complex goals in unpredictable environments is risky. Yet all too often the people closest to the task are not asked to explore and contribute to the total solution. Major IT projects fail, and millions are wasted, because CEOs and senior managers allow themselves to be managed and to carry the monkey for the delivery of these major, and sometimes transformational, projects.

There is a better approach, whereby not only is the project risk reduced, and the business benefits tested en-route, but where the monkey is moved to the back of those most able to explore the risk and recommend the solutions.

Project managers typically measure the success of a project by its meeting their project metrics. Yet often successful projects do not deliver business success. A new type of cross-functional team needs to be established to explore the white space risks, to identify real organisational integration issues, and to deliver fast-track business benefits. By moving responsibility to these new teams, the monkey will be shifted, the risks will be contained, and the business results will be better.

Why does the CEO have the monkey on his or her back for failed projects?

In Kenneth Blanchard and William Oncken's book One Minute Manager Meets the Monkey the authors tell managers not to take on problems if the problems don't belong to them. They tell them how to give back these monkeys, thus increasing production and reducing stress. Typically the monkey for major project implementations - projects that have enormous white space risk and integration risk - lands on the back of senior managers, and even the CEO.

MAKING CRM STICK

The Standish Group's studies of the past few years document a 70% failure rate for IT projects. Some 30% fail outright, and another 40% drag on for years, propped up by huge cash infusions until they are finally shut down.

In a recent survey conducted by KPMG more than half of the major companies questioned admitted that they have experienced failed IT projects in the past year. The research, involving 134 listed firms in the UK, Europe, the US, Australia and Africa, found that the average cost of failed projects was US$10m. One firm admitted that a single project failure in 2002 had cost it US$200m.

This research raises two vital questions for CEOs and senior managers:

- Why are they holding the monkey for such projects - which have such an appallingly poor likelihood of success?

- Why do these projects have such an appalling record?

They do not have to hold the monkey, and in fact if they let it go the chances of project success will improve!

You can get this monkey off your back AND significantly increase the chance of delivering success from major projects by understanding some simple techniques. These techniques are not magic; they are just not commonly practiced. Why should they be? The project teams are happy to manage the boss and leave the monkey right there - on your shoulders.

It is time to put the monkey back where it belongs. Remarkably, this will not only bring you relief but it will also grow your team and produce superior results, especially for major transformational projects such as large-scale IT projects.

Why projects fail - according to project managers

It is certainly not fundamental technical problems that cause most IT project failures. The wave of failed enterprise resource planning and customer relationship management (CRM) projects in the past few years have not come about because of problems with the technology. Almost all have resulted from a failure to mesh the project effectively into the business, and to implement the business process changes required to reap the benefits.

MAKING CRM STICK

What does that last statement mean? According to traditional analysis it means this, taken from a highly respected UK online IT management journal: "The reasons why we keep ignoring these lessons cuts to the heart of what is probably the biggest single issue facing business IT today: the disconnect between the IT function and the rest of the business in most organisations."

The gap in alignment between IT and business strategy is certainly an issue, but solving it will not necessarily reduce major project failures. (For a framework and method to solve the Business-IT Alignment gap see our website www.digitalinvestor.com.au and the menu item "Business-IT Alignment").

If we ask the experts themselves, the project managers, we get another view. According to a UK survey of project managers the major reasons for IT project failures were:

- Missed deadlines (75%)
- Overrun budgets (55%)
- Poor communications (40%)
- Inability to meet project requirements (37%)

And perhaps even more interestingly the main success criteria were given as:

- Meeting milestones (51%)
- Maintaining the required quality levels (32%)
- Meeting the budget (31%)

The surveyed project managers were very experienced managers, having taken the lead in integrating large systems in Times Top 100 companies across the finance, utilities, manufacturing, business services, and telecommunications sectors.

Therefore, things are transpiring as we suspected - project directors measure the cause of failure and success of major projects from an implementation perspective, from a delivery milestone perspective and from a sense of pride as a project manager. These are all internal perspectives. We could even position these indicators as lagging indicators, although they are commonly perceived as leading indicators. Even at best, if you find it hard to consider these traditional measures as lagging indicators, they are definitely only hygiene factors.

MAKING CRM STICK

But all of these factors combined can only measure whether a project has been delivered successfully - and even then they are barely capable. However, no combination of these factors will measure if a project has delivered success - that is delivered business success. Therefore, most remarkably, the traditional analysis does not yield any insights.

Improving project management skills in doing better what the surveyed project managers are already doing will not necessarily yield better business results. More training for project managers will not get the monkey off the CEO's back for failed major projects.

Major projects fail because we don't know everything until we get to the end

I don't want to let this one slip by you, so let me say it again. Major projects fail because we don't know everything until we get to the end.

So we need to do things to help find out what we don't know before we get to the end.

It can be done, and, most remarkably, by getting it done it also moves the monkey off the back of the CEO and senior managers. Because traditional project management techniques focus on fine details and activities they tend to narrow people's attention onto progress and recommendations and partial solutions on the track to the final result.

In paying attention to the details, two global project-killers often go unseen and therefore unheeded (1) the integration of the final components, and (2) the identification of important elements of the white space between project streams.

The integration issue is important because even if all the right things have been anticipated, their integration often has not. It is very hard for management to predict all the activities and events that will need to be brought together in the final implementation.

The white space refers to those things that are critical to a project's success yet are not identified as issues additional to the actions and tasks that are being managed in detail.

The result? Project teams, including large IT teams, perform well and deliver a project successfully. Unfortunately, although the project is delivered successfully, it does not deliver success to the organisation. The unresolved issue in large-scale project delivery is how to move from successful delivery to delivering success, and the unspoken issue is how to move the monkey off the senior management's back.

Moving from successful delivery to delivering success

In analysing successful delivery, as against delivering success, what is most often found is that management and their project teams have jumped to a larger transformational solution than is prudent. They have often done this because of impatience and a lack of respect for a process of taking transformation through pilot benefit delivery projects.

In many instances I have witnessed management reject these pilot projects as being simply more planning, or accuse them of being time-wasting or brand them as half-baked. In these organisational cultures once an end goal is seen the managers then leap in and dismiss everything other than taking the most direct path to the fully-blown goal as being indecisive and wimpish.

The solution is to go back to ABCD and to have patience in learning how to deliver transformational projects by backing bite-sized mini-projects which deliver rapid benefits. The ABCD of project implementation is as follows:

- A is the current state of the project environment - from where the organisation is starting;

- B is the intent, the goal, the organisational vision of the end-result of executing and implementing this project - this is, the vision of delivering success;

- C is the set of constraints that may restrain or guide or shape the way in which the project is delivered. Here in C we should also identify the white space risk; and

- D is the development of rapid benefit prototypes - mini-sized rapid implementation modules which test the project assumptions and deliver real business benefits.

The D-type Monkey Moving Business Benefits projects (M2B2) are a series of mini-projects that deliver a vision of B, what the overall project is intended to deliver as business benefits. They are not traditional inter-disciplinary mini-projects where different streams collaborate to investigate and resolve project implementation issues. These M2B2 projects deliver the real outcomes that build confidence in the ability of the total project to deliver success.

Why are senior managers carrying the white space and integration risk? Because they rush past the careful consideration of the D-type mini-projects and head straight for the B goal. In the rush to prove how macho they are, at the end of the day, these managers incur massive losses to their companies and shareholders. The absolute legion of failed big-bang IT projects, with the billions of dollars washed down the drain, speaks to those inclinations.

Moving the monkey to the people with the knowledge

Consider how large projects are often run - specialized teams are formed to tackle major streams of work to deliver the project, and these teams run in parallel towards the final cut-over date. Figure 1, below, illustrates this typically parallel team approach.

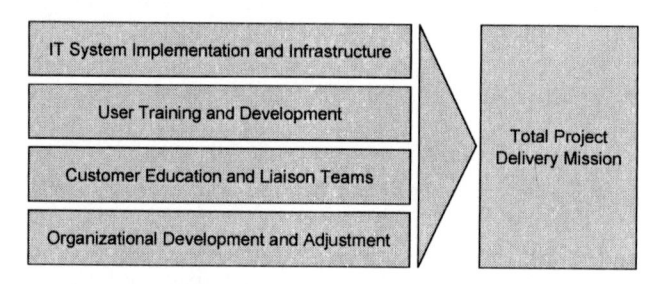

[Diagram: Four stacked boxes labeled "IT System Implementation and Infrastructure", "User Training and Development", "Customer Education and Liaison Teams", "Organizational Development and Adjustment" pointing to "Total Project Delivery Mission"]

Figure 1: Typical project streams building towards a final integration

The recommended M2B2 approach tasks additional cross-functional teams with implementing mini-versions of the final outcomes. They may do this by focusing on a small subset of customers, a subset of the organisation, a subset of the functionality, but importantly they aim to produce a business result. See Figure 2, below.

In producing a business result these teams will discover the missing white space items, and learn of the integration risks and challenges first hand. These M2B2 projects, as part of the D step of management, test the criteria and constraints that have been identified in the C step of the ABCD process. In testing the constraints and criteria, they also extend the boundaries of those criteria and in parallel reduce the risk by increasing the understanding.

MAKING CRM STICK

Because each M2B2 project gets progressively larger in scope, as the confidence grows, they continually scale-up the white space issues and integration issues as the project progresses. And incidentally, these M2B2 projects also scale-up the delivered benefits.

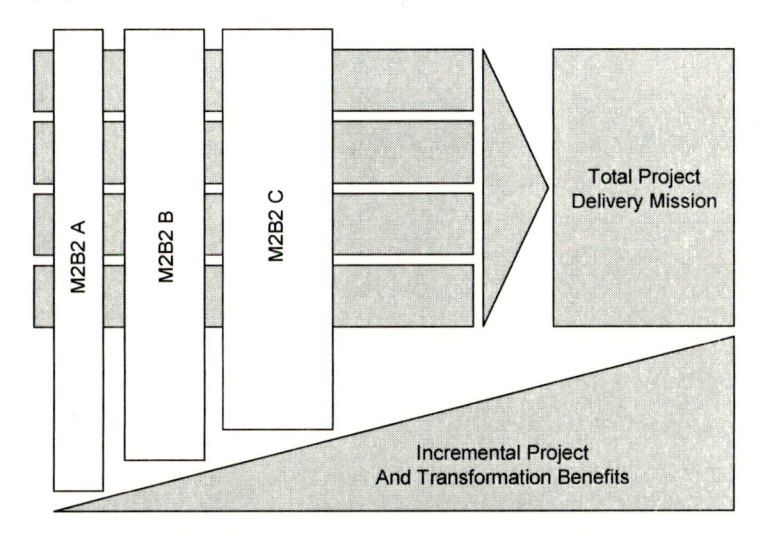

Figure 2: Delivering incremental business benefits from vertical projects

The benefits are very simply stated: by using these M2B2 teams important issues are identified at the earliest possible time in the project lifecycle.

We all know that issues identified early are easier to correct than issues which are hit later in the cycle. The issues which we want to surface are those often hidden challenges associated with integration of the work streams and things which have just been lost in the white space.

Typically, a M2B2 team will comprise members from each major workstream and from the beneficiaries themselves e.g. in a business the business users would be part of the team, and perhaps even carefully selected customers.

Rather than being horizontal and project-task oriented, the M2B2 teams are vertical and success-outcome oriented.

They should be timetabled for short-term results in comparison to the total project schedule. Typically the project goals should be achievable in no more than 90 day timeframes, along the lines of the Cisco model for rapid

MAKING CRM STICK

delivery projects.

Part of the skill in getting the best incremental benefits, and in reducing the risk, is to know how to select scope and scope the M2B2 projects. As a guide, an experienced management team needs to look across the areas of the horizontal effort, and think about the nature of the organisational change, and then pick the areas of white space where they see red flags. That selection process description is not very scientific, but it also lies at the heart of using the full knowledge of the organisation to bring to bear on white space and integration issues for major projects.

You need to think about where the greatest cross-integration risk lies, and focus a vertical M2B2 project down through that vertical. The real challenge for CEOs and senior managers is to let go. To let go of the desire to control and own the risk, and to let go of the monkey they subconsciously pride themselves on wearing on their backs. Letting go of the white space risk, and integration risk, is an art not a science. Giving people space to manage the white space and reduce integration risk in complex projects is a management discipline.

The difference between monkey-moving projects and typical cross-functional teamwork

Major projects, structured as in Figure 1 with horizontal streams, often also do include cross functional teams in their project plans. Although cross-functional teams and reviews are used, these groups are not typically tasked with producing mini-results. More likely, they are meeting to resolve inter-stream issues associated with the mechanics of project delivery. This will certainly ensure that the project gets delivered successfully, but the evidence shows that these teams are not able to improve the chances of delivering business success.

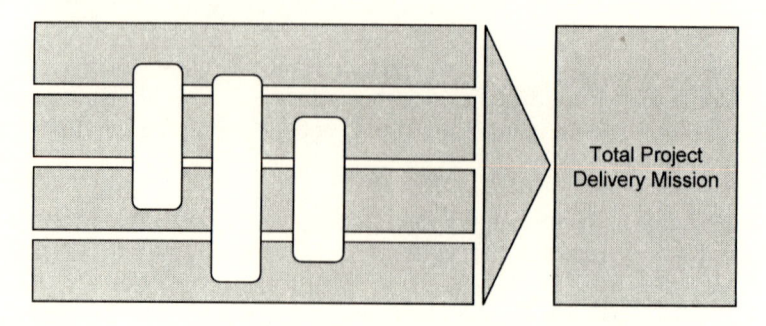

Figure 3: Typical project cross-stream teams

In the best case they will be trying to theoretically conceive of the white space risk - typically expressed as trying to watch out for things that might fall through the cracks (between the major teams). But unfortunately goal generation and scoping for these types of projects does not provide a platform to bring together the dual unknowns of white space risk and end-point business integration issues.

The essential goal for a M2B2 project is to produce real business benefits. The primary goal is not to solve project implementation issues - that is a means but not a goal. And this difference in goals is the essential difference in the M2B2 approach as compared to the typical cross-functional project implementation tasks.

This is illustrated in Figure 3, above, where typical cross-stream project teams are represented by the vertical ovals. This graphically shows the difference in philosophy between traditional cross-functional teams and M2B2 teams. The typical cross-stream teams are not formed as a result of the ABCD business planning process, nor as a result of scanning across the white space for the transformational organizational integration challenges.

Summary

By implementing Monkey Moving Business Benefit fast-track projects CEOs and senior managers move the responsibility for identifying white space and integration issues to those closest to the action.

Because of the progressive nature of these M2B2 projects the internal fit of the organization - the way it is aligned behind the business strategy and project goals - will be bought into a step-wise alignment with the transformational project outcomes.

The M2B2 approach is really part of an organizational change program requiring selecting, sequencing and timing interventions to achieve results. It has the added benefit of moving to those who are best able to act, the responsibility to identify the white space risks and the integration challenges in delivering real business benefits from the project.

By being selected and given responsibility to run a M2B2 project a manager is clearly being given responsibility to confirm or challenge the real world benefits of the major project. These managers are being charged with the challenge of closing the white spaces.

MAKING CRM STICK

In terms of selecting M2B2 projects, the selectors must be skilled at scanning the environment, understanding the implications of change across the organization and choosing appropriate scope and objectives having regard to the organizations wider strategy.

By moving the monkey, and at the same time getting faster to real business benefits, major projects are sure to succeed more often because you will know a lot more about what you don't know before you get to the end of the whole project.

Copyright 2004 by Walter Adamson. All rights reserved.

MAKING CRM STICK

Gaining Visibility and Commitment to Technology Projects - Part 2 – Douglas Arnstein

Developing the Project Plan

The Project Plan is the document used to manage project execution. It defines the project 'What, Why, Who, When, Where, and How'. It is a text document (not to be confused with a Microsoft Project Plan) which states how the project intends to achieve its objectives. It helps other internal and external organizations understand what they need to do and when in support of the project.

Although the project manager has primary responsibility for producing the Project Plan, it should be developed as a partnership between the business and technology organizations.
A well-drafted Project Plan would include the following sections.

1.0 Introduction

This section details the background and purpose of the document, its structure, the intended audience, and the reader's obligations. One of the obligations should be to require formal approval from project stakeholders and that should be directly stated.

2.0 Project Charter

The Project Plan will be distributed to a wider audience than may have participated in the Project Charter and stakeholder analysis exercises. For this reason, incorporate the completed Project Charter in its entirety in this section. This gives project newcomers a brief, comprehensive overview of the project and sets the stage for the rest of the Project Plan.

3.0 Milestones with Projected Dates

This section uses a combination of significant events and the list of key deliverables developed in the Project Charter and sets forth projected beginning and ending dates for each. This information sets expectations as to when components of the project work are to be started and completed. At this early stage of the project, these may merely be best estimates based on the preliminary Work Breakdown Structure (see 11.0 WBS).

4.0 Resource Plan

This section describes the project organization and how the project will interact with the day-to-day organization. Every organization is unique in the way it organizes projects, and this section will reflect those particulars. At a minimum, one should provide specific role and responsibility information for the project sponsor, the project manager, the project core team, any management oversight or steering committees, and required business and technical resources. List each resource role, the responsibilities of the role, the skills required, and the projected start date. A project organization chart could also be included.

5.0 Scope Management and Change Control

Change is inevitable. Change can hurt the project. The Scope Management and Change Control section documents how the project will manage change. It is critical to identify the project's process for submitting, logging, approving, and adopting change requests. By defining this process early, the same rules are communicated to all project participants.

6.0 Quality Plan

Stakeholders provided feedback regarding project quality during the stakeholder analysis. The core team should be able to come up with other ideas. Generally, quality can be defined for an end deliverable, such as the software product, or it can be applied to a process. From a deliverable perspective, quality can be measured in several ways; developing reusable code, specifying throughput performance, or requiring the software to conform to organizational standards. As for process quality, it can be defined as how the project will conduct a given process so as to produce quality results.

7.0 Risk Management Plan

This section articulates the project's early understanding of risk. The project size and complexity will be the main drivers of this activity. The objective at this stage is to identify the threats to 'avoid' by formally building tasks into the project execution processes to eliminate the probability of the risk occurring.

8.0 Communication Plan

To promote project visibility throughout its life cycle, it is necessary to communicate, communicate, and then communicate some more. The Communication Plan documents the information the project will capture and disseminate about project activities. Depending on the practices within the organization, some of it may be pre-defined, yet other forms may be dictated by the wishes of the stakeholders. Give the stakeholders what they want the way they want it. This simple action will elicit their support for the duration of the project. The Communication Plan should also include project document standards and information about the online project document repository location.

9.0 Communication Matrix

This matrix is a visual representation of the information collected and disseminated as documented in the Communication Plan. It is a simple tool to develop, easy to read, and it conveys a significant amount of information. The information presented is the stakeholders, the communication vehicles, the frequency of the distribution, and the media type of the distributed information.

	Freq	Media	Project Manager	Project Sponsor	Product Manager	IT
Status Reporting (meeting outcomes, action item log, issue log, project schedule	Weekly	Electronic	X		X	X
Milestone Progress Report	Bi-weekly	Electronic	X	X	X	X
Vendor Communications	Upon Receipt	Paper	X	X	X	
Status Meeting	Weekly	Conference	X		X	X
Steering Committee Meeting	Monthly	Conference			X	X

10.0 Deliverables / Responsibility Matrix

This matrix has the same format as the Communication Matrix, but is focused solely on deliverables. The purpose of this matrix is to document for each deliverable the project stakeholder or participant responsible for creating the deliverable, actively supporting the creation, reviewing it, and approving it.

	Freq	Project Manager	Project Sponsor	Product Manager	IT
Project Plan	1/5/05	P	SA	A	A
Business Requirements	2/28/05	R	A	P	A
Technical Design	4/15/05	R	R	A	P
Code and Unit Test	7/31/05	R		A	P
Etc.					

Key:
P = Primary creator
A = Approver of outcome
R = Reviewer of outcome
S = Support of del. creation

11.0 WBS (Work Breakdown Structure)

Even if it is a preliminary draft, include the WBS in the Project Plan. The more information presented, the better stakeholders will understand the impact to their respective areas. Identify assigned resources to the extent possible. Use the WBS to populate the Milestone start and end dates in section 3.0.

Finalizing the Project Plan

Depending on the number of project participants and stakeholders, it may require several reviews to cover the entire document with everyone. During these reviews, listen carefully to the feedback and negotiate appropriate changes to the document. Upon completion of the reviews, update the document identifying the revisions, and re-distribute the Project Plan for approval. All stakeholders should approve the Project Plan in writing. Post the signatures in the project repository. It is now a matter of executing the plan.
I carry the Project Plan with me and refer to it often throughout the project. I use it to keep participants focused on the agreed upon project mission, objectives, and processes.

2004 © Douglas Arnstein, Absolute Consulting Group, Inc. All rights reserved.

MAKING CRM STICK

Effective Use of a Program Management Office in CRM and Other IT Projects – James Butler and Andres Salinas

Background

Many organizations struggle to assess whether they are receiving the projected benefits from their Customer Relationship Management (CRM) and other information technology (IT) investments. In addition, they have difficulty determining whether their budgetary [and personnel] resources have been allocated appropriately to achieve the maximum yield on this expenditure. This paper will outline how a Program Management Office can help ensure organizations receive the maximum return on their CRM (and other IT) investments.

The CRM Investment

Most organizations spend significant portions of their budgets on CRM initiatives. Given both the significant costs of CRM expenditures and the opportunity for added revenues and cost savings that CRM technology can ultimately deliver, projects should be scrutinized carefully using a sound approach and methodology. Like all IT efforts, the CRM initiative of any organization must follow an efficient, organized, and finely tuned process to maximize the benefits of the investments and to remain competitive, provide customer value, and support the high-level goals of the organization.

In addition, like other IT efforts, the CRM initiative should support the institutional strategy. It should be documented in a Business Case Assessment (BCA) or Case for Change that articulates how the initiative supports the strategy, depicts the business need and objectives, estimated costs, resource requirements, anticipated benefits, among others. Such assessments are typically presented to an executive body for approval. Some organizations have taken steps in this direction through their capital budget review process and the requirement by their budget office to submit a full project proposal (including cost benefits) prior to the release of funding for the development stage of a large capital development project. The process of preparing and validating a business case against an overall strategy ensures that individual projects, when pulled together, support the enterprise goals and overarching mission. The benefits identified in the BCA document are the key project objectives, and success in realizing those benefits is a measure of the CRM project's success. When a business case is made that a CRM project provides an opportunity to increase sales revenue, improve the customer experience, improve efficiency or reduce expenses, the organization should expect that successes will be validated upon completion of the CRM project. The BCA should be used to measure success during the post-implementation monitoring phase of the project.

Given the size of most CRM investments and their importance to the organization, it is imperative that a Program Management Office (PMO) is established to ensure the organization obtains the expected benefits, reduces redundancy, communicates to all interested parties and ensures the efforts continue to support the business case. Among other things, the PMO should be charged with managing the CRM investment, just as an investment firm manages the company retirement account. Is this analogy, the staff retirement account represents a significant amount of money and requires knowledgeable dedicated staff to make sure it is growing appropriately and is protected. The PMO is the team responsible for overseeing the CRM (and other IT) investments and managing the IT portfolio of programs and projects.

Program Management Office

Some companies create Program Management Offices (PMOs) to ensure that their organizational objectives are aligned with the goals and associated metrics of the many projects they have underway. PMOs monitor project costs, keep projects on track and provide the overall guidance for a portfolio of projects, commonly referred to as a Program. In addition, PMOs are responsible for portfolio management, developing a project methodology and an enterprise communication plan, monitoring/tracking IT expenses, facilitating executive-level reviews, and providing the services of professional project managers. The expense of establishing a PMO is typically more than justified by the savings it provides by ensuring that projects remain within scope and focused on the overall strategic goal, utilize repeatable processes, and align with related and dependent efforts to synchronize efforts. Finally, to achieve the best results, the PMO should have support at the highest level of management and be positioned appropriately in the organization chart to establish authority and report freely on the status of initiatives.

So, now we know that the creation and effective operation of a PMO is essential to the success of any organization in the midst of a CRM (or other IT) transformation or any organization seeking to more efficiently manage a portfolio of projects. But what else does it deliver, and what are specific components of a good PMO. In addition to establishing a Project and Program management discipline across the organization, the PMO also enables senior management to closely monitor and report on the progress of multiple initiatives. Other key benefits to an effective PMO include:

- Consensus among executive sponsors and other stakeholders about Program and Project objectives, the management approach, the allocation of resources, roles and responsibilities, and required commitment levels.

- A strong program management infrastructure that promotes sound and effective communications, decision-making, issue resolution and risk mitigation.

The establishment of a PMO begins with the development and socialization of the Program Management Charter Document. This charter document outlines all the key elements required for the successful implementation and operation of the PMO.

The primary elements of a Program Management Charter (and the PMO) include:

- Program and Project Organizational Structure: Defines the program and project team members, the executive sponsors, steering committee members, and other key stakeholders.

- Roles and Responsibilities: Defines the expected roles and responsibilities of everyone assigned to projects and programs across the organization.

- Issue Management: Defines how issues are captured, documented, assigned, tracked, and resolved throughout the project lifecycles of all initiatives in the organization.

MAKING CRM STICK

- Risk Mitigation: Defines how critical issues and risks are captured, documented, assigned, tracked, and mitigated throughout project lifecycles, and provides a framework to prioritize and appropriately group all risks, and proactively develop mitigation activities.

- Escalation Procedures: Defines when issues are to be escalated, the mechanisms by which they are escalated, to whom they are escalated, and how escalated issues are tracked.

- Reporting Procedures and Tools: Defines the expected project reporting procedures and tools for the project lifecycles. This includes executive dashboards to track the defined Key Performance Indicators (KPIs) of multiple projects and programs. KPIs will include measures used to track progress against expected gains from IT investments.

- Internal and External communications: Defines the internal and external stakeholder audiences for projects and programs, as well as the message, frequency, and mode of communications they will receive.

- Change Control: Defines how the scope of all projects and programs will be managed. Specifically, this includes establishing the Change Control Board (CCB) and the process for introducing changes to the baseline scope, identifying the members of the CCB, how the proposed changes will be analyzed and prioritized, and how changes will be documented and sanctioned.

- Project Introduction Framework and Processes: As outlined in the Business Case Assessment (BCA), this provides the framework and procedures for introducing new projects and programs to the organization. The framework includes the decision variables (budgetary, strategic, compliance, etc.) that will be considered when deciding if a new project should be initiated.

PMO Manager

Typically, the PMO head has extensive experience in IT program management, is at the senior management level, and facilitates regular meetings with the executive steering committee and review board to review the IT budget, provide updates on project progress, and review and prioritize new IT requests based on business needs. Most executive teams already receive high-level reports of the company's projects on a regular basis. The head of a PMO should manage at the next level of detail, and be dedicated to this effort. Project Definition/Business Case Assessment presentations should be provided to the committee by the sponsoring Business Managers and IT Support Managers. Executive committees should also provide the strategic vision for the CRM initiative based on requirements that support the objectives of the organization. The PMO should support this committee and ensure that they have the proper data to make informed decisions pertaining to CRM and other IT expenditures.

Project Management

Project management is the function that turns a vision into reality. It is a set of processes and procedures that define a goal and create a plan to implement that goal.

Professional project managers are trained in meeting management, facilitation, change leadership, project management methodologies, and negotiation/issue resolution. They dedicate their time to supporting the Business Manager and IT Manager, who are usually occupied with operational activities. Project managers are responsible for gathering all pertinent information to generate the CRM project deliverables and adhering to the identified methodologies and plan. Project managers report to the PMO and are responsible for cross-enterprise communications with other project managers.

Project Methodology

To establish scope and define objectives, all projects should begin with a Project Definition and Business Case Assessment document, prepared in a standard format and approved by the organization's senior oversight body. This document should provide management with information that shows how the CRM project fits within the strategic plan and should factually show how it supports the objectives of the line of business. The approved document is the foundation for launching the project and, later, for measuring its success.

PMOs are responsible for establishing and monitoring the use of proven project approaches and methodologies that span the entire CRM project lifecycle. Approaches and methodologies should bring all appropriate resources together to ensure the success of the project. Almost all project teams require integrated representation from the user community, work practices, information technology, training, and project management.

MAKING CRM STICK

PMOs also serve as resources for standardized project documents. They typically produce and maintain a project library containing templates, samples, and archives of project documents (e.g., status reports, RFPs, issue/action logs, requirements documents, etc.) to guide project managers in documenting and reporting on their efforts. This practice is used by most management consulting firms to provide consultants with a consistent and organized approach to their work, increase the efficiency of their project management efforts, and ensure that all necessary information is gathered throughout the consulting project life cycle.

Project Manager as "General Contractor"

A project manager's role in implementing a CRM or other IT project is similar to that of a general contractor in building a customer's dream house. The contractor must first understand his customer's definition of "Dream House," then set parameters. These two steps are key to understanding how to build the house and develop a construction plan.

Understanding the customer's definition of "Dream House"

The contractor must ask a series of questions to get the customer to describe, in detail, the house. More information and detail makes it easier to develop a model and plan that matches the customer's expectations.

Establishing the parameters of the "Dream House"

The next step is to understand the parameters, or scope. The contractor must obtain information about the amount of money the customer wants to spend, the timeframe for the house to be completed, any constraints, or dependent activities.

These two steps, if performed correctly, give the contractor enough information to start designing the "Dream House." The contractor usually pulls an existing blue print that is similar to the existing engagement and implements the necessary modifications or customization. The modified blue print is reviewed by the customer to determine whether the contractor accurately understands the vision.

Project management requires that the same initial steps be taken to identify and understand the client's project goals and the scope of the project prior to implementation.

> The "blue prints" used by project managers are called project plans. The process and procedures are defined in the project methodology used to guide and manage the project.

Role of the Project Manager

The project manager manages the project based on the goals, objectives and scope that are defined in the initial phases of the project. The project manager is the spokesperson to senior management as well as to the project team. In many cases, the project manager is the glue and guiding force of the project that ensures the integration of a comprehensive and cohesive project team.

The role of the project manager is:

Leader - "GOIFCOCTD - Get out in front, cross over and connect the dots."

Negotiator - Successful negotiators "Care but don't care too much".

Budget Administrator – Budget and expenditure control is required.

Facilitator - Meeting facilitation is a key tool for project managers.

Coordinator – The project plan is a good tool to coordinate work efforts across the team.

Communicator - Communication throughout the project to Executive Sponsors, Steering Committee, Project Managers and the Project Team. (Memos, Meetings, Project Plans, Voice Mail, Email, etc.)

Enterprise Service & Communication

A PMO should use standard reports and all project managers should provide the status of their initiatives to the manager of their respective organization. The PMO should also provide a consolidated view of all initiatives to the organization's budget office and management. The reports allow the PMO to identify common themes at the enterprise level, provide guidance and offer solutions, and identify potential redundancies in different project plans. Standardizing—yet keeping flexible—the project approach, deliverables, and methodology allows the PMO to avoid project overlap, appropriately phase common priorities, identify dependencies, and keep projects moving in unison to meet the institutional goals.

Manage IT Expenses

The PMO should be responsible for managing and tracking the CRM project's (and other IT projects') budget. This requires monthly monitoring of the expenditures to ensure the expenses remain on target. In addition, PMOs should establish a process to measure and track the benefits obtained from projects. In short, the PMO should be generally tasked with ensuring that CRM and IT expenditures support business needs, continue to be justified, and are an appropriate percentage of overall business expenditure.

In addition to managing costs, the PMO should be aware of future projects and technology and their potential impact on IT expenses. The Business Case Assessment process, utilized during the organization's budget season allows Business Managers, together with their IT Support Managers, to request future enhancements or functionality. This also allows the CRM Manager and other IT Managers to identify required maintenance releases or infrastructure upgrades necessary to support new projects or the existing environment.

What Makes a Successful CRM Project

A key success factor for all CRM (and other IT) projects is proper communication between stakeholders. Poor communication has been the downfall for many projects. Professional project managers acknowledge this risk and utilize tools and techniques to increase communication, such as facilitated work sessions, project methodologies and standard templates to gather and share information. The PMO's first step in defining a successful project is to make sure all participants understand the purpose of the CRM initiative.

Know what you want.

Knowing what you want is not as simple as it sounds. Defining and achieving the desired outcome requires a solid governance structure, organization, teamwork, research and above all strong communication skills. In order to ensure a successful project, organizations must be willing to create the detailed blue prints necessary to show the builder (project managers and project team members) what is expected at completion. In our house construction analogy, there is a significant amount of detail that is necessary to complete the blueprint. Communicating the desired results for a CRM or IT project requires the same effort.

Communicate your desired results

Most business initiatives require the integration of several departments such as, data processing, audit, legal, business users, and senior management. The level of involvement depends on the nature of the project. Project communication plans and definition documents help identify stakeholders and others who should be consulted on the project. Communicating requirements, desired results and benefits is one of the most difficult tasks of a project. This is why it is imperative that organizations establish PMOs and follow sound project management methodologies.

The best way to communicate requirements is to have a detailed understanding of the desired results. A good project manager will use a methodology that will help the team design a plan to reach the project goal. This process will allow business executives to develop a business case assessment of the endeavor in order to share the benefits of undertaking the project. In some cases, the executive team may discover that the cost of the initiative out weighs the benefits and thus decide to scrap the plan or make changes to make it worthwhile.

Set expectations

Good project managers listen to the project sponsor to identify their expectations and break the project vision into manageable activities. This helps manage the expectations of all parties involved. Project costs and timelines may require executive sponsors to scale down to a CRM solution that meets critical needs but is not the ideal solution (i.e., moves from a Rolls Royce approach to a Lincoln). A principle of good project management is to identify expectations at the project outset to avoid costly changes once implementation is underway.

Current Environment

Many large companies have benefited from the establishment of an integrated project approach and could achieve further benefits by implementing additional industry-standard project management practices. Large companies create an information technology strategic plan which

MAKING CRM STICK

provides the executive strategic direction for the company. This strategy is usually supported by a number of programs and projects. At first, it appears that all projects support the common strategic vision; however, some projects may not be represented by a Business Manager. Projects operating in isolation can begin to stray from the original intent and suffer scope creep. In some cases, projects will overcome common hurdles on an individual basis. This leads to non-standard solutions, or a silo approach, to common issues. These solutions may conflict with other projects. For example, in the area of information management, the absence of overall metadata standards will force individual project teams to create their own standards that may or may not be compatible with other initiatives. This shows the desire to meet the project timeline but it also distracts the project resources from their documented mission. A common approach between projects can lead to a higher degree of understanding of project requirements and will reduce the potential for overlapping activities. If for example, a CRM project team begins gathering business and technical requirements, and another IT project team starts by gathering only technical requirements for their project, then the two projects will likely not be able to determine if they have conflicts or overlaps, and comparisons will become difficult.

Successful projects should identify benefits during the early stages of the project lifecycle. These benefits need to be stated in the form of measurable objectives that allow management to track whether benefits have actually been realized. If a project is approved because it will improve effectiveness and efficiency, then quantifiable results must be documented. For example, a target metric may include the reduction of the average customer handling time by CSRs. This is a benefit that can be tracked and measured. The project manager is responsible for assisting the Business Manager and the CRM Manager with identifying and documenting such metrics.

Without a centralized view of the organization's multiple projects, there is a strong likelihood that duplicating, and possibly conflict projects may be underway in different areas of the organization. Indeed, many large organizations have an impressive number of initiatives underway at any given moment. The problem is that they are largely disconnected. Many have disparate processes for performing the same kinds of related functions hat may contribute to the productivity of specific staff or units, but do not lead to improved divisional, departmental or institutional productivity. A well-managed PMO will help alleviate these risks.

Conclusion

CRM and other information technology efforts play an important role in most customer facing organizations, and often consume a large portion of the operating budget. The level of importance and the size of these investments warrant a dedicated staff to track and manage these investments to ensure the organization realizes their expected benefits.

A Project Management Office can be more effective with visible support from senior management. Placing the PMO at a level in the organization that provides an enterprise view of the business and IT department will assure that they have access to the proper level of management, and will facilitate active communication pertaining to CRM and other IT investments. This will also equip the PMO with the authority necessary to complete their mission and with the dedicated resources to provide positive value to the organization. In addition, it will ensure CRM and other IT investments are properly measured and that their expected benefits are realized.

2004 © James Butler and Andres Salinas. All rights reserved.

MAKING CRM STICK

Why Planning Fails in Middle-Sized Enterprises – Walter Adamson

Most plans fail

Most strategic plans fail to deliver their goals because there is insufficient focus on implementation. In particular, insufficient attention by the leadership team on the management of strategic change.

If the plan is an incremental one compared to the previous plan, and the organization has well-developed change management in place, then the risk of failure should be low.

Where well-developed change management processes exist as a general practice in an organisation an even more radical plan has only moderate risk of failure.

However for most middle-sized enterprises the risk is high because:

- they develop a strategic plan in response to a threat, a "reinvention strategy;" and,
- they do not have deliberate, effective change management processes in place.

In these latter circumstances my rule for the best possible chance of success is for the CEO to establish a Strategic Change Leadership Team to guide the implementation of the strategic plan.

MAKING CRM STICK

The role of the Strategic Change Leadership Team

This Strategic Change Leadership Team needs to be focused on the implementation of each element of the Strategic Plan. It is responsible for appointing sub-groups to carry out specific tasks and assignments.

The Team reports to the CEO or the Board and must hold itself responsible for setting the program and meeting the implementation targets. In this way it becomes the creator and overseer of the "program office" for the implementation of the strategic plan.

Part of the Team's early role is to not only set out the program as a set of projects but also to seek to clearly link the implementation activities to business benefits.

These benefits should be apparent from the Strategic Plan - but that is not to say that mapping them to particular projects is always straightforward. Nonetheless, that mapping work is an important initial job for the Strategic Change Leadership Team.

It is also highly desirable that the Team plan a series of pilot and mini-projects which are aimed at delivering the business benefits of the change program. By seeing through these mini-projects the risks and unknowns of the larger project will come to be better understood. Then the plan can be adjusted against those outcomes in a cycle of continuous improvement and risk management.

Action for the CEO

The CEO should appoint a Strategic Change Leadership Team. He or she should assign the Team to directly manage the most critical actions from the Strategic Plan, or have task-groups appointed to overview specific tasks.

All the members do not have to permanent; they might come and go according to the type of change being led. For example, changes to a specific business unit or market may require a particular specialist, changes to channels may require another and changes to recruitment strategies another - perhaps including outside experts.

A key requirement for success is that the Team has to have senior leadership heavily committed to it and the changes. One excellent demonstration of this commitment is by appointing a senior executive to lead each sub-team e.g. a strategic reinvention sub-team for a particular market or geography.

Ultimately the whole management structure and system should provide for continuous leadership of strategic change. That is, it should bridge effortlessly between the current organizational strategy and the detailed plans and operations to execute the strategy. By this method the lessons learned by the Strategic Change Leadership Team about the organization and its systems and people, can be captured into further incremental and ongoing action to ensure the organizational capacity is built to change, learn, innovate and adapt.

Vision, mission, and values statements as implementation tools

To further reduce the risk of failure during the implementation of change CEOs should consider more seriously the role of vision, mission and values statements.

Successful entrepreneurs running middle-sized companies very often question the practical value of vision/mission/value statements. On the other hand many other entrepreneurs build their companies around strong values and vision, and they clearly create shareholder wealth from that fabric. Therefore the doubts of one set of entrepreneurs contrasts with the behaviours of the other entrepreneurs who act out their values and vision.

What is apparent is this: where there are shared values which are integrated into the organisation, whether explicit or implicit, then powerful outcomes can be achieved.

In times of change, and when implementing change, there is a need for CEOs to be explicit, to write down and discuss what before may have been implicit.

Your people should understand the operating values of the organisation. They also need to come to terms with the ways in which others' values can be integrated to assist the changes. This process can then be used as a tool to assist in implementing a new strategic plan by building greater understanding of behaviours.

How is this to be done? Producing statements of values, mission and vision is a beginning, but some would say the easy part. The action and wealth creation comes from their implementation.

MAKING CRM STICK

And here lies a great danger. Because paradoxically, the production of a "values statement" with no further implementation program can actually lead to skepticism and diminution of organisational capability.

What this means is that as a CEO you are better not to embark on this journey if you do not intend to follow it through to conclusion. Producing a values statement but not living it or "walking the talk" will lead to a negative impact on strategic change.

If you and your leadership team do not give attention to deployment, to living the values, to benchmarking and improvement, then in times of change your staff will rapidly dismiss the statement of values as a meaningless gesture, perhaps "another fad".

However, when created and deployed in the right way vision, mission and values statements can be leveraged in the following way. And by doing so, in my opinion, CEOs will:

- Significantly help shape and focus their organization, and,
- Create a perceived natural worth around the statements, and,
- Ultimately deliver extra shareholder and employee value.

Actions for the CEO

Use the vision/mission/values statements as a template for all items and actions that come before you, and the Leadership Team, for decision;

Most importantly use them in discussions of issues and decisions with leaders at all levels and with all staff. Let them be used in daily life!

Encourage, or at least don't be defensive, if people challenge the words and meaning. Help them understand the meaning through discussion. The real value is in the discussion not in the words on paper. It is important to maintain the objectives without too much change but be open to changing the words if it helps ease confusion. In fact I would go as far as to say to encourage your people to challenge the statements - because in that way they will become committed by seeing you and your leaders being involved and passionate about their meaning. Forsake the ritual for meaning.

Encourage and demonstrate the use of the statements as a guide in meetings with all divisions and business units of your organisation. Judge and decide on actions by reference to the statements and in particular where difficult and strategic choices have to be made;

Have those reporting to you formally report on how they are developing and implementing strategies based on the statements - on a regular basis;

Benchmark each and every value, and put improvement programs in place to take the values forward and to integrate behaviors across the organization. The benchmark results and the design of interventions must be a regular agenda item of each leadership team meeting;

Assess individual and collective behaviours regularly to ensure that they are in line with the espoused values (including your own behaviour);

Lastly, when walking the floor ask people not "Are we making money today" but "Are we meeting our values today? (And by the way can you please tell me if I and the leadership team are meeting your understanding of our values?)"

Conclusion

CEOs can greatly increase the chance of success of strategic change initiatives, even those induced by anxiety or shock, by appointing Change Leadership Teams, and concurrently paying serious attention to using vision, mission and values statements as implementation tools.

Copyright 2004 by Walter Adamson. All rights reserved.

MAKING CRM STICK

MAKING CRM STICK

The Challenge of Knowledge Transfer in the New World of Outsourcing and Offshore CRM: The effective transfer of system administrative knowledge requires a formal program where all parties have specified roles and responsibilities – Javad Maftoon and Daniel T. Murphy

"The real news about CRM is its decidedly mixed reputation in the tech world. Some studies show that half of all CRM projects never work out, despite the hundreds of millions of dollars companies sometimes spend on them." (Wall Street Journal)

"Prediction: Through 2006, more than 50 percent of all CRM implementations will be viewed as failures from a customer's point of view." (Gartner Group)

INTRODUCTION

Ask any CRM consultant, and they can identify a dozen known points of risk in a large-scale complex CRM implementation. They will mention the need for stakeholder buy-in and the need for a perspective on the future-state customer experience. They will emphasize that the proposed solution should have a quantitative business case and a balanced set of future-state features that benefit the customer, the employees and the enterprise. The list of risks and mitigating factors is growing longer every year.

One of the reasons why the list grows longer is that we are getting smarter about the risks. In the past, we were simply less able to articulate the risks. The landscape is now littered with failed and partially-failed CRM implementations, and luckily, we have learned a few things along the way. For example, ten years ago, who was really worried about getting stakeholder buy-in at the beginning of a project?

But there is another reason why the list of risks and mitigating factors grows longer. It is because we increasingly embrace complexity. For example, ten years ago, how many companies embarked on the multi-phased, multi-dimensional, cross-border CRM implementations that we see today? If things aren't complex already, we are now moving into a more advanced phase of IT outsourcing and utilization of overseas assets. And the points of risk grow greater still. In the old days, a consulting firm built a CRM application and handed it off to the post-go-live owning organization. With the big CRM suites (e.g., Siebel, etc.), the owning organization was usually the client IT organization.

In recent years, things have started to change. These days, it is very common for a consulting firm to build a CRM application, and, rather than handing if off to a client's IT organization, the hand-off is made to a third-party outsource provider. The latest trend is for the outsource provider to be an offshore entity. The result is that the level of risk has intensified – and many of the risks have been conveniently overlooked. Knowledge Transfer is just one example.

KNOWLEDGE TRANSFER

Knowledge Transfer has always been a challenge. End-users must be taught the requisite skills and knowledge so that they may wield the new tool set. Management must be taught how to leverage the new technology to make better-informed business decisions. System Administrators must acquire the necessary skills and knowledge to support the new technology. It is this third category of Knowledge Transfer that is the focus of this white paper – the transfer of knowledge from the solution development team to the support team that will take ownership and administer the system in the post-go-live state.

The team that builds a system is rarely the team that will own the system after go-live, and there has always been a high-level of anxiety around the hand-off between the builders and the owners. As a comparative example, think about building a house. The contractor has anxiety over whether the construction will be well-received by the home owner, or whether the home owner will have an endless punch list of things that need to be fixed before they sign off that the work has been completed. The home owner worries about all of the things that could go wrong after the contractor has been paid (e.g., the roof that may leak, the foundation that may crack).

MAKING CRM STICK

Unfortunately, the deployment phase is destined to remain one of the most challenging phases of a project for the foreseeable future, especially with the added complexities of outsourced and offshore IT. In the old days, the integration vendor needed only worry about the client's internal IT organization accepting delivery of a CRM solution. These days, it is very likely that the integration vendor will be making a hand-off to another vendor. The level of anxiety for both the delivery team and the receiving team is moving to a new level. The stakes are high on both sides. The developers are worried that, if the system doesn't work as expected, they will be criticized by the receiving team. The receiving team is worried about signing the receipt for a system that will break down. The root cause of the anxiety is the money – the professional services fees that are at stake for the development of a working system, and the fees that are at stake for the outsourcing company to be able to support a system with minimal staffing. With the profit margins narrowing on each side of the fence, anxiety is heightening.

When there are multiple vendors involved in the CRM solution handoff, practitioners should beware that the situation can easily go awry. When budget pressure has caused the overlap time between the developing and receiving organizations to be minimized, practitioners should be especially concerned.

As if the deployment phase of a project is not scary enough already, we now have the added complexities of outsourcing and off-shoring. Coming out of the recent recession, we have seen a marked increase in the movement of projects offshore. A common occurrence is that a CRM solution is built onshore (or mostly onshore), and then handed off to an offshore entity for post-go-live ownership. When the development team in Baltimore needs to prepare the ownership team in Bangalore to take over a large CRM system with complex workflow rules, visibility rules, integration points, etc., the level of stress becomes acute. This added complexity presents further risk for the project to have an unsuccessful outcome.

THE CHALLENGES OF OUTSOURCING AND OFFSHORE

We were recently involved in a large-complex CRM implementation that required a complex system hand-off, and an off-shore component. We spent some time in advance thinking about the challenges we were facing. We also talked to our consulting colleagues who had recently faced similar challenges.

MAKING CRM STICK

Managing Anxiety - Let's be honest, there is a very high level of anxiety in making a solution hand-off from one consulting company to another. Integrators are reluctant to hand off their solution to an owning organization. The owning organization is typically terrified of taking the hand-off. As described above, the developers worry about criticisms of the solutions that they architected, constructed, and (supposedly) rigorously tested. They worry that, as soon as the solution is handed off, they are open to the criticisms of the receiving organization. They worry that, after hand-off, they will no longer be in a position to defend their reasons for configuring the solution a certain way or for architecting a certain workaround. This is a natural anxiety that everyone is a bit afraid to acknowledge.

Foreign Language – This may not seem like a big deal at first glance. However, training System Administrators and Support staff who speak a foreign language is considerably more difficult than training end-users who speak a foreign language, mainly because the technical terms are not at the trainer's fingertips (e.g., What's the word for 'workflow' in Chinese?). These days, most outsourcing providers claim that their System Administrators and Support staff members are fully prepared to attend training in English. In reality, the challenge of transferring system knowledge to non-English-speaking learners is still significant.

Logistics – Distance learning has certainly made the world seem like a smaller place. On most CRM and ERP implementations, a large percentage of end-users acquire their new skills and knowledge virtually, via various synchronous and asynchronous technologies – web-based training (WBTs), Webex and Centra sessions, etc. Yet, Project Managers are still hesitant (justifiably) to rely solely on distance learning for System Administration and Support training. "Nice work! Now let's pack it up and take it to India!" It isn't as easy as it sounds. The logistics of planning, developing and delivering an offshore training program is a challenge.

Teach Who? – The outsourcing and off-shoring components have had some rippling challenges as well. These days, it does seem that the System Administrators and members of the future-state support organization are being identified later in the game. Rarely are the future owners present during the Requirements phase, the Design phase or the early days of Development. This is yet another planning challenge for the Project Manager.

Criteria and Timing for the Hand-Off – We have found that it is rare that the criteria for solution hand-off are articulated at the beginning of a project. This is a huge source of anxiety. Nobody seems to have an agreement on the timing for the hand-off and how the hand-off becomes official. The lack of specific criteria allows imaginations to take over. The development team may believe that the hand-off of the system is completed on the day of go-live, or when the receiving team has been trained. The receiving/owning organization may believe that the development team has a responsibility to provide support during a transitional period. But how long is the transitional period? What is the duration of co-ownership of the system, before the hand-off becomes official? Should the development team be available for support en masse, or is a skeleton crew sufficient? Will the development team provide support on-site or by phone? All these questions should be answered well in advance of the deployment phase of a project.

Roles and Responsibilities – Who is responsible for Knowledge Transfer on the developer side? Who is responsible on the receiving team? Who has responsibility for arranging the logistics for the Knowledge Transfer sessions? Who will develop the training and supporting materials? Who will conduct the training? Who will attend the sessions? We have found few instances where these questions are answered early in a project. "We'll figure that stuff out later. Right now, we're up to our elbows in configuration, and we don't have time for anything else." Human beings are not comfortable with not knowing. The result is that most project stakeholders will make their own assumptions about roles and responsibilities. "Oh, Knowledge Transfer? The PMO guys own that." Clearly articulating Knowledge Transfer roles and responsibilities in advance will reduce a great amount of anxiety in the late stages of the project.

The Quality of System Administrator Training – For several reasons, the time and effort spent on training the System Administrators and Support staff will be less than the what is spent on end-users – mainly because the population is typically small in number. Usually the system developers are assigned to train the future System Administrators and Support staff. This approach works well when it is managed with an appropriate level of rigor. It is okay for the training program for System Administrators and Support staff to be less formal than the training program for end-users. But it is not okay for this training to be cursory or half-baked.

Remember – The System Administrators and Support staff members are the future owners of the application. They are key stakeholders who can make or break the project. The training program for this audience should be built based on sound adult learning theory (e.g., adults learn by doing) and should include a series of instructional 'cycles' of instruction to ensure the transfer and retention of skills and knowledge. A trained instructional designer should be included in the effort to ensure that these cycles are built in, and the training must be evaluated (e.g., using a Knowledge Transfer Feedback Form) and improved after each iteration. Finally, the transfer of knowledge to the owning organization should be documented in writing:

- Topics Covered
- Session Dates
- Release Team Members (Knowledge Transferred By)
- System Staff (Knowledge Transferred To)
- Documentation Completed and Certified? (Y/N)
- System Administrator Staff Signoff
- Signoff Date

THE KNOWLEDGE BROKER

As a mitigating approach to the challenge of Knowledge Transfer in an outsourcing/off shoring environment, we have recently been successful at taking what we have called a Brokerage approach. We assign an independent impartial third-party Knowledge Broker to take responsibility for facilitating Knowledge Transfer between the development team and the post-implementation ownership team. If the development team is a Big Five integrator, and the post-implementation ownership team is the in-house IT organization, the Broker role can be played by a third-party consultant. If the hand-off is from Big Five integrator to Big Five outsourcer, the Broker can be a member of the in-house IT organization.

The Broker brings impartiality to the table – a meditative and arbitrative mindset that helps diffuse the anxiety behind the hand-off of the CRM solution from one party to the other. When the Broker brings their Knowledge Transfer toolbox to the table, the message becomes clear – that Knowledge Transfer is indeed a 'program' where all parties have roles and responsibilities, there are proven tools from the toolbox are used, and all parties derive the benefits of having a systematic approach. The Broker approach makes clear that Knowledge Transfer is a program with work activities that all parties must step through together.

Here are some of initial questions that the Knowledge Broker should be asking early in the project to initiate the discussion of Knowledge Transfer:
- Have project sponsors (business unit sponsors, IT sponsors, outsource

organization sponsors, onshore sponsors, offshore sponsors) been identified at the executive and middle-management level? Have these roles been communicated throughout the organization?
- Has the target go-live date and the full scope of technology and process change been communicated to the system's future owners?
- Will the future-state owning organization need to reorganize, re-skill, or recruit new staff?
- Have the future-state System Administrators and Support staff been identified by name?
- Does the integrated project plan include tasks for writing the Service-Level Agreement(s) for the new system(s)?
- Are the new System Administrators and Support staff assigned/budgeted to attend training on the new system? Are they participating in system development?
- Has anyone created a detailed Knowledge Transfer plan? How many activities are in the plan? Ten? One hundred? Five-hundred? Has the plan been incorporated into the integrated project plan (IPP)?
- What jobs in the IT organization will change in the future-state?
- What new jobs will need to be put in place? Have the hiring requisitions been created?

IN CLOSING

The effective transfer of system administrative knowledge does require a formal program where all parties have specified roles and responsibilities . . . especially in today's world of outsourcing and off-shoring. In case you have only skimmed the paragraphs above, let us offer the following simple advice: Find out who holds all of the information about the new systems, processes, business rules, etc., that are being constructed. Find out who will be responsible for these things in the future. (If the answer is 'We don't know yet', be aware that you have a problem.) Make it a requirement that these stakeholders all read this paper. Make them read it twice. On your project plan, specify two days during the design phase of your project where these people must spend two days in the same conference room. Make it a requirement that everyone must attend. Make it a requirement that the group must produce a list of roles and responsibilities, and a detailed Knowledge Transfer plan using Microsoft Project. Accomplish this much, and you will have increased the probability that the hand-off will be a smooth one, and that your project will have a successful outcome.

Copyright 2004 by Daniel T. Murphy and Javad Maftoon. All rights reserved.

MAKING CRM STICK

MAKING CRM STICK